The Bible Explains Creation

Dr. Charles R. Vogan Jr.

Copyright © 1996, 2007 Charles R. Vogan Jr.
All rights reserved

Second Edition

1 2 **3**

Scripture taken from the HOLY BIBLE, NEW INTERNATIONAL VERSION, Copyright © 1973, 1978, 1984 International Bible Society. Used by permission of Zondervan Bible Publishers.

ISBN 978-0-6151-4571-6

Cover photo courtesy of Robert Gendler

Ravenbrook Publishers

A subsidiary of
Shenandoah Bible Ministries

www.shenbible.org

Contents

Preface — 5

Part One: Introduction

   Why is Creation important? — 9
   Different Creation theories — 17
   The current situation — 34
   A new method for understanding Creation — 45

Part Two: The Bible's explanation of Creation

   The *Method* of Creation – Miracle — 61
   The *Means* of Creation – Command — 82
   The *Pattern* of Creation – Wisdom & Understanding — 101
   The *Proof* of Creation – Eyewitness — 115
   The *Agent* of Creation – The Spirit of God — 138
   The *Joy* of Creation – Blessing — 148
   The *Builder* of Creation – Christ — 156
   The *Goal* of Creation – God's Glory — 168
   The *Test* of Creation – Judgment Day — 176
   The *Window* of Creation – Revelation and Faith — 185

Part Three: How the Biblical writers used the Creation account — 201

Part Four: How to present Creation — 227

Appendices:

   A historical survey of Creationism's response to the findings of modern science — 243
   How to determine what is Truth — 275

Preface

Of all the issues that the Bible talks about, perhaps the one that causes the most confusion is the Creation account in Genesis. Some people simply refuse to believe it. Others accept it to a certain extent, saying that it is symbolic of deeper scientific realities than its child-like simplicity would have us believe. Still others are convinced that it's an accurate account of what literally happened.

The problem about the Creation debate is that most people have been looking at bits and pieces of the issue, whereas we can never know what really happened until we get hold of a great deal more information than what we've been working with. It's about time that we examined a bigger picture of Creation. Instead of scrutinizing certain details of the process, we need to back up and look at the whole picture. There are certain fundamental questions that we must ask. For example, what was the point of Creation? What was God doing there? What were the methods that he used? What were the results?

If we only use science to understand our world and its beginnings, we will inevitably get a skewed world view. The results of scientific research don't begin to fulfill the deeper needs of the human soul, nor do they match the facts of a universe that obviously includes more than matter and energy and scientific laws. Evolutionists have closed their eyes to spiritual concepts and therefore will never know what is really going on around them in the world made by God.

Many Creation scientists are also making that mistake, as if they have accepted the atheist's belief that science is the best way to understand our world. It is not. The Bible *does* answer these fundamental questions for us, however, in ways that fit the facts perfectly.

But the information on Creation that we will find in the Bible is bigger than the issue of whether evolution is true or not. We have to keep in mind that the scientists have misled us for centuries. The issue isn't just whether God created the world in six literal days or long eras of time, though we will have something to say about that. The issue is much bigger than that. The universe is like a house: we aren't going to look only at the bricks that make up the wall of God's house, but the foundation as well, and the framework and the overall structure and surroundings. There were powerful realities moving at Creation that set the stage for all of history; we will see these realities again and again, because this is the way our God always works and always will work. Once we see those realities, then the smaller details of how God made the world will be answered as well. (But, to give you a preview of what's to come, the Bible very plainly teaches that God *did* make the world in six days – as *we* understand them – and he did *not* use evolution to create the universe or life!)

This book arose out of research for a doctoral dissertation on the subject of Creation. Since Creation is something that many people, both inside and outside of the Church, are very interested in, I felt that it would be appropriate to offer my findings to the general reader. But surprisingly little help came from Creationists over the past two centuries of debate! Most Creationists apparently haven't seen how powerful our accepted Christian doctrines can be in explaining Creation; they have, for the most part, satisfied themselves with "bread and water" when there was a rich feast waiting for them in God's Revelation. Therefore the ideas presented here are mainly my own, though hopefully they will reveal a deeper message about Creation in the pages of Scripture. My purpose is to convince you that the Bible *does* explain Creation in a satisfying way – much better than does any other source.

Part One:

Introduction

Why Is Creation Important?

There has been a tremendous battle raging in recent years over the subject of Creation. The opponents – scientists and religionists, teachers and politicians – are fighting for the right not only to be heard, but to be in sole possession of the field of battle, and the routing of the enemy. They have waged war in Congress and state governments, in academic institutions from universities down to grade schools, and even *within* churches! We've been able to follow the fight in the movies (for example, remember Spencer Tracy's portrayal of Clarence Darrow of the Scopes "Monkey Trial" fame?), in the newspapers, and in innumerable books and magazine articles. Furthermore, the battle has raged for about 200 years and doesn't appear to be letting up.

These people, who have invested so much time and money to destroy their opponents' arguments, are obviously fighting about something serious. Not only that, since the battle continues from generation to generation with no apparent winners, there must be something terribly complex and mysterious about the subject. Why is the subject of Creation so important to people? And why is it so difficult to get to the truth of the matter?

Creation is about how the world first got started. You wouldn't think that this would be so important to us now, since we have our lives to live, and more important current issues to solve – like poverty, crime, and other matters. But actually Creation is *very* important: if we knew how the universe came to exist, we would have the answers to a great many important questions in life, answers that would have a tremendous impact on how we live our daily lives.

We have to know these answers. For example, if you would move to San Francisco or Japan, no doubt one of your first questions to the real estate agent, as he or she showed you houses to buy, is whether these houses were constructed to withstand earthquakes. You have to know that because you could very well be faced with tremendous property damage in the future. But you couldn't necessarily tell whether the house was built to withstand earthquakes by looking it over from the outside. You would have to rely on the real estate agent's knowledge of how the building contractor made it in the first place.

In the same way, you would show the same kind of wisdom if you asked about the origin of the world. Was it by accident – or by design? If there is no God, and the universe just fell into place according to evolving laws of physics and chemistry, what does that tell me about the meaning and purpose of life? On the other hand, was there a God who made the world? If so, what was he after? How do I fit into his plans? And one of the wisest things you could ask is this: *how* did he do it?

Everyone wants to know who they are, why they are in the world, and what place they fit into in the scheme of things. Adolescents grapple with these issues as they mature; hopefully they will find workable answers by the time they become adults, so that they can take responsible and useful places in our society. Unfortunately, many don't: either they become tremendous problems to society (criminals, freeloaders, dysfunctional families), or they struggle through life unhappy and unfulfilled with the lot that fate seemingly cast them into. There are a lot of people struggling and searching for answers to their personal problems and never finding them.

Evidently people are desperate for the answer to the origin of the universe. For example, our government is spending billions of dollars on ultra-sophisticated electronics, both on our planet and out in space, to search for signs of life elsewhere in the universe – or at least some clues as to how it all began. Physicists are spending just as much money on particle accelerators to analyze the smallest parts of matter, hoping that they can come up with the fundamental "theory of everything" – an equation that they can then use to understand and predict everything in the universe, including life itself. There are many other searches going on right now, great and small, all over the world, as people strive to answer the questions of *who we are* and *why we are here*.

Let's look at some of the fundamental issues behind the Creation question. The reason that the problem of the origin of the universe is so important to solve is that it will give us answers to the issues that have burned in people's minds since the beginning of history.

Is there a God?

After all, what everyone really wants answered is, did God make the universe or did it fall together on its own? Our biggest problem in trying to answer this question is that one can't see God, and one can't easily tell that the world came into existence because of something that God did.

Evolution claims that we can explain everything that happens by means of simple laws and mathematics, without bringing God into the picture. Is that claim true? Each generation of scientists adds to our store of knowledge, and it does appear that we are getting a better understanding of our world – and, as one scientist put it, there seems to be "nothing for a Creator to do." [1] And if there is no God, then the universe obviously doesn't need a God to operate – and then neither do we. So you see that it's very important to nail down this issue at the very beginning.

If there is a God, however, and he did make the universe, we immediately have all sorts of answers and, unfortunately, many more problems to solve. For example, we would know that this universe *needs* God if, in fact, it couldn't come into existence without him. We would also know that God is bigger than we are, and he can just as easily destroy the world as well as make it. We could also make a pretty astute guess that he had a plan in mind at the beginning, and he made the universe according to that plan. He's probably waiting for the time when he will stop everything, take it apart and analyze it, and come to some sort of judgment as to how well his creation met his original expectations.

---

[1] Stephen W. Hawking, *A Brief History of Time From the Big Bang to Black Holes*, introduction by Carl Sagan, Bantam Books, 1988, x.

Some of the problems that immediately face us are these:

First, how did he make the universe in the first place? There don't seem to be any clues left lying around; everything appears to run like clockwork without him now – or at least that's what the scientists tell us.

Second, unless he wrote something in the sky for everyone to read (which it appears that he didn't!), how are we to know what his original plans were? What are *we* here for? Are we to live in ignorance of his plans, assuming that whatever we want to do in life is Okay with him, and that everything will turn out well for everybody in the end?

Third, in spite of the fact that he created the entire universe, including ourselves, we still seem to know remarkably little about this God. Rocks and trees don't tell us much about him. For proof, look at the many theories about God that you find around the world in different cultures.

One more thing that we'd all like to know is, will we see more of this God from now on? Did he simply wind up the universe at the beginning, as the Deists tell us, and stand back to let it spin on its own? Or does he still involve himself in his creation – and if so, how? This has a practical side, because people want to know if they can pray to this God! Does he answer prayer? If so, how does he do it – by overruling the laws of his creation or by means of those laws (that is, through Providence)? And last, is God responsible at all for the way the world has turned out for the last few thousand years? Is the Creator responsible for sin and suffering and death? Can he do anything about it?

What is man?

Naturally we want to know as much about ourselves as possible – we are our favorite subject! But it makes a great deal of difference whether we were created by God, or are the product of an evolving universe.

First, we need to know whether we are here for a reason – to fulfill God's purpose, whatever that might be – or whether we just happened for no reason at all. If for a reason, then we had better be about our business or we will be caught unprepared before the Judge! A businessman expects profits from his employees or they will be fired. God, if he made us to serve a purpose in his world, will be very upset if we haven't been about his business making a profit for him.

Second, there has always been a persistent, nagging thought in the heart of man that just won't go away: there *is* such a thing as right and wrong. We don't know where we got such a thought, but it would make sense if God created us. It would mean that he himself is holy, that he expects his creatures to be holy, and that he will reward the righteous and punish the wicked based on their actions in the world. Every society has a code of ethics. Even those who don't know anything about the Bible or the Creation account have governments and laws, prisons and punishments, social and cultural ethics that all of its citizens are expected to live by. Is this from Creation? Or are we making up something that really isn't necessary, something that is relative, something that we can easily change, or get rid of, if we have the desire or nerve to do it?

Is the Bible reliable?

The one reason that the Creation debate has been fought so fiercely and for so long is that the Bible says very plainly how the world began. Unfortunately, it's true that many people don't have any trouble ignoring the Bible's account; science gives them all the answers they need in life. But many other people can't turn their backs on the Bible so easily. After all, if there really is a God, and the Bible is his book, can we afford to ignore his own description of what he did at the beginning? Are we free to doubt the Almighty and the Judge of all men?

The bottom line is this: did it happen as the Bible said it did, or is science a better judge of what actually happened? In other words, is the Bible reliable? Can we take it at its bare word, or do we need to "doctor" it up a bit before it's good enough for modern man? Often people think that the Bible is a naïve explanation for immature cultures, whereas our modern, sophisticated culture that has been trained by science can only use the Bible for "devotional" purposes now, not for scientific or historical fact.

But if you think about it, that's not being honest about the Bible. If we can't trust it in some things, what makes us so sure that we can trust it in "safer" subjects? For example, if a scientist lied about his experiments in order to get fame and fortune, we would never trust him again in the future, no matter how penitent he was. We'd rather get someone else's opinion, someone whom we know has always been trustworthy.

You must realize that the Creation account is not the only subject under severe scrutiny in our century! Miracles, historical events, prophecy, dating, famous Biblical characters – modern scholars have doubted the genuineness and accuracy of all these things in the Bible. As we shall see, Creation is so tightly interwoven with these other matters that when you doubt one, you essentially have to throw the whole thing out!

It's a spiritual world

There's another purpose for studying the subject of Creation, which is this: we will be able to see what our world is made of. Scientists understand this need very well. They have done a wonderful job in the last several hundred years; they have analyzed the world, searched out its workings, formulated its laws, and laid the foundations for using that knowledge for the common good of humanity. Because of their hard work, we now have cars and computers and telephones and medicines and spaceships and innumerable other things that none of us want to do without.

But there's more to the world than physics and chemistry, if the Bible is true. Put some different glasses on, and look again. Imagine that you are an explorer in a new land. What if you could see new laws, new realities, in our universe that scientists can't see? What if you made discoveries of such a nature that your descendants would be *spiritually* blessed as a result of your discoveries? If you could see the landscape of God's world so clearly that you could avoid sin and death, would that be worth something to you?

So, Creation, according to the Bible, was a much bigger event than most people think. Great foundations were laid there, foundations for the great works of God yet to come. Tremendous spiritual battles rage over our heads; eternity hangs in the balance for every one of us. What we do and say has eternal consequences, because of the way the world was made. What we are now, and what we do now, will be a springboard for what is yet to come in future ages.

The trouble is that a purely materialistic, scientific outlook misses all of this. Someone who takes this approach to life knows nothing about God, nothing of the bigger realities that God created in the beginning. All he can see are the physical foothills that stand in the way to the tremendous spiritual heights beyond his clouded vision. Therefore he claims, in his ignorance, that there is no such spiritual reality, in spite of the fact that the Bible says there is.

The search for the Creator

That's the debate about Creation. I hope you can see that the subject is *very* important – for everyone. The intellectuals aren't the only ones who need to solve the problem. They won't stand in your shoes for you on Judgment Day – you have to answer for yourself to the God who made you. What will you say then, if the Bible was right and you paid no attention to its explanation of what you were made to do? How will you account for a precious opportunity thrown away?

The solution is to find out *now* what the answer is. That's what we want to do in this book: to find out how we were made, and what we were made to do. Then with that knowledge we will be able to live in such a way as to please our Creator on Judgment Day.

Different Creation Theories

It's unfortunate that people won't listen to the truth; it would save them so much trouble and heartache if they would! We are too inclined to ignore the truth (though we know in our hearts that it *is* the truth) and invent some other "truth" more to our liking. It's a fact that we love to give our opinions on things instead of listening to someone who really knows what's going on.

The Bible has the truth about Creation, but most people aren't listening. That self-inflicted ignorance has been going on for a very long time. Man from the very beginning knew how the world was made. But because he preferred a different God than the One who demands that man be holy, he invented innumerable gods in the place of the real God, and invented a new scheme of what is right and wrong so that he could get away with murder and do whatever he wanted to do. Paul tells us this in Romans:

> For since the creation of the world God's invisible qualities — his eternal power and divine nature — have been clearly seen, being understood from what has been made, so that men are without excuse. For although they knew God, they neither glorified him as God nor gave thanks to him, but their thinking became futile and their foolish hearts were darkened. Although they claimed to be wise, they became fools and exchanged the glory of the immortal God for images made to look like mortal man and birds and animals and reptiles. Therefore God gave them over in the sinful desires of their hearts to sexual impurity for the degrading of their bodies with one another. They exchanged the truth of God for a lie, and worshiped and served created things rather than the Creator — who is forever praised. Amen. (Romans 1:20-25)

And because answering the question of Creation is the first step to dealing with all the other issues of life, getting *that* wrong meant that nothing else is working out for us as planned either. This is God's world; and if you don't get in line with his created order, you will always be out of step and at cross-purposes with the Creator. Nothing you do will work in the long run if you're always at odds with the true God. We have seen this many times throughout history, as civilization after civilization has created their own gods and come to ruin in the end.

Many Creation stories have come down to us from the history of various cultures. Most of them are pure nonsense. Some of them are pretty sophisticated, and it would take a lot of effort to prove them wrong. Since we're really only interested in our own times, we will limit our scope here to the theories that are popular nowadays, in our modern western culture.

Evolution

Believe it or not, the theory of evolution, scientifically speaking, has been around for at least a few hundred years. It was known long before Darwin. A man named Lamarck had a theory of evolution that came very close to Darwin's. Charles Darwin (in 1859) formulated his own theory, however, with some important changes that seemed to better explain the facts, and so he gets the credit for discovering the modern theory of evolution.

Evolution in its broadest sense has to do with more than biology. Physicists insist that the entire universe has "evolved" from the Big Bang (when there was only a "soup" of sub-atomic particles) into its present state of planets and galaxies and rocks and people. Biological evolution deals with how life appeared on the earth.

On the whole, however, evolution means that something changes in form or function, and becomes something new as a result. It may take seconds, or eons. The change takes place because of outward circumstances – perhaps there are more foxes for some reason, and rabbits with more powerful legs will survive as a result and the ones with weaker legs will die out. Or the change happens because the thing itself is on the roll, so to speak, and *must* change because of internal forces: a gas cloud that swirls in space will gradually congeal into separate planets over a few millions of years due just to the laws of physics working things out.

Evolution depends on the fact that the change is entirely understandable, once all the facts are known. We don't need anything from outside the system to explain how it happened. The change occurred because of the way the thing is made, or because of precise circumstances. In other words, the future of a thing is literally locked up in its present makeup.

The famous example of evolutionists will serve us here. At some point in time, a fish presumably left the water and started walking on land. At least two things had to happen for this event: the fish had to have lungs, and it had to have legs. (I realize I'm condensing the progress of millions of fish, years, and gradual changes into a single example, but since the results *are* with us, I think we can use this fish to make the point.) Evolution states that, as the fish's ancestors splashed around in the shallows, those who showed gradual changes in their gills were slowly able to swallow air from outside the water and use it. And those who showed gradual strengthening and restructuring of their fins into leg-like limbs, became more adapted to life in the shallows. Finally this fish, the result of all those small changes, found that it could walk out on land and breathe the air – it didn't need the water anymore. This is the theory of evolution, pure and simple. Every step is logical, understandable, and predictable.

If we know everything about its present state, and know all the tiny and great forces around it that interact with it, theoretically we can then predict exactly what will happen to it in the future – where it will be and what it will look like. That's the theory of evolution: things change according to known laws and forces of the material world.

The evolutionists need a theory like this to account, for example, for the innumerable forms of life on earth. How did all this happen? There must have been one or more primitive cells in the early oceans, and from them came (in a very precise and understandable way) new forms of life, and from them still others, until we now have a myriad of life forms around us. But they insist that it can all be accounted for by the internal structure of the living things themselves, and the surroundings. They don't want to bring God into the picture at all.

You must understand that pure evolution is a scientist's delight. It works only with material things, with the laws of physics and chemistry and mathematics, and deals only with what we can know through our physical senses. The question of whether there is a God or whether he had anything to do with Creation is of no interest to evolutionary scientists. Why should they be concerned about God when there is no need for him in their equations?

Of course the present state of the evolutionary theory is far from perfect. Scientists don't have all the answers, and they can't reconstruct how the world came into existence because they are still missing most of the data that they would like to have. What they *do* have are the theories, the mathematics, the physical laws and principles. With these they can describe, on paper at least, how the universe happened, step by step.

The problems with evolution are many:

First, we may be impressed with their theories and mathematics, but we mustn't forget that a piece of paper will sit still for anything these days. There was a great deal of work done over the years on the blackboard that was quietly put aside because they themselves knew it didn't match reality. The little that they are showing us in their books is only what they want us to see, out of all the work that they scrapped over the years that they would be embarrassed about now. [2] Even now, there are

---

[2] "Even within the community of particle physicists there are those who think that the trend toward increasing abstraction is turning theoretical physics into recreational mathematics, endlessly amusing to those who can master the techniques and join the game, but ultimately meaningless because the objects of the mathematical manipulations are forever beyond the access of experiment and measurement." David

still some theories that have been proven wrong that fill the textbooks of our students.

Second, few evolutionists are agreed about the theory of evolution. Some hold to it enthusiastically, some have reservations, and some admit that the only reason they still use it is because there simply isn't any other good alternative around. There are also different kinds of evolution, according to the scientists, because no one theory accounts for all the facts: for example, some scientists believe that living organisms change drastically in sudden leaps, instead of enduring gradual changes over great periods of time. So, which experts are we to believe? Obviously somebody has it wrong!

Third, pure evolution leaves no room for God or the spiritual world. I said before that evolutionists don't care about God, but actually they would be forced to admit that there can be no God if evolution is true, or at least that God is unnecessary. This means that they are going to have tremendous problems trying to explain certain basic realities of our world – for example, morality, the value and meaning of life, the tragedy of death, the hope for a future life, and of course the persistent feeling that there really is a God, in spite of what the scientists tell us.

Evolution and God

Many people feel that they are caught between a rock and a hard place; they can't in good faith turn their backs on the Bible completely, yet they can't ignore the "facts" of science either. So they have come up with an ingenious solution: God made the world, it's true, but he did it by using evolution.

Lindley, *The End of Physics: The Myth of a Unified Theory*, Harper Collins Publishers, 1993, p.19.

This is known as "theistic evolution." People who believe this think that they have solved their problems, but they really haven't solved anything. The fact is that they lost their nerve in the face of cold, hard data from the scientists. Who wants to play the fundamentalist fool? For ages the Church has had to back up in embarrassment as scientists repeatedly found perfectly natural answers to what Christians thought were miracles. For example, for a long time the Catholic Church was reluctant to admit that Copernicus was right – that the planets (including earth) revolve around the sun, not the sun around the earth, in spite of the fact that her own scientists provided many proofs to support it.

Who would doubt that truth today? Yet in every generation the scientists find new explanations for events in our world, and it looks as if there is little or nothing left for the Church to claim for herself. For instance, do we really have a soul? Brain research seems to be on the verge of answering that question conclusively – and Christians aren't going to like the answer. Is there anything sacred anymore? Is there anything that science can't help us with, that we still need the Bible and God for?

Theistic evolution, therefore, backs up as far as it can without giving up God in the process – at least in theory. Go ahead, its followers say, discover whatever you want out there – it's really God doing it, though you don't see it. God used the Big Bang to bring the universe into existence, God used billions of years and natural laws to form galaxies and planets, God arranged for the first living cell in the primitive oceans, God carefully guided the evolution of living things until, billions of years later, we now have man and all the other creatures.

Pure evolutionists laugh at this theory. Take the word "God" out of it, and the world doesn't look a bit different. Why add a religious superstition to the theory of evolution, they claim, when it doesn't change a thing? Evolution *means* predictable change, according to existing material circumstances. If someone insists on adding God to the picture, then we aren't talking about evolution –

because if God does *anything at all* to the situation, then evolution didn't happen but Divine Creation.

For example, let's go back to our fish crawling on land. Evolutionists claim that its fins changed into legs because of slow (or maybe abrupt, the theorists disagree on this) changes in its ancestors, which made it easier for them to live in the shallows. They can describe the changes and the genetic process behind it. Theistic evolutionists say that God directed those changes. But if that's true, what was it that God directed? The scientists have it all figured out; it's all a very natural process, and they could duplicate it if they had the right conditions. So where do we need the hand of God in this picture?

For some reason the theistic evolutionists ignore this criticism and hold onto their theory like a comforting blanket. It makes them feel better that God is involved somehow, though they don't feel obligated to tell us exactly how he is involved. The most that they can say about God, however, is that he is someone we can believe in if we want to (though there's nothing in the way the world works that would force us to that conclusion), and we can get happiness by thinking about him in this evolutionary world of ours. That's not much to go on, is it? A God like that can't do much for us when we need help.

Natural Theology

There was a famous book written in 1736 by a man named Joseph Butler, entitled *The Analogy of Religion, Natural and Revealed to the Constitution and Course of Nature.* In it he assumes that God made the world; to assume that God didn't is just a waste of time, Butler says, because it doesn't fit the facts of nature. And if this is true, it must be the same God that we learn about from Scripture; and if so, then surely he left his characteristic footprints in his Creation. In other words, there ought to be signs in the natural world that the same God rules there as does in the Church.

This idea ruled supreme for a long time in Western culture. It made perfect sense: the God of the Bible is a God of law and order, a God of consummate wisdom, a God of purpose and meaning, a God of goodness and plenty. He would surely make his universe along the same lines. This means that we ought to be able to examine nature and find reasonable proof that God did, in fact, create the world.

This of course fits in nicely with some well-known passages of Scripture – for example,

> The heavens declare the glory of God;
> > the skies proclaim the work of his hands.
> Day after day they pour forth speech;
> > night after night they display knowledge.
> There is no speech or language
> > where their voice is not heard.
> Their voice goes out into all the earth,
> > their words to the ends of the world. *(Psalm 19:1-4)*

And we've already looked at Romans 1:19-25, which teaches us the same thing: namely, that we can learn a lot about God by looking at his masterpiece. Only a willful, ignorant sinner would miss the lessons written large in Creation around his feet and over his head.

This principle is also known as the "argument from design." The argument is this: when you look at how the world works, and how it is made, it's obvious that things have a purpose, a built-in design to enable it to achieve its intended goal. For example, when we study the eye (a classic example in natural theology), we can't help but see how remarkably designed it is, how each part fits together perfectly to achieve the act of seeing. Surely that wasn't accidental! If just one minor detail was missing out of the thousands that are involved, we wouldn't be able to see at all. This leads us to believe that Someone made the eye, and he intended us to be able to see with it.

You've probably heard of the "Divine Watchmaker" – the idea that the universe is like a complex watch, made in intricate detail and obviously made for a purpose, which means that we simply have to assume a Creator behind it all. There is no way that such a beautifully made universe could have come together by chance with no design in mind, and no purpose for it all.

Natural theology is perhaps the easiest way to defend the idea of Divine Creation, and many people with or without scientific expertise eagerly search the natural world for "proofs" of God's handiwork. For a long time the atheists couldn't successfully argue against it – because there is no denying the fact that there is design and purpose built into everything. Scientists from the last century, for example, who didn't want to believe in God the Creator, nevertheless had no proof against the idea. That's why books from that century that dealt with Creation usually homed in on the argument from design: there was no good argument against it.

In our century, however, the game has changed. Scientists have discovered yet deeper levels of existence in the atom as well as the expanding universe. They have managed, for example, by means of physics and brain research, to successfully analyze laws and principles of our world and the mind of man that used to be mysterious and thought to be beyond our understanding. Not only have they mastered the principles involved, they have demonstrated their knowledge by an amazing stream of inventions that make the everyday life of modern man so powerful and comfortable in comparison to that of past ages.

This deeper knowledge of modern science has made atheists very bold. They are no longer impressed with the argument from design. They can show us, for example, that "design" and "purpose" were mathematically necessary as the universe came together according to natural law. In other words, the matter in the universe wasn't an inert pool of stuff that God had to stir up and form into objects; rather, atoms and the laws that jostle them around are already "building blocks" that fit naturally into the things we see around us today. Physicists can *show* you the atom's characteristics that make it form complex objects, and mathematicians can *show* you the equations that predict that such "creations" must happen on their own. Scientists now believe in design: not imposed from the outside, by God, but built into the system already from the beginning. Design is now a proof of the universe's self-sufficiency, not of God's hand.

So, what was once the Creationist's strongest argument has been blunted by scientific advancement. Evolutionists now *like* the word "design," but they are using it in an entirely different sense from those who want to give God glory for Creation.[3]

Early Creationists put too much importance on the argument from design; of course it was only a matter of time until science became sophisticated enough to be able to challenge that idea. What is needed now is what the Creationists should have done a long time ago: while arguing from design, they should also have argued from Scripture. The Bible says a lot more about Creation than how well designed it is.

The fundamental weakness of natural theology is this: it is primarily focused on physical evidence, and that's not enough to prove the point. For example, in a court of law, physical evidence is often brought forth to "prove" that the defendant committed the crime in question. But, as we have often seen, physical evidence can be interpreted many ways. Perhaps the man's gloves were left at the scene of the crime. To the prosecutor, that's "proof" that the man did it. But the defense attorney may point out that another person who wanted to harm the defendant actually planted those gloves there. Who is to say who is right? When all we have is the evidence, the conclusion that naturally comes to mind may or may not be true. This is often the case with many other issues in life.

When we look at how complex and beautifully made the world is, we naturally think that God had to have made it. But now science is

---

[3] "Symmetry principles have moved to a new level of importance in this century and especially in the last few decades: there are symmetry principles that dictate the very existence of all the known forces of nature." "I have been referring to principles of symmetry as giving theories a kind of rigidity ... We are on the track of something universal – something that governs physical phenomena throughout the universe – something that we call the laws of nature. We do not want to discover a theory that is capable of describing all imaginable kinds of force among the particles of nature. Rather, we hope for a theory that rigidly will allow us to describe only those forces – gravitational, electroweak, and strong – that actually as it happens do exist. This kind of rigidity in our physical theories is part of what we recognize as beauty." Steven Weinburg, *Dreams of a Final Theory*, Vintage Books, 1993, p.142, 147.

telling us that there is an equally valid conclusion! Who is right? How will we *prove* that one is right and the other wrong? You see, we need more than just evidence to move the argument along from guesses and feelings; we need other kinds of facts.

The Gap Theory

Another idea that people have come up with to explain Creation is known as the "gap" theory. The claim is this: between verses one and two in Genesis 1, there was a vast geologic time period between two worlds. God made the first world as recorded in verse one, and then destroyed it – which is what the phrase "without form and void" means. Then verse three begins with the "second" creation of the world, in which God made a new world over the ashes of the first one. If you think about this, it isn't as nonsensical as it may first appear. Why else would it say first that God "made the heavens and the earth," and then immediately say that "the earth was without form and void"? Wouldn't that naturally suggest a first Creation followed by a wholesale destruction?

An excellent representative of the "gap" theory was G. H. Pember in his book *Earth's Earliest Ages: A Study of Vital Questions*. He was not content to simply explain the mysterious phrase "without form and void" in Genesis 1:2 as the initial state of Creation, a kind of original "soup" out of which God raised his universe. Instead, Pember describes a first earth peopled with an original race of sinners, led by diabolic forces that eventually forced God to destroy the entire planet in punishment. The only "proof" that he had for this sequence of ancient "history" is a series of deductions.

> **First**, since there evidently was "chaos" in verse 2, this means that it must have been the remains of a first earth.

> **Second**, its destruction would *have* to have been the result of sin, since God does not capriciously destroy his own Creation without good reason.

Third, as we know in our present world, sin is the result of rebellious sinners. This means then that the first world was populated with wicked sinners, no doubt led by Satan, who lived in such rebellion against their Maker that he felt the need to destroy it all and start over again with the world we now live in.

One favorite passage for those who believe in the "gap" theory is Isaiah 14. Here is a description of someone who was glorious at one time, the "morning star," who boasted that "I will make myself like the Most High." Then he was "cast down to the earth" in punishment. All this seems to point to Satan; surely this is a glimpse of some "prehistory," of events that happened before the present earth was created – perhaps during those chaotic days of Genesis 1:2. That would neatly explain how Satan was already evil by the time Adam and Eve were made.

This is all very romantic, and no doubt many people believe in it because it holds so much appeal to the imagination. But we have to be more careful than that when interpreting Scripture. Just because one can see the *possibility* of two separate worlds in Genesis 1:1-2, doesn't mean that such a thing is actually true. We can just as easily read it like this: verse one is the general introduction to the topic of Creation, and verse two is the beginning of the details of the story. In fact, this is the more natural way to read it, because nothing in the rest of the Bible even supports the idea of two earths in the beginning!

The "explanation" of Isaiah 14 doesn't hold water either. The prophet tells us that this is about "the king of Babylon." (Isaiah 14:4) Just because the character there claimed to be equal to God doesn't mean that we *must* assume this is about Satan (especially when the Bible doesn't say anything about that!). Babylonian kings were known to claim that they were gods; for example, in Daniel we read the following account:

> The royal administrators, prefects, satraps, advisers and governors have all agreed that the king should issue an edict and enforce the decree that anyone who prays to

any god or man during the next thirty days, except to you, O king, shall be thrown into the lions' den. (Daniel 6:7)

The point is that we can't just make up an elaborate and clever theory to support an idea that the Bible doesn't clearly teach. The "gap" theory is only a guess about a mysterious verse; we aren't allowed to go rummaging through the rest of the Bible to find wild interpretations that would make our guess in Genesis sound more believable.

But the main reason that the "gap" theory was created was to somehow make sense of what modern geologists have discovered. They teach us that the world is obviously billions of years old; it took the mountains and oceans and continents eons of time to form, and they know exactly how it all happened. Furthermore, the fact that fossils exist is another proof that the earth has been around for a long time. Fossils take millions of years to form, as the story goes. Most people believe this. But how are we going to square these "facts" of geology with the Bible's account of Creation and be faithful to the rest of the first chapter of Genesis?

One easy way out of this dilemma was to create a long period of time within the Creation account, without disturbing the six days of the creation of the present heavens and earth. In other words, let's have an earth that took millions of years to form – the earth that Genesis 1:1 describes. Then let's have God "destroy" that earth (verse two) but not too completely – its mountains and oceans and fossils will still exist as the foundation of the "new" earth. Then in verse three is the account of how God took the remains of that first earth and built a second one on top of it, in six days, just as the text describes. Thus the "gap" theory. Supposedly it neatly explains how the earth can take ages to form, yet it accounts for a miraculous new Creation on top of the old one.

However, we are still faced with the six days of the rest of the chapter! If that's literally true, we have a miracle on our hands that isn't easy to fit into the "gap" theory. What I mean is this: if it only took God six days to make the "second" earth, why then do we need the "gap" theory to explain the facts of nature that geologists insist must take place over billions of years? If God can easily make the "second" earth in six days, why didn't he do the same with the "first" earth instead of working through geologic eras? If he has to work through geologic eras, then why did he switch methods on the "second" earth and do it miraculously in just six days?

And if the six days of the "second" creation were only symbolic of long eras (as many people believe), then why did God go through the bother of creating and destroying a "first" world (a theory that we need to account for the time it takes to make mountains and continents) and then *remake* a world through those same normal evolutionary processes? In other words, if the "second" earth was made through natural geologic processes, why do we *need* the "gap" theory in the first place?

As you can see, the two "creations" don't fit together in this theory. One or the other has to go. And we will also see that the problem that the "gap" theory was designed to solve – the geologic "evidence" for long ages of time in the making of the earth – is itself under suspicion.

Scientific Creationism

This twentieth century movement is actually the direct descendent of classic natural theology. Whereas in the nineteenth century the Creationists would have been following Butler's lead, in our century they follow, for example, Henry Morris and the *Institute for Creation Research*.

First a little history. Evolution made such a clean sweep through the intellectual West that, by the beginning of the twentieth century, very few Christians were willing to admit that they believed in the literal interpretation of Genesis 1-3, and certainly no one was comfortable challenging geology's claim of an old earth. But one interesting holdout was the Seventh Day Adventist Church. Prompted by a supposedly direct revelation of its visionary founder Ellen G. White, who claimed to have been transported back to the time of

Creation and witnessed the event, the SDA laid the groundwork – all new – for the twentieth century phenomenon of Biblical Creationism.

The SDA's principle spokesman was George McCready Price, a normal school teacher who was self-taught in geology. His main work was *The New Geology*, published in 1923 by the SDA publishing house. The way he approaches the subject of Creation has been closely followed by modern Creationists (not of the SDA Church) such as Henry Morris and John Whitcomb in their famous book *The Genesis Flood*.

Scientific Creationism's main points are, first of all, that the Genesis account is literally true: the Lord did make the earth in six literal days, through a miracle. Second, it's possible to show, scientifically, that the earth was made as the Bible says. Or to put it negatively, there's nothing in nature that scientifically disproves or contradicts the Genesis account. The Creation account and the physical evidence are in perfect harmony.

As you can see, this is a new twist on natural theology. Before, the focus was on design – what else can we assume about such a well-made universe except that God made it that way for a reason? Now, Creation scientists are tackling the very concepts of modern science that atheists claim disprove special Creation – they are demonstrating that, on the contrary, those concepts fit in very nicely with the idea of Creation.

Scientific Creationism has two great strengths: **first**, it uncovers the weaknesses of the theory of evolution. Evolutionary science is absurd, and it's about time that someone showed us why. Evolution claims that there is only one way to interpret the physical evidence – its way. Scientific Creationism very clearly shows us another way to look at things using the same scientific principles and tools that evolutionists use and respect, only with much different results.

Second, Scientific Creationists are proving that a person can be a good scientist *and* a good Christian – the two systems of belief are not mutually exclusive. For a while, the evolutionists had most people thinking that, in order to do good science, one would have to give up much of the Bible – or at least be ready to explain a lot of it away. Now we are finding out that this won't be necessary; the God who made the world also wrote the Bible, and there is more agreement between the two than people thought.

Unfortunately there are some weaknesses in using *only* Scientific Creationism to understand Creation.

> **First**, its followers tend to focus primarily on science and very little, if any, on the Bible itself. To prove my point, notice the speakers at their many conferences. They are almost always trained in the sciences, with doctorates in their respective fields. Their presentations are scientific in nature. What they are trying to do is show how scientifically accurate a Creationist perspective is. But the trouble is that they can't get too technical because their audience usually consists of "laymen" assembled in church buildings! Once in a while a speaker will draw our attention to a Biblical passage, but that's *not* the general thrust of today's Creationist movement. In fact, some Creationists feel that it's counterproductive to introduce the Bible into the discussion – they want this movement to be scientific, not religious! [4]

> **Second**, much of the work of the Scientific Creationists focuses on the Flood of Genesis 6, not on Creation itself. There's a good reason for this. The Flood is what made our earth look as it does nowadays; great mountains, continents, rivers, and other geologic

---

[4] "... Most creationist books treat the subject of origins from the Biblical point of view, as well as the scientific, and, therefore, are not appropriate for instructional purposes in the public schools ... The purpose of *Scientific Creationism* is to equip the teacher to treat all of the more pertinent aspects of the subject of origins and to do this solely on a scientific basis, with no references to the Bible or to religious doctrine." Henry Morris, *Scientific Creationism*, Creation-Life Publishers, 1974; p. 3.

features are the remains of the universal Flood, and probably resemble their original created forms very little. While this is interesting, however, it doesn't contribute much to our main point: that is, is the Creation account of Genesis 1-2 accurate? But since there isn't much to go on scientifically as far as Creation itself goes, most of their research centers on the Flood instead. That's not very helpful.

Third, by limiting our study to the scientific issues of Creation, we are going to miss huge spiritual issues that are no less real. That is, in fact, what happens among Scientific Creationists; they aren't dealing with the massive realities in God's world. But since that "missing element" is the topic of *this* book, we'll reserve our comments on that until later.

The Current Situation in the Creationist-Evolutionist Debate

The past helps to explain the present, and the nineteenth century success story of scientific achievement well accounts for our society's present anti-Creationist, pro-scientific world view. The dynamics of the struggle transformed the Western world from a culture that at least respected the Biblical statement, to one that now does not even consider it. Thus, what we see in our present Creationist movement is not an effort to maintain a slowly ebbing faith, but a heroic comeback after two centuries of doubt and confusion.

Our situation right now is the culmination of many streams of development, and we are in a unique position that requires new answers. What past generations apparently did not realize, and that we *must*, was that the old methods of countering unbelief do not work with the new atheistic scientific threat. We, the descendants of those older generations, have inherited the results of their lack of spiritual skill at meeting the threat of materialism. At least one problem that we have was pointed out long ago by Hugh Miller in a prophecy that, though written in 1854, sounds embarrassingly relevant in our day:

> But ere the Churches can be prepared competently to deal with it [*i.e., the developmental hypothesis*] ... they must greatly extend their educational walks into the field of physical science. [5]

> When ... the higher philosophy of the world was metaphysical ... the battle of the Evidences was fought on metaphysical ground. But, judging from the preparations made in their colleges and halls, they do not now seem sufficiently aware ... that it is in the

---

[5] Hugh Miller, Ibid., 43.

department of physics, not of metaphysics, that the greater minds of the age are engaged.[6]

... the clergy, as a class, suffer themselves to linger far in the rear of an intelligent and accomplished laity — a full age behind the requirements of the time.[7]

Therefore, in order to catch up with *our* time, we must first take stock of the situation that we find ourselves in.

- **First**, evolutionary scientists now have the tools and information that they need to prove their point in a society that is sold on the materialistic world view. We must not underestimate their position of power in our society. They have the schools, the government grants, and the support of public opinion. They also have facts. Creationists have long lamented that, because they do not have access to adequate funding, they cannot do the research that anti-creationist colleagues are able to do.[8]

And their facts are imposing. For example, NASA launched the COBE satellite in 1989 to detect background radiation that, according to the physicists' equations, ought to be there if the Big Bang theory is true. They predicted the type and extent of the fluctuations of the radiation if the universe had, in fact, come into being billions of years ago – if their theories were true. The COBE satellite revealed that the ripples *were* there – and exactly as the math predicted they would be. What other conclusion can you draw from the evidence except that the physicists seem to know what they are talking about?

---

[6] Ibid., 44.

[7] Ibid., 45.

[8] Numbers quotes Duane Gish, an ICR staff member, as saying, "It is our dream and fervent hope that some day we will have the facilities, the personnel and the funds to carry out bench-type research right here in the Institute." Numbers, 286.

Results such as these are causing such strong defenders of the faith as, for example, R.C. Sproul and others to shy away from a public statement on how to interpret Genesis 1-3.[9] On so momentous a topic as origins, we would expect a firm position *against* the spirit of the age and in favor of Biblical cosmology – yet there is definitely a reluctance to do so among many in educated Christian circles.

The fact is that evolutionary scientists stand in an increasingly strong position, and it is getting nearly impossible to even carry on the discussion with them, let alone prove them wrong about anything. All they have to do is revert to the mathematics that prove their point, and they have lost virtually any Christian who has not had that kind of training. Who is to prove them wrong? How *can* we, when their system has been so successful in defining the principles of matter and energy?

---

[9] In a letter dated June 23, 1994, Sproul answered a supporter who requested his stand on Creationism, and commented in particular on Hugh Ross's controversial *Creation and Time* which proposes a model of theistic evolution (a work which Sproul previously publicly endorsed): "I do appreciate the contribution Dr. Ross brings to the ongoing debate regarding the earth's age. I believe the issue is more complex than some make it." In another communication from Sproul's office (Feb.24, 1995), in response to a question on his Creation position, an associate states, "As far as creation goes, Dr. Sproul evaluates the evidence from all sides. He does not deny special creation, a creation termed *ex nihilo* (out of nothing). There was only God and He brought corporeality into existence. This was done by divine fiat. Is 'yom' in Genesis 1 literal 24 hour days, or is 'yom' an extended period of time? This, for Dr. Sproul, is still under investigation. Most Christians hold to a 24 hour period, while some believe in extended periods of time. Let the debate continue." Indeed! Finally, in a review of Sproul's book *Not A Chance*, John Byl notes that though Sproul has here the perfect opportunity to steer the discussion away from science's concept of chance to the Scripture's plain teaching about Creation, he conspicuously refuses to do so. "One gets the impression that Sproul has no problem with big bang cosmology, as long as we do not attribute the big bang to chance." *Christian Renewal*, Oct.24, 1994; 16.

The two hottest areas of scientific study today that challenge the Biblical doctrine of Creation the most are in particle physics and brain research. Particle physics deals with the most elemental level of existence, the very makeup of the atoms that constitute the entire universe of matter. If scientists can correctly analyze the constituents and workings of the foundation of existence, they feel that they will have the "theory of everything", or the "final theory" which can be applied to the rest of the universe. As Weinberg claims, "whether or not the *discoveries* of elementary particle physics are useful to all other scientists, the *principles* of elementary particle physics are fundamental to all nature."[10] If, therefore, they can discover the fundamental laws that govern the building blocks of existence, they have at their disposal the ability to understand and predict everything else in existence – without the need for mysteries and gods.

Brain research is also threatening our understanding of what it means to be human. We thought Darwin's evolutionary explanation of man was dangerous enough; now the medical experts are finally probing the human brain to the degree that they know what sections constitute our personalities, our behavior, in short what makes us peculiarly human as opposed to lower life forms. Richard M. Restak, a neurologist who wrote *The Modular Brain*, explains consciousness as not a particular location of mental activity in the brain (a common model that provides Creationists with a seat for the soul), but a working together of different areas in the brain to provide an effective *simulation* of a control center. Consciousness is the effect of many "modules" of the brain, easily located and understood by themselves, working together to create a complex montage that we experience as a focused mental

---

[10] Weinberg, Ibid., 57.

awareness, rather like focusing red, blue and green light together to form white light. "Consciousness must be understood as a very special *emergent* property of the human brain."[11] If this is true, then what makes us unique is the way the physical centers of the brain *interact* with each other – not a special spiritual element, such as the soul. This seems to strike at the very root of the nature of man and his relationship to God, since the Bible says that our existence is fundamentally a spiritual reality.

- **Second**, the Church still has no statement that clearly defines the event of Creation. That is, when one claims to be a conservative Christian, that commitment does not require any definite stand on how to interpret Genesis. Basically we have handed the problem over to the scientists to solve; we are waiting to see if they will find conclusive evidence that will settle the issue about how literally we should take the Genesis account.

This seems strange when one considers that conservative Christians have developed well-defined procedures for approaching most other Biblical topics. Myth versus history, forms of literature, the genuineness of prophecies and the Gospel accounts, all these are areas in which we have definite things to say. Yet Creation is still a mysterious topic for which we have no clear guidelines.[12]

---

[11] Richard M. Restak, *The Modular Brain*, Charles Scribner's Sons, 1994, 135.

[12] A distressing example of modern Christians sounding an "uncertain note" on this subject of Creation is found in a modern edition of the Bible: "Did God create everything in six literal 24-hour days? Certainly an all-powerful God could have. Yet is that what the text really says? Is that what other evidence points to? Scientists and theologians who have examined both the Bible and assorted scientific data don't agree on how we should interpret the meaning of 'days.' As a seeker, you may wish to study this issue further. The good news is that God, the creator of the universe, wants a relationship with you even while you're trying to sort this out!" *The Journey: A Bible for Seeking God and Understanding Life*, Willow Creek

There are currently many different Creation accounts among Christians, which has been the case for at least two centuries. The theories range from a slightly theistic form of full-blown evolution, to the 4004 BC, six-day literal interpretation of Genesis – with many variations in between. This certainly points up the fact that we evidently do not see any theological necessity for a particular interpretation.

Evolutionists have noted the confusion and inadmissible fantasizing of Creationists as they struggle to maintain both a scientific respectability and a Christian testimony. Ronald L. Ecker, for example, makes it a point to document careless and inappropriate statements that Creationists have written in their works. Morris attributed lunar craters to the possibility of "continuing cosmic warfare" between spiritual powers,[13] and the disturbance between stars and planets to the warfare between good and bad angels;[14] Segraves stated that UFO pilots are "fallen angels and followers of Satan" disguised as aliens and preparing the way for the antichrist;[15] supernovas may result from the "continuing cosmic warfare between Michael and his angels and the dragon and his angels," speculates Morris.[16] But these assertions cannot be backed up in any way by the Bible, and have no scientific merit as well. They can only

---

Association, published by Zondervan Publishing Company, 1996, note on Genesis 1:31; 6.

[13] Henry M. Morris, *The Biblical Basis for Modern Science*, Baker Book House, 1984, 182-184; cited in Ronald L. Ecker, *Dictionary of Science & Creationism*, Prometheus Books, 1990, 32.

[14] Henry M. Morris, *The Remarkable Birth of Planet Earth*, Bethany House, 1978, 66-67; cited in Ecker, ibid., 149.

[15] Kelly L. Seagraves, *Sons of God Return*, Pyramid Books, 1975, cited in Ecker, ibid., 168.

[16] Morris, *The Remarkable Birth of Planet Earth*, 66-67; cited in Ecker, ibid., 188.

cause damage to the Creationist cause. It is embarrassing to find them so carefully and publicly catalogued by an evolutionist.

What we need is a solid, demonstrable statement on Creation of a nature that can be supported consistently from the Bible. It is not threatening to our position that evolutionists do not accept the testimony of the Bible, because a key point in our theology is that they are *obligated* to accept it, and will eventually be sentenced by God for not accepting it. It is important to state our position clearly from what we have been given, and let God determine the outcome.

- **Third**, the Church has left scientists out on the front line of battle, bearing the burden of defending the truth of the Genesis account. For example, the Institute For Creation Research makes a point of admitting only trained scientists to its board. Creationist speakers who make the circuit among churches display their scientific degrees and expertise; their approach is almost always a scientific presentation of the Creationist's case against evolution.[17] Books on Creationism focus predominantly on the scientific issues, almost never on the theological issues involved in Creation.

There is something terribly unhealthy about this strategy. It points out graphically that the Church has no

---

[17] Case in point: in an advertisement for an upcoming Creation conference, the Origin Science Association, which purports to believe that "it is through Scripture that we should gain understanding of the world in which we live, including its origins", lists the following session titles: "How Mt. Saint Helens has Challenged Traditional Geologic Teaching", "The impact of a new formulation of design theory on the study of biology", "Catastrotectonics: A Summary of a new Flood model", "What explains the fossil record better, conventional or creation geology?", "Exciting research problems in creation geology and paleontology". The speakers had academic training in paleontology and biology. Nowhere on the program was there listed any specific input from the Bible or theology, nor from persons specially qualified in such areas.

confident spokesmen available to tackle the Biblical data. It reveals that Christians are allowing the anti-Creationist scientists to select the field of battle – limiting the discussion to interpretation of physical evidence instead of spiritual realities. It says, in clear terms, that science is the arbiter of the truth of God's works, not the Bible! And scientists, whether Christian or pagan, are the "high priests" of truth who alone have the ability to "know the mind of God" on this issue of Creation. What layman can contribute anything of value in a discussion that is beyond his training or abilities?

In leaving the issue for scientific experts to resolve, we will inevitably have results that compromise our Christian world view. For example, D. Russell Humphreys, in his book *Starlight and Time*, claims that there is a relativistic answer for the puzzle about light appearing to come from billions of light years away in a universe that is actually only a few thousand years old.[18] In other words, God "had" to create the universe according to accepted principles of relativity – which essentially makes Einstein the interpreter of God's Word. As if relativity principles antedated Creation! Apparently Humphreys puts no stock in the efficacy of God's spoken Word to perform miracles out of nothing.

Whatever the answer of origins is, it must be information accessible to any and all of God's people – whether they have been trained scientifically or not. If the scientists are right and the answer can only be understood by means of specialized scientific disciplines, then it is no use continuing to probe for the Bible's explanation. But if the Bible has the answer, then it is not a matter for scientists alone to elucidate – it will require spiritual skills and insights instead.

---

[18] D. Russell Humphreys, "Creation Week: A Possible Scenario", *Starlight and Time*, Master Books, 1994, 31-38.

- **Fourth**, modern atheistic science is beginning to turn back to old pagan religions. It seems ironic that a discipline that boasts of being completely materialistic would seriously dabble in religion of any sort. But modern physicists have been discovering an affinity for the ancient Eastern religions; it seems that the two streams of thought present remarkably similar world views.

First the religious side. The similarities between Eastern religions and the procedures of modern science, its findings, and its developing world view due to relativity and quantum mechanics has been repeatedly pointed out by the practitioners of those religions:

> In its competition with other world religions such as Christianity and Islam for the attention of the modern world, Buddhism claims that it deserves special consideration because its approach and teachings are compatible with those of modern science. A number of Buddhist leaders have repeatedly stressed that Buddhism is scientific because it has no notion of an absolute deity, an immortal soul, or a first cause, and because all its teachings are based on universal laws. In its methodology, Buddhism is said to be experimental in that the Buddha called upon his followers not to accept his teachings merely because he taught them, but that they should first test them to see if they were efficacious. Moreover, the Buddhist apologists also claim that such Buddhist teachings as the doctrine of non-self, universal flux, and the cyclic theory of evolution are all scientific in nature, and that therefore Buddhism is indeed a religion suitable for modern humanity.[19]

---

[19] *Abingdon Dictionary Of Living Religions*, Keith Crim, Gen.ed.; Article on "Buddhism," K.K.S.Chen, Nashville: Abingdon, 1981, p.136.

The scientists are starting to see the world in the same way, though few of them would admit to religious affinities. There is a growing consensus among scientists that the universe resembles a living thing, through which the principle of evolution rules from top down. John Gribbin plainly states that "I believe that the Universe – like all the universes – is literally alive."[20] And this statement comes from a trained astrophysicist! The entire universe, in his belief, is characterized by principles that we are already familiar with in the biological world; and the fact that organic life arose from such a universe was a natural result – as much as expecting a particular kind of young from the same kind of parent. Kafatos and Nadeau go one step further. They see, in the quantum theory, the scalar nature of consciousness itself. Because quantum theory states that an event is only real when it is observed, the authors extrapolate that idea to the entire universe: the existence of everything depends on itself.

> What we are suggesting is that if complementary relations [*i.e., the quantum concept of **observed phenomena being the only reality***] are enfolded into the life of the universe throughout all scales, and become recognizable in mathematical physics as we approach the event horizon between part and whole, it could well be that complementarity will also be useful in comprehending relations on the largest of scales and understanding the emergence of patterns at all levels characteristic of our universe.[21]

---

[20] John Gribbin, *In The Beginning: After COBE and Before the Big Bang*, Little, Brown and Company, 1993, 252.

[21] Menas Kafatos and Robert Nadeau, *The Conscious Universe: Part and Whole in Modern Physical Theory*, Springer-Verlag, 1990, 168-169.

In other words, since quantum mechanics requires an observer, and since scientists do not want to invoke God as the supreme Observer of his universe, they therefore make the universe conscious of itself – which is what makes existence *per se* possible across the universe. This compares remarkably well to the Eastern religions' concept of the all-pervading Mind in which every part of existence shares the cosmic consciousness.

Even more bizarre theories are finding their way into scientific circles. In a recent work entitled *Beyond the Big Bang: Ancient Myth and the Science of Continuous Creation*, the author Paul A. LaViolette (a scientist involved in research on cosmic dust) claims to have found not only the foundations of modern quantum and relativity theories in the religions of ancient civilizations, but also that modern scientists are actually somewhat incorrect in their theories – and the ancient mystics hold the necessary corrections that LaViolette claims to have discovered in their writings. He uncovers the supposedly scientific nature of Egyptian mysteries, the Tarot cards, astrology, and the Atlantis myths, and attempts to demonstrate the unity of the ancient mind in its understanding of the workings of the universe, putting forth concepts that modern scientists should take seriously.[22]

The reason we point out the trend in modern science to call up the spirits of old religions is that *they* accuse Christians of introducing the subject of God into *our* science. But what is fair for one is fair for the other.

---

[22] Paul A. LaViolette, *Beyond the Big Bang: Ancient Myth and the Science of Continuous Creation*, Park Street Press, 1995.

A New Method For Understanding Creation

Perhaps now you can see that we have a critical problem on our hands. Science is getting more sophisticated and harder to challenge. Christians are divided about how to respond to the issue of Creation. Some of today's top defenders of the faith, in fact, are defecting to the other side – they have essentially given in to science's bold claims and they no longer believe in the Bible's account.

What is needed is a new way of approaching this problem. Experts in the art of thinking often recommend that, when you are stuck on a problem, taking a fresh start with new ideas will often break the deadlock. In this matter of Creation, my suggestion is that we start using a new source of facts that is certain to shed light on the subject – the **Bible**.

That may sound strange, but unfortunately it's a fact that almost nobody has been using the Bible as resource material in the Creation debate. I know that many writers and speakers quote Bible passages in their presentations, but they don't seem to know what to do with these passages. It's like a child who picks up a loaded gun without knowing how to use it, and he doesn't realize the power in his hands. We will look later at what power there is in the teachings of the Bible, and then we will see that these ideas are little appreciated in our day even, it seems, among Creationists.

Something is wrong

Christians have ignored the Bible's testimony for too long in the Creation debate. Here are some proofs that we are terribly negligent in this area.

- *Today's Creationism isn't convincing very many people.* I'm sure that the Creationists would like to think that they're making headway, but unfortunately there are serious charges being made against them. Notice that the majority of people in our country who claim to be Christians still don't believe in a literal interpretation of Genesis 1-2. Even many of those who are ultra-conservative in how they read the rest of the Bible are skeptics when it comes to Creation. [23] Scientists have done too good a job of convincing people that the Bible is scientifically illiterate and naïve when it comes to science.

What are the charges that evolutionists make against Creationists? **First**, that they aren't doing good science. Science consists of research, and it takes a lot of money to do that research. The entire community of scientists benefits from the research that is done. But Creationists suffer greatly from a lack of funds as well as public support, which means that their work happens more in the library than in the laboratory – that is, they can do little experimental research. As long as that's true, they probably won't be taken very seriously by the rest of the scientific community. Furthermore, most of their time is spent defending a theory for which there can be no scientific evidence – that God made the world. That doesn't help their respectability in research circles.

---

[23] Ronald Numbers, a recent chronicler of the history of Creationism, notes that "most Christians remained untouched by the revival [*that is, of modern Creationism defined and developed by the Institute For Creation Research and related groups and their publications*] and even millions of evangelicals, from Billy Graham to Jimmy Lee Swaggart ... continued to subscribe to old-earth creationism." Ronald L. Numbers, *The Creationists: The Evolution of Scientific Creationism*, Alfred A. Knopf, Inc., 1992, 299. Recently even one of the "defenders of the faith" of such stature as R.C. Sproul has come out publicly supporting the idea of "Big Bang" cosmology.

Second, that they aren't being honest with their roots. Creationists are making a huge assumption right from the start – that God created the world exactly as Genesis says – and then trying to prove that assumption through science. But the primary reason that Creationists believe that God made the world is because of what the Bible says. That's a religious source, not a scientific one. Everyone knows that. Many Creationists, however, refuse to admit that their scientific work is based on their religious convictions because they're afraid to: once you do that, the atheists easily reject it *because* it's religion, not science. [24]

Third, that they don't have the experts on their side. It appears that Creationists have a hard time finding big-name scientists to support their ideas. They especially lack support in the area of geology, which is an embarrassing thing because it's in geology that they have the most startling things to say to the world. But it's not true that they don't have *any* scientific experts; the reason people align themselves with Creationism isn't for scientific reasons, but because they take God's Word seriously – because this isn't mainly a scientific issue. Some good scientists are still willing to do that.

---

[24] For example, when the legality of forcing Arkansas public school teachers to teach Creationism in the schools came before the State Supreme Court, the Court ruled against the Creationists because their argument was obviously based on religious principles, not just scientific data. This statement was in their ruling:

> The evidence establishes that the definition of "creation science" contained in 4(a) has as its unmentioned reference the first 11 chapters of the Book of Genesis. Among many creation epics in human history, the account of sudden creation from nothing, or *creatio ex nihilo*, and subsequent destruction of the world by flood is unique to Genesis. The concepts of 4(a) are the literal Fundamentalists' view of Genesis. Section 4(a) is unquestionably a statement of religion, with the exception of 4(a)(2) which is a negative thrust aimed at what the creationists understand to be the theory of evolution.

Fourth, that they spend most of their time impressing churchgoers instead of other scientists. This *is* a serious charge. In other words, much of their efforts go into church seminars on Creation, where the average person in the audience has little scientific training. As scientists, however, they have accomplished very little if they only manage to convince those who have *no* training in science. If they really mean to prove that a Christian can do better science than an atheist in God's world, then they need to make that point with other scientists. People who know almost nothing about science aren't good judges of the scientific correctness of Creationists. Besides, in order to impress the non-scientific community, Creation scientists have to strip away the hard-core science that would prove their point in order to make it understandable – so they really don't prove anything as a result.

Fifth, that they hold to wildly different theories and sometimes even absurd theories. It ought not to be, but out of zeal for the cause, Creationists too often put forth theories that are neither scientifically correct nor Biblically correct. For example, some have stated that angels may be responsible for various kinds of astronomical events in the universe. Now there is nothing in the Bible that says that, and such a statement will only make the scientific community roll its eyes. If they are going to do science, let the Creationists do *good* science – not medieval superstitions for which there is no evidence.

Of course none of these charges are serious enough to disprove Creationism. Creationists do need to take them seriously, however, and tighten up loose ends so that the charges will no longer have any foundation. But it's still true that their present methods of trying to prove the Bible's account seem to be making little impression not only in the general public but also within the church at

A New Method For Understanding Creation

large. We need to rethink our strategy and examine where we are going wrong.

- ***There are huge categories of reality that nobody is talking about.*** It's always a red flag to me when nobody is talking about the really important things in life. For example, just to give you a preview, the Bible states emphatically that the world was made by command. That one theme opens us up to a wide range of subjects that describe the real world – including kingdom, morality, the static nature of Creation, Judgment Day, and so on. Yet neither Creationists nor evolutionists even raise the issue. Command is part of the fabric of the universe, but nobody seems to see the importance of it. The reason for this fatal omission is that when you insist on looking at everything through the microscope instead of the Bible, of course you won't see such things as command and miracle and the other great categories of Creation.

This means, then, that whatever world view that scientists give us is going to be seriously distorted, if not actually misleading. Keep in mind that they seem to be the high priests of our modern society; everyone is depending on science to analyze the world and tell us how to take advantage of it for our pleasure and profit. Yet the lessons that we learn at the feet of scientists are materialistic – they talk about what we can see and touch with our five senses, that's all.

This isn't realistic at all. Everyone knows that a well-balanced, functioning society requires much more than bare materialism. People need a sense of value and worth. We also need justice, because too many people want their half out of the middle, so to speak, and they don't mind cheating or even murdering their neighbors to get it. We need some way of dealing with our consciences. We also want to know about God, because we need to have a successful relationship with our Maker – one in which we are fulfilling our responsibilities toward him and have some hope for the future.

This means that scientists need to step aside and let those experts lead our society who have answers to these kinds of problems. In fact, the Church does have people with these kinds of answers. But in a society that is so heavily dominated by science, their voices are hardly heard and almost never heeded. Thus our problems will remain unsolved; we have the wrong "experts" working on them.

- ***Creationists and evolutionists are contradicting the Bible.*** Perhaps the strongest proof that evolutionists are wrong is that the answers they come up with are in flat contradiction to the Bible. A true Christian will never accept some of their statements, even though he may not understand *why* they are wrong, simply because they are flying in the face of a higher authority. Our faith in a God who knows what he is doing is stronger than our faith in fallible man, who always has to change his theories to fit the obvious facts, if not change the facts to fit his theories!

But Creationists also contradict the Bible at times, which means that Christians need to be more careful about what they are doing. In their zeal to support the Bible's claim about origins, they mustn't sacrifice their precious Biblical doctrines in order to have a science that the world will be more willing to accept. For example, I don't believe that Creationists are doing justice to the doctrine of miracles; they are afraid that the world will reject the idea, and flatly refuse to accept the kind of science that allows miracles whenever God wants to do them. In one instance, many Creationists, in order to dull the effect of the tremendous miracle involved in the

A New Method For Understanding Creation

Flood, claim that the event occurred because of a passing asteroid, or some other natural event. They just can't bring themselves to say what the text says – that God simply worked a miracle and unleashed a tremendous amount of water without depending on natural causes!

The reason for believing in the God of the Bible is that he can do what no other god can do. Creation scientists need to learn the lesson of letting the Bible speak for itself instead of trying to make it more scientifically acceptable. The astonishing feats that God did, that the Bible records, is the basis of our faith in him. We will find that those amazing works are far more interesting and valuable to us than anything that science can offer us.

One reason that scientists often carelessly contradict the Bible is that they are, at the moment, regarded as the interpreters of all truth in our society – both in the Christian camp and elsewhere. Everyone looks to them for the truth, and nobody dares question their research and accumulated wisdom. But as we have already seen, we need a different kind of leadership if we are going to solve the more important issues of life. Science can't give us justice or meaning in life. If those who know God and are familiar with his ways and works were once again held in esteem in our society, then the scientists themselves would be more careful to do their work in light of the truth of the Bible, instead of arrogantly doing away with the Bible or contradicting its truth.

- ***The argument from design is not enough.*** We have looked at the struggle between evolutionary science and Creationism, and noted some of the strengths and weaknesses of both. In particular, we have seen the primary methodology of the Creationists – that is, using the argument from design. In the present century, this argument has taken the form of extensive scientific work done, for example, by Morris and others at the Institute for Creation Research.

There is nothing wrong with the argument from design. It is, and always has been, a powerful argument for the cause of Creationism. Its great strengths are, first, that it allows us to avoid the absurdities that arise from purely naturalistic explanations of the world (e.g., evolution), and second, it very naturally leads us to the Bible's plain statement that the infinitely wise and powerful God as described in the Bible was responsible for what is so plain to see in the design and structure of the world. And the Creationists are doing valuable work in this area, not only exposing the fallacies in the evolutionary arguments, but constructing a new way of doing science that acknowledges the role of the Creator who interacts with his world at all levels.

However, the root problem with the scientific approach is that the event of Creation was comprised of much more than merely physical elements and forces. In the debate on Creation, both evolutionists and Creationists have narrowed their study primarily to scientific investigation, thereby hoping to unravel this complex event. That strategy is both helpful and misleading. Helpful, because it trains the minds of the experts on the physical evidences of Creation and helps us (generally) to better utilize the scientific principles of the world for our material benefit. Misleading, because it imposes unnecessary blinders on man's mind as he examines God's works, and prevents him from seeing fundamental aspects of Creation that science cannot uncover but are, nevertheless, very real.

Adequate in some respects, natural theology has severe limitations that become obvious when it is used as the sole interpreter of the Creation event. While the virtuosi would be amazed at the infinite wisdom and power of a Creator who could create such variety and complexity that they saw in the world, there were other truths about God, and his relationship to the world, that they could not see without the special revelation of the Bible. For instance, a scientist cannot detect, through his instruments, that the objects under his inspection were made by command – a fundamental concept that explains a great deal about how and why the world works the way it does, and the reason behind the role that God assumes toward his creation. There are a great many more foundation stones of our world that cannot be seen or understood in any sense by the use of natural theology – even by a sanctified use of science.[25]

In addition, the argument from design has lost its cutting edge with modern scientists. Before this century, any scientist who denied that God was the maker of the universe could be successfully backed to the wall with the demand to explain the complexity and obvious functionality built into the world; he could not, because

---

[25] Furthermore, even the argument from design has come under attack from an unexpected direction. Kitcher notes that the present generation of Creationists are not utilizing the idea nearly as strenuously and confidently as their eighteenth and nineteenth century counterparts did. "Invocation of the word 'design,' or the passing reference to the satisfaction of 'need,' explains nothing. The needs are not given in advance of the design of structures to accommodate them, but are themselves encompassed in the design. Nor do we achieve any understanding of the adaptations and relationships of organisms until we see, at least in outline, what the Grand Plan of Creation might have been ... Leibnitz developed the theme with a striking analogy. Any world can be conceived as regular ('designed') just as any array of points can be joined by a curve with some algebraic formula.

"Why are contemporary Creationists silent about the Design? Because things did not go so well for their predecessors who tried to show how each kind of organism had been separately created with a special design. They found it hard to reconcile the observed features of some organisms with the attributes of the Creator. Contemporary Creationists have learned from these heroic – but fruitless – efforts." Philip Kitcher, *Abusing Science: The Case Against Creationism*, MIT Press, 1982; 138.

his science did not provide him with the models or principles that could successfully explain such design. In this century, however, the advances of science have provided the scientist with just that – the ability to explain, if not by demonstrable occurrences in nature, then at least in theory, the arising of the design. If we challenge them now with the design argument, all they have to do is pull out their calculators and show us that design is inherent in the system, it is required for the system to exist – in other words, that the thing fell together, in this design, by sheer determinacy, which they can predict and demonstrate with their math. They are still wrong, but now they have the ability to turn the old argument around on us. This is what makes our present situation so unique in history. The argument from design now only impresses those who already accept its necessary premise that there is a God.

The limitations of natural theology become apparent when Creationists, who mistakenly rely on only that method, fail to adequately address the claims and advances of evolutionary science. For example, the problem of morality is repeatedly raised by Creationists and scoffed at by the evolutionists. Christians know that the theory of evolution in some way helps lay the foundation for godlessness and immorality, but they do not know how to present their argument in a convincing way. Evolutionists, on the other hand, easily dismiss this claim with scorn, without having to present hard evidence to disprove it (when in fact the evidence clearly supports the Creationists' claim), because both evolutionists and Creationists capriciously limit themselves to the scientific playing field.[26]

---

[26] For example, Gallant quotes from a statement by the Creation-Science Research Center (San Diego, California) to the effect that their research proved that evolution "fostered the moral decay of spiritual values, which contributes to the destruction of mental health and ... [the prevalence of] divorce, abortion, and rampant venereal diseases." He later passes off this possibility with a careless understatement of the

What we want to do at this point is set aside natural theology for now, along with the attendant helps that science can offer, and examine new concepts that more fully develop the theme of Creation. Only by looking at this additional information will we get a complete, usable picture of the actual makeup of the universe and its peculiar standing before its Creator.

An assumption

Before we start looking at the Bible's explanation of Creation, however, we have to make an assumption. Now before someone raises an objection about making assumptions, may I point out that everyone makes assumptions! It's just that not everybody is honest about it. Even "objective" scientists make assumptions before they start work every day. For example, scientists assume that they can discover all the pertinent truth about an object by using physical instruments, their physical senses, and the scientific method. The only reason they assume that is because they *want* to! But as someone pointed out,[27] the decision that they made isn't necessarily accurate or useful – nor is it called for, in light of what the world really is. This approach may well be putting blinders on so that one *can't* see the whole truth.

Our assumption here is this: there is more involved in the universe than science, with its limited instruments and methods, can ever show us. We all know that, of course, but many people are afraid to say so out of fear that scientists will attack them with demands that they prove that assumption *scientifically*. But we can't prove it scientifically; that's the whole point. There are some things that science can't help us understand. The thing that many don't recognize,

---

facts: "... the wave of disenchantment with the 'godless materialism of science,' and what many regarded as its misuses *[!]*, that swept into the 1970s and is still with us." Roy Gallant, "To Hell with Evolution," *Science and Creationism*, ibid., p. 283, 305.

[27] See Phillip Johnson's book, (*Reason in the Balance*, Intervarsity Press, 1995) which states that modern society's decision to enforce naturalism in professional circles wasn't based on fact but sheer caprice.

of course, is that there are more ways of knowing the truth than by way of the scientific method – and those ways will give us hard facts that are just as true and reliable as science gives us. (See the **Appendix** for five *other* ways to determine what is truth.)

You probably realize that our assumption is opening the door to the spiritual world. That's what we're trying to say here: that beyond the reach of telescope and microscope are huge spiritual realities like God, the soul, Heaven and Hell, morals and ethics, reward and punishment, wickedness and righteousness, Kingdom and rebellion, glory and Judgment Day. Science will never see these things; it can't, since it's using the wrong instruments to look for them. Scientists operate by rules that purposely shield them from these realities, and that actually lead them away from the spiritual world. If ever we are to know the truth about God and his works, we must lay aside those tools that were never meant to do the job and pick up new ones.

But let's not waste our time looking in the wrong places – like philosophy and psychology and other disciplines that claim to understand the meaning of the universe. The Bible has this truth that we need to know. It claims to be the *revelation* of God and his works – which means that it reveals the true God to us, and shows us *how* he does things and *why* he does them. There are many reasons we have for accepting its claim, not the least of which is that we have found that it's the only explanation that fits all the facts of life perfectly!

What we will find in this revelation is that Creation was mainly a *spiritual* event, so much so that it was the perfect introduction to the great spiritual works that fill the rest of the Bible. We will see that subjects like God's Kingdom, the process of salvation and redemption, prophecy, the Spirit of God, and Judgment Day are the walls and framework of God's "house" that rest firmly on Creation and depend on it heavily. What God did at the beginning, in other words, he *kept* on doing through history, and will *continue* to do it to the end of time. It's all one house.

And since it was a spiritual event, we will see spiritual elements in the story – that is, if we take off our blinders and put on the special glasses that God gives us to wear. Physical eyes weren't made to see spiritual realities, so it's no wonder that people don't usually see what's really going on in Genesis 1-2. God knows that, of course, and he has graciously provided the means of seeing spiritual truth. Unbelievers may claim that this is blind faith – that we mustn't be so naïve as to believe something that we can't see or know through physical senses. But again, the proof is in the pudding: what we will see in the Creation passage is, in fact, the perfect explanation for the world we live in. The Bible fills in the gaping holes that science can't explain for us with satisfying answers that work.

What we want to do in this book, then, is build up a more complete picture of God's universe. So far, scientists have only drawn a wall or two of God's house and a window here and there, so to speak. But with the Bible we are going to see much more: the foundation, the entire framework, the walls and roof, and the yard around it. There is no sense in limiting ourselves to bits and pieces of the picture – the things that science gives us – when the entire answer is lying right here before us in the Word.

There are certain simple doctrines in the Bible that, to a Christian, are of supreme importance. If these aren't true, then we have nothing to put our hope in. We know these doctrines well, because they are everywhere in the Bible. All the things that God did in history, in both the Old and New Testaments, depend on these doctrines. The Lord Jesus Christ taught them and used them in his ministry. The Apostles built the Church of Christ upon them.

What we haven't done, however, is take these simple doctrines back to the Creation account in Genesis. If God has always done things in a certain way, can't we assume that he did things in the *same* way at the beginning of the world? If God is unchanging, shouldn't we see those same doctrines in Genesis that we see in the rest of the Bible? We can. And those doctrines will clearly explain what happened at Creation in a way that no scientific theory has ever done.

What we will discover is that the Bible's explanation is a much better way of describing the universe than anything that man has come up with so far. With man there are different ways of looking at things, and each way is useful to him in only a limited sense. For example, you've probably heard the story of three blind men who met an elephant and tried to describe what they learned about it: one described it as a long, thick trunk; another as a massive leg; and the third as a narrow tail. None of them knew what the whole animal was like, so each was actually wrong in a way. But when God looks at something, he sees it as a *whole*, the way it really is – he isn't limited by our shortsightedness. When he explains Creation to us, it's the best explanation that can possibly be given; nothing can improve on it, and nothing can add to it in any way. There is no better way of describing the Creation event than the Bible's account of it – the *entire* Bible.

Part Two:

The Bible's Explanation of Creation

The Method of Creation – Miracle

Miracle is at the heart of the Creation account. If we take Genesis 1-2 at its simplest level, just as it reads, God would have had to make the world through a series of miracles in order to fit the description we have there.

Of course the evolutionists deny that a miracle ever happened. Their scientific explanation of the beginning of the universe has nothing to do with miracles. Atheists despise the very idea of miracles. Unfortunately, the Theistic Evolutionists – those who believe that God made the world through evolution – also despise miracles, although they're a bit more dishonest about their beliefs. They will admit that God *could* have created the universe through miracles, since he's certainly powerful enough to do that; but they claim that he chose to work through natural means instead, not through miracles.

The real problem here is that many people don't understand the importance of miracles *throughout the Bible*, not just in the Creation account. Miracles are a foundation stone in God's Kingdom; the Church of Christ, for example, would never exist if it weren't for miracles. God prefers to use miracles whenever there is important work to do – mainly because there isn't anybody else or anything else in this world that can meet the needs of his people satisfactorily.

Our problem, in these modern times, is that science has crippled us to the point that we can't accept the idea of miracles at all. We know too much. On the one hand, science has done us a great service: what people of past ages considered miraculous, we know better now that such "miracles" are really natural events. For example, many cultures used to think that gods were behind the tremendous forces of nature; now we know the explanation behind lightning and hail and hurricanes – there are no gods involved. But there's such a thing as going too far. There have been genuine miracles in the past which can't be explained in any way, not even by the most sophisticated scientific theories. The miracles of the Bible are good examples. If we let scientists talk us out of them, we won't have any God to believe in!

What we want to do here, then, is find out what miracles really are, and how important they are to the whole scope of God's works – recorded all through the Bible. Then we should be able to go back to Creation and see why God created the world through miracle – because there is no other way that our God *would* have done it to make the kind of world we live in.

What is a miracle?

There is so much confusion about what a true miracle is that I have a feeling that's the reason behind people not taking them seriously in the Bible. So, we must be very careful to define what a miracle is:

A miracle is God doing something by his own hand, apart from natural means.

In other words, in order to achieve his goal, he purposely *avoids* the normal processes that we would have to use if we were trying to reach those same goals. He goes around the physical laws and gets what he wants out of nothing and without going through intermediate steps. He *does not* rely on anything in this world when he's doing his work of creation.

An example will show the difference between his miracles and our work. When we want bread, we know that there are certain steps that we must go through to get it: plow the ground, sow the seed, kill the weeds and insects, harvest the grain, grind the grain and make the bread, and distribute it through the food service channels so that people can buy it at the store. We can't leave out any of the steps. We are bound by our limitations: because we are physical creatures, we *must* obey the world's physical laws if we want to get someplace in life.

When God makes bread, however, he just skips all the intermediate steps. He isn't bound by physical laws as we are. He simply reaches out and creates it out of nothing – and in a way that defies the natural order of things. For example, he sent down manna on the Israelites in the desert. (Exodus 16) There was nothing in the world that could explain such an event: in fact, the method that he used was, and still is, unknown to man! To this day nobody knows how he did such a thing.

We can't do what God did there in the desert, nor can we understand *how* he did it. In order to understand something and duplicate it, we need to see the steps between the initial idea and the finished result. Scientists like a full description, from beginning to end, of how a process happened. But God skips all the steps in between when he works a miracle; there are no instructions that we can follow.

Jesus did the same thing when he fed the multitudes with a few fish and loaves of bread. (Matthew 14:13-21; 15:32-38) Although he started with something small, he fed thousands with it; he obviously didn't rely on any principle or power of the physical world in order to perform the miracle. It was a miraculous feat that we can't duplicate ourselves, despite all our scientific knowledge.

If you study God's miracles that the Bible records, you will notice that every one of them are like this. God skips the steps between the beginning and the end. When he wants something, he simply makes it out of nothing, with his bare hand, without using anything in this world. He reaches out of Heaven and touches the earth, making something where there used to be nothing. We will see the vital importance of this point below.

Of course science can't understand such a thing as a miracle. Science deals with laws, with cause and effect, with processes and step-by-step procedures. Science is at a complete loss to explain an event that just skips the intermediate steps. It can't understand a process that ignores natural laws and has no need for raw materials. Science can do nothing to help us understand the works of God. It's simply out of its depth here, and always will be.

We can explain how *we* do what we do; but God does things that can't be explained or understood. Even more: even if God described to us how he did it, we wouldn't understand him. We could never do it ourselves because it takes the mind and power of the Creator (who needs nothing to make something) and we just don't work like that. While God omits the steps that we need to accomplish our goals, our science, on the other hand, *depends* on those steps. And because we must go through the steps, we require resources – energy, raw materials, physical laws, chemical reactions – to accomplish our goals. God, on the other hand, requires nothing to accomplish his goals.

The miracles that God did stagger the imagination. They were not sleights-of-hand that could eventually be understood and explained (not even by sophisticated twentieth century science!) but monumental "violations" of natural law that can't be explained in any way. God raised the dead, split apart rivers and seas, brought the walls of a city down in sudden collapse at a trumpet blast, flooded the entire earth, rained down fire and destruction from the sky, turned water into wine, gave people the ability to walk on water, healed lepers instantly with a word – the list goes on and on.

The events that are recorded in the Bible were the genuine article. They were actual miracles that God really did – there is no question he did them, because he provided witnesses to testified to the fact. The Bible isn't talking about superstitions here, or old wives' tales, or fables. These aren't ignorant savages who made claims about natural events which our modern science is able to explain away with naturalistic concepts. We ourselves know that those events, if they actually happened as recorded, would have to have been genuine miracles and did not rely in any way on normal scientific processes.

If we were there, for instance, when Peter stepped out on the water (Matthew 14:29), the thing would have astonished us as well. We would no doubt have started looking for something under the waves that would be holding Peter up! But the disciples were no fools; they knew that they were witnessing the impossible. Another example: there was no mistaking, for instance, the act of turning water into wine (John 2:1-11) *in the way Jesus did it*: any person from any age in history, no matter what their level of scientific expertise, has to admit that such an act was a miracle.

What miracles are not

The reason we were so careful to define miracles the way we did is that people often have a wrong idea of what a miracle is. And if we get this wrong, we are going to believe things about God himself that aren't right.

Many people think that God works under the same system of laws that we do. Since he made the universe to work a certain way, he would therefore use his own laws to do what he wanted in the world. For example, many scientists who admit to a belief in God also believe that he made the universe out of the cosmic "soup" at the Big Bang, using the familiar laws of physics. The gradual progress from the "Big Bang" to the present universe can all be easily explained, because God used principles that we are already familiar with. That is, there are no such things as miracles. In fact, any "miracle" that may happen is only an event that impressed someone who is scientifically illiterate. Science, in their view, is the only way to understand the universe.

Another view, however, is that God does do miracles – impossible-looking ones – but never something that is contrary to natural law. For instance, he would take a process and speed it up so fast that it *looks* like a miracle to us, though really there's nothing impossible about it. For example, when Jesus turned water into wine, he did what happens all the time in our natural world – he only speeded up the process a good bit.

Or (and this is a popular way that people often use to explain how God works) what God does looks impossible but really he used a law that we haven't yet discovered through science. In a few centuries we ourselves will probably learn about it and then *we* will be able to do it too. In other words, God uses laws that we don't know about yet, but they are still natural laws in the universe.

These theories sound plausible enough, but actually there are two huge problems about them: **first**, the reason people believe these things about miracles is that they can't accept anything that is contrary to natural laws. They believe in scientific laws so much that they feel that God himself must obey them. They feel that the human mind must be able to understand *everything* that happens in the universe; if not now, then at least when they get to Heaven and have the chance to question God about his methods. No impossibilities, please!

What they fail to realize, however, is that there is a great deal of difference in what the Creator can know and what a creature can know. Though we were made in God's image, we aren't therefore God! The Bible says that there is only one God; he alone is full of glory, he alone knows the end from the beginning, he alone made the heavens and the earth. Our proper response is to worship this awesome God – not to claim our equality with him in any way.

What this means is that we will never see the Creation as God sees it. It all belongs to him in a special way; it lies under his hand as his subject, a physical world resting in his spiritual hand, ready for whatever he wants to do with it. His command creates and molds and subjugates it; he judges its structure and purpose; the Spirit opens the lines of communication between God and the world. To us, however, the universe will never be more than matter and energy: already formed, operating by law, changeable and useable only if we follow those laws.

God works with his world in a *different way* than we work with it:

> "For my thoughts are not your thoughts,
>   neither are your ways my ways,
>   declares the LORD.
> As the heavens are higher than the earth,
>   so are my ways higher than your ways
>   and my thoughts than your thoughts.
>   (Isaiah 55:8-9)

Second, their explanation of miracles doesn't fit the facts. Let's take the miracle of Jesus changing water into wine. Though that process *does* happen every day in our world, it takes the natural world months to accomplish it – the rain making the vine grow, which bears fruit, which man then crushes and ferments into wine. But how did Jesus do it? With a word. That's all. One minute it was water, the next it was wine. Nothing touched it, it happened instantly, there was no fermenting process – what was chemically simple water became, in an instant, a completely different chemical substance. We have witnesses who testified to this impossible feat. There was no way to explain that event in any natural terms. Nor will there ever be.

Therefore, it's important how we define miracles. We don't want to take away from their impossible nature in order to leave science an open door. Many think that if miracles are just speeded-up natural laws, or yet-undiscovered laws, then nothing impossible has ever happened in the universe. And if *that's* true, then the Genesis account *isn't* true: science will eventually be able to explain to us what really happened at Creation. But if a miracle (which we know has happened many times in history, from eyewitness accounts) is the direct touch of God's hand, bypassing nature, then Creation couldn't have been a natural event.

Miracles are impossible

Of course miracles are impossible. People stumble over them in the Bible, claiming that "such things don't happen in our world." Since they can't imagine *how* a miracle could occur – that is, how one could get from water to wine, for example, without doing anything to it at all – they therefore claim that such a thing didn't happen.

But that's why we were careful to define miracles as we did. Of course we don't understand it – we need to use means, and God doesn't. Remember, a miracle is when God does something directly, *apart* from natural means. When we see it this way, it makes perfect sense that we will never understand how a miracle occurs. But they happened nevertheless; there were witnesses. Therefore, God did something extraordinary which we need to take seriously.

Impossibility is a key feature to the works of God. When he reached down and touched the earth through miracle, the impossible always happened. It got to be so typical of how he worked on earth that people identified him with the impossible: "With man this is impossible, but with God all things are possible." (Matthew 19:26) "For nothing is impossible with God." (Luke 1:37) This was for a reason, of course: people know that there are certain things that can't happen unless God, the miracle worker, overrules natural events and does it himself. And if their hearts are set on the things of God's world, they hope in and depend on this miracle-working God to do what they can't do.

Miracles are a stumbling stone for unbelievers; they can't accept the fact of miracles, and they certainly don't want God interfering in their lives in such an unpredictable and uncomfortable way. Their gods work through nature, through scientific means – like Baal in the Old Testament who sent spring rains when his worshippers sacrificed something to put him in the mood (a natural event which would have happened *without* the sacrifice, I might add!)

But instead of stumbling over the impossibility of God's work, the believer is assured, by that very characteristic, that he is dealing with the true God. It's a sign that Jehovah is working; anything short of a miracle would never meet our needs. Baal can't begin to help us with our real problems. For example, Jesus proved that he was both Creator and Redeemer by the miracles he performed:

> When John heard in prison what Christ was doing, he sent his disciples to ask him, "Are you the one who was to come, or should we expect someone else?" Jesus replied, "Go back and report to John what you hear and see: The blind receive sight, the lame walk, those who have leprosy are cured, the deaf hear, the dead are raised, and the good news is preached to the poor. Blessed is the man who does not fall away on account of me." (Matthew 11:2-4)

You see what he uses to prove his calling? Only the God of the Bible can do such things. Only the One who has the authority and mission to save souls can prove his claims with impossible miracles. Let any other "savior" try to do what Jesus did! They can't do it. So we know who to believe in, who to go to for help, who to fear, and who to serve by looking for the One who did the impossible on earth. *That's* the God we want!

The importance of miracles in the Bible

We must keep in mind that the miracles of Creation aren't out of place in the Bible. The whole book is about God's miracles; and what God did in the beginning, he kept doing through the rest of history. In fact, whenever he has important work to do among men, he resorts to miracles – from Creation to Redemption – because nothing else will do the job for him. Miracles are a natural part of the entire message of the Bible.

For example, when God wanted a world and yet there was nothing in existence except himself, he literally made a world out of nothing. Likewise, when Jesus needed bread and fish to feed thousands of hungry people and yet there wasn't food for them all, he made it out of virtually nothing. The same God takes the same approach to a same kind of need. Notice too the blessing in both places: God blessed the land creatures to make them prolific, and Jesus blessed the few loaves of bread to make it multiply for the needs of thousands. Obviously we're dealing with the Creator in both instances.

If you study the particular points of history when miracles occurred, you will find that circumstances were at a crossroads, so to speak. Left to themselves, men and nations would have gone right on in their ignorance and sin. God, however, wanted something different to happen – and the only way to steer events into a new direction was to step in with a miracle, from outside the world, and force things to turn out differently.

For example, after Jesus rose from the dead and ascended into Heaven, he sent his disciples out into the world to spread the Gospel of the Kingdom of God. Left to themselves, the apostles no doubt would have interested some people with this strange story of a Savior – as it did the Athenian philosophers (Acts 17:16-33) – but their new religion would have simply taken its place alongside the many other religions of that day. But when Peter and John spoke to the crippled man at the gate of the Temple (Acts 3:1-10) and healed him immediately of his life-long illness, it astonished people. Here was a religion worth looking into! As a result, crowds followed them everywhere, and the Church grew rapidly across the Roman Empire. People *wanted* a living God who demonstrated his power and love through such miraculous impossibilities. So, just when the Church needed to capture people's minds and hearts, God sent miracles to confirm the message of the apostles.

Miracles also supplied the things that people needed, when there was no other source of help. The widow of Zarephath, for example, found flour and oil miraculously renewed daily when all of Israel around her suffered from famine. (1 Kings 17:7-16) And, as we've already seen, the Israelites found food and water in a desert where there was no hope of finding it without a miracle. (Exodus 16-17) When the world can't provide what we need, God provides through miracles.

The thing to remember is that miracles serve a purpose. They weren't magic tricks to impress people. They weren't illusions (try telling one of the Israelites in the desert that the food he found every day for himself and his family was an illusion!). They weren't fables that add nothing to the spiritual message of the Bible, as modern skeptics claim. Without miracles, history would have gone from bad to worse, many people would have done without vital resources that they needed, and there would have been no Savior for God's people. Miracles are literally the foundation of God's works among us; we have never been able to do without them.

We want a God of miracles. Who of us would be satisfied with a God who can't help us when the world is against us? Who of us would appreciate a weak God, a God who can't manage the world's forces, a God who can only hope as we do that things will turn out better? Everyone I have ever heard of that called on God in times of trouble expected him to come down in irresistible power and rescue them! What we want is a God who can do the impossible, who can literally move mountains out of the way for the sake of his people.

A crippled scientific world-view

Perhaps the greatest service that science has provided for us is this: it has taught us how the world really works. When the sun rises, we don't show ourselves to be fools and worship the coming of a god – it's just the result of the earth turning its face toward the nearest star. But this comfort that we get from scientific explanations can prevent us from seeing spiritual realities. Science actually cripples us spiritually, if we insist on looking at God's world only through our physical senses and scientific instruments.

There are several reasons that people who depend only on science to understand the world don't like the idea of miracles:

> • *First*, we're afraid that if we allow for miracles, then we can't do good science. Scientists depend on the fact that the world is predictable, fixed, and controllable. Miracles, however, seem to open us up to the opposite kind of world – a world where the impossible happens, where God steps in from nowhere and does something that we're not expecting. How can someone claim to be a scientist who believes that impossible things happen in the natural world?
>
> But there is nothing about God, or his works, that will keep a person from being a good scientist. Just because scientists can't see God in the telescope, or trace his steps with a microscope, doesn't mean that he doesn't exist. The rules of science don't necessarily force us to cut God out of the picture! That's just being dishonest: there are other sources of truth which teach us about God and his miraculous works, sources that are just as reliable – perhaps even more so – than our scientific

instruments and principles. We can't just deny the miraculous because we don't have a scientific category for it! Besides, we have undeniable evidence that miracles *do* occur in our normally stable physical universe. A good scientist would want to know about such things, to help fill in his world view.

- ***Second***, people don't like the implications of a miracle. If God can so upset our neat little world with a word, if he can sidestep the laws of science so easily at his pleasure, then this means that everything in the world lies open to his hand to do whatever he wishes with it – including ourselves. He can make and destroy our world at his pleasure. He can create out of nothing, and do what we thought couldn't be done. This means, of course, that he really is the King of kings that he claims to be, and we are by nature his subjects.

- ***Third***, we know very well that just one genuine miracle, proven beyond all doubt to have actually happened, would be enough to bring about the collapse of modern scientific theory. We would have to rewrite our science textbooks. It would mean that there really is a God, that he does work as he wishes in our world apart from, as well as through, scientific principles, that miracles are not only possible but the way he *prefers* to work in our world, that the world is not proceeding along strictly scientific and physical lines, that everything depends wholly on him, that the world's beginning was most certainly miraculous and its end will be equally miraculous and catastrophic, that there are value and meaning to all physical things and therefore there will be an accounting before the Judge of all the earth in the future. All of this follows if miracles are real. In other words, a single miracle, proved beyond all doubt as actually having happened, would mean that the entire Bible is true and reliable, and we would therefore have to change our world view and prepare to meet God. And since most people don't like that idea at all, they purposely turn a blind eye to miracles for fear that this God might be real.

Creation was a miracle

Creation was obviously a miracle, if we take the Genesis account as it stands. The Bible presents it *as a miracle*. It offers no scientific explanation for what happened, and it doesn't leave any opening for a scientist to gain a foothold. The way it presents the event is with a child-like simplicity, assuming that God did what he said he did. There is no hint in the text that the writer expected us to take it in any other way than what it plainly says.

Every single piece of information in the account is a separate miracle. Let's look at them all together, and you will see that it certainly isn't a natural way of starting a universe, and none of it agrees with our modern scientific explanations!

- There was **nothing** except God before the world was made.
- God **commanded**, and all things came into being.
- Different parts were created on different **days**.
- The whole work took **six days**.
- He **blessed** each living thing to make it prolific.
- The Lord rested on the seventh day, making it **holy**.
- There were two special **trees**: the tree of the knowledge of good and evil, and the tree of life.
- Man was formed from the **dust** of the ground.
- Man and woman were made **righteous**.
- Woman was taken out of the **side** of man to be his helper.
- The devil, in the form of a **serpent**, deceived Eve.
- When Eve ate of the tree of the knowledge of good and evil, her eyes were **opened** and she knew she was naked. Adam experienced the same thing.
- In the day they ate the fruit, they **died** spiritually and were doomed to die physically.

- The two were *expelled* from the Garden of Eden and the way to the Tree of Life was *barred* by an angel.

There is no way that a modern, scientifically-minded atheist would accept any of these details as they stand. They are miracles contrary to the natural world; they assume huge spiritual realities that science knows nothing about. In order to accept that such things really happened, one would have to have a faith born in Heaven, with a perspective that can see bigger things going on than science can provide.

Obviously the Bible expects us to believe in the reality of spiritual principles, spiritual powers at work that override and guide physical events: the reality of God, the reality of sin and death, the reality of holiness and of pleasing God, the reality of dark powers who work against God, and so on. The Bible expects us to take hold of the entire picture, all of the parts of the story, not just the physical laws that scientists would primarily be interested in. This is what makes Christians believe that there are greater issues being discussed here than just how the physical world began.

Furthermore, other Biblical passages assume and depend on the fact that Creation was a miracle. For example,

> For in six days the LORD made the heavens and the earth, the sea, and all that is in them, but he rested on the seventh day. (Exodus 20:11)

> For in six days the LORD made the heavens and the earth, and on the seventh day he abstained from work and rested. (Exodus 31:17)

> For he spoke, and it came to be; he commanded, and it stood firm. (Psalm 33:9)

> By faith we understand that the universe was formed at God's command, so that what is seen was not made out of what was visible. (Hebrews 11:3)

> But they deliberately forget that long ago by God's Word the heavens existed and the earth was formed out of water and by water. (2 Peter 3:5)

As you can see, the Bible never gives us any reason to believe that Creation didn't happen exactly as it says in Genesis. The reason that the Bible never questions the "how" of Creation is that the miracle described in Genesis is not only probable, but *necessary*. If we eliminate the possibility of miracles, the entire Kingdom of God would collapse – since all of God's creative works were done through miracles. Creation *had* to be a miracle, because events that followed it depended on the world being made, for instance, by means of *command* – clearly a miraculous method.

For example, a literal six-day creation is the very foundation of the Sabbath laws. The point of the Sabbath is to take one day out of seven to rest, *as God did* after Creation. This Law is part of the Decalogue and is of supreme importance to God's people. It would have been a devious interpretation, and a dangerous example, to invent a Sabbath ordinance like this from a creation that supposedly took eons. If the Creation took only six days, however, this Law is perfectly understandable and fitting. And since the Christian Sabbath is the spiritual extension of the original Law (Hebrews 4:9-11), it would behoove us to step carefully here: the Law, and our salvation in Christ, literally depends on the foundation of Creation and *how* it was done.

Another area that would suffer seriously if the miraculous element of Creation were removed is the way that God worked in other instances recorded in the Bible. If we can't accept the fact that he created the world as Genesis literally claims, then that would throw all other miracles of the Bible into question. These other miracles are actually lesser displays of his power than the first creative act.

When God used Moses to inflict the plagues upon Egypt, Pharaoh's magicians recognized that they were dealing with a power that was above, and therefore overruling, natural or earthly powers: "This is the finger of God." (Exodus 8:19) They knew what they were up against: a person *can* know how the physical universe works, if given enough time and resources; he *can't* know how God does his miraculous works, no matter how much time he works to understand it, because God bypasses the forces and material of this world and creates out of nothing. The Egyptians had never seen this kind of power and strategy before; they knew they were looking at the Creator's work, not the work of any earthly power. Man just can't fathom a miracle.

> As you do not know the path of the wind, or how the body is formed in a mother's womb, so you cannot understand the work of God, the Maker of all things. (Ecclesiastes 11:5)

Miracle is not evolution

At this point we need to compare the two models of miracle and evolution, and it will become evident that they are two entirely different ways of looking at things – they simply can't coexist. In Figure 1 is the classic understanding of the process of evolution:

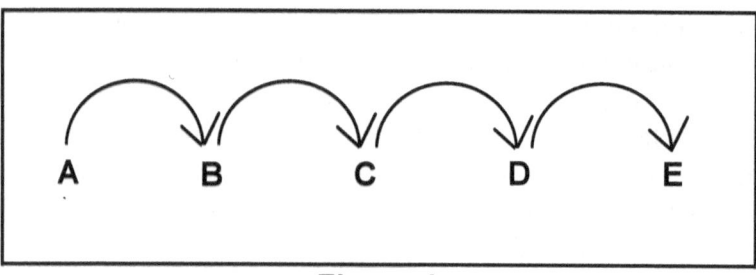

Figure 1

The main characteristic of evolution is that each step leads, naturally and logically, to the next step. A grows into B, and B grows into C, and so on. One can trace the steps that an organism took to go from the beginning of its existence (A) to its present form (E). The only way to account, for example, for Step B is to assume that there was a previous Step A that *could* bring about Step B with its peculiar characteristics. A moth's coloring, for instance, could change from white to dark because its genes have the capability of dark coloring under the right circumstances. There's no place for miracle here.

Figure 2 is a diagram of creating by miracle.

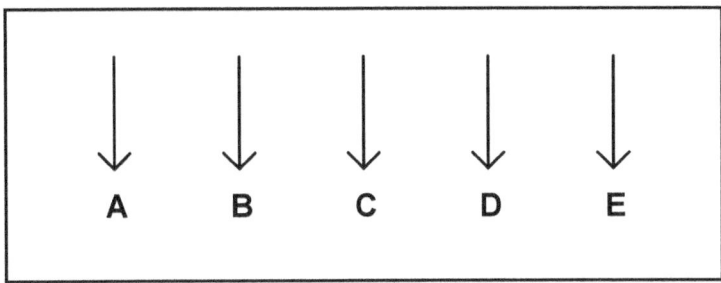

Figure 2

In this model, every step came about by a direct Divine act that brings it into existence. For example, God made the amoeba, the trout, the bear, the dinosaur, and the dog. The five creatures share the same world – like pieces to a puzzle forming a coherent picture – but there is no reason to believe that one creature changed into one of the others, (just because they share common characteristics doesn't logically lead to the conclusion that one changed into the other! – there *are* other logically acceptable options, especially when we have evidence that says so). Nor do we *have* to believe that they all descended from a common ancestor just because they share characteristics (especially when nobody can produce the ancestor!).

Since a miracle doesn't follow natural steps — since God skips the natural means and does the work directly with his own hand — obviously miracles and evolution are not the same thing. Either one or the other happened, but not both.

Why did God use miracles?

Why would God resort to miracles to make the world? Why would he not have used natural processes, as the evolutionists and physicists claim, to let the world evolve into its present form?

- *There was nothing to start with.* For some reason there are even Creationists who overlook this point. At the beginning, there weren't even the laws of physics in existence to make a world with – contrary to what some

Creationists have claimed! There was nothing but God. "By faith we understand that the universe was formed at God's command, so that what is seen was not made out of what was visible." (Hebrews 11:3) So, since at the beginning there was nothing, whatever God did at this point would *have* to be a miracle.

This of course is directly contrary to the claim of many scientists that matter and energy have always existed, and the universe naturally and predictably formed out of the soup of subatomic particles after the Big Bang. But even scientists bog down when they try to imagine what it might have been like at the point *before* the First Instant, that split second behind the Big Bang: they can't conceive what might have preceded that moment. The reason they can't is that man is unable to conceive of nothingness: that could never happen in the material universe which, they say, exists apart from God and therefore is eternal. But nothingness is exactly the impossible situation that God had at the beginning – which is why he resorted to a miracle to make the universe.

- ***The material requires the spiritual.*** We will look into this point more closely later, but for now we can put our finger on what happened at Creation by saying that **the material world was born at the hand of the Spirit**. We can't truly understand the physical universe apart from God's spiritual work, because he built the material universe to rest upon a spiritual foundation. Scientists who focus only on the material side of the universe right away run into an insurmountable obstacle when they try to explain where morals and emotions and progress and value came from if, as they claim, the universe is only made of matter and energy. And how about the widespread belief in God himself – where did that come from? How can we even imagine a spiritual Being if there is no spiritual side to the universe? Pure matter can't breed the spiritual; it's the other way around.

Physical realities are only the outward shell that gives form to the underlying spiritual reality. It's like the body which reflects the soul inside – the soul expresses itself in the world by means of the body. The Spirit gave the world its reason for existence, and he works out his eternal plans there, on that level. Without the spiritual, the material means nothing, just as without the soul the body is dead – or soon will be.

- *Future needs depend on this beginning.* The way God made the world gives us valuable insights into the way he intended to work in other special times in man's history. At critical junctures, when the needs require more than man or the world can provide, God will step in with resources from Heaven to meet those needs.

We can use Israel's Exodus experience as an example. In order to free them from Pharaoh's grasp, lead them for forty years in the desert, feed and water them, and protect them from their enemies, God performed a series of miracles the nature of which so greatly impressed them that they remembered the experience ever since then. In each situation the people had great need, but they had nowhere to turn – there was *no* help in the desert. God's answers came in creative steps, making resources where there were none naturally.

This exactly fits the way he created the world in the beginning. In both places we see the same God doing things the same way – because *only in this way* can he support his people. If we missed the point in Genesis, we should at least notice how he keeps on turning to the same methods in his future works.

- ***Everything must depend on him.*** There was no Big Bang at the beginning. Scientists resort to this because they think the universe depends on itself as it unfolds into stars and galaxies and planets and animals and plants and humans. The root idea of evolution is that physical matter has within itself the ability to change and fill the universe with life and movement and solar systems. But according to the Genesis account, the world *can't* depend on itself for what it needs, least of all for its very existence – it wasn't made to be self-sufficient. Everything depends completely on God.

God made everything according to a special plan. Thus stones are what they are because God made them that way. They can no more change into something else without God's direct command than they can sit up and talk on their own. (Except, of course, if God commands them to – remember John's threat about changing rocks into Abraham's children! – Luke 3:8)

Evolutionists like to use anthropomorphic expressions when they talk about living things (including non-thinking plants and inanimate matter). That is, it's as if evolving creatures know what they must do to fit in with the world, and therefore they change accordingly – as if animals can think it out as well as the evolutionists have! Scientists are forced to say things like "the fish's fins changed into legs *so that* it could walk around on land" – as if fish and fins somehow *know* what to do next! Of course evolutionists apologize for having to talk like this, but even they can't escape the conclusion that the creatures of the world need a wisdom that's beyond them in order to get along in the world. Though they don't admit it, they know in their hearts that every creature depends on the constant care of its Creator:

> The eyes of all look to you, and you give them their food at the proper time. You open your hand and satisfy the desires of every living thing. (Psalm 145:15-16)

Miracles in the eternal plan

The miracle of Creation laid the foundation for the future works of God. At the very least, the marvel of a complex and yet organic whole has astonished people throughout the ages and caused them to worship a God who could make such a masterpiece. But there was more than that in God's plans when he made the world. His plans extended to the family of Abraham, their travels in and around Palestine, and eventually to the culmination of that plan in the birth of the Son of God. All these events needed a world in which God had complete control and had the freedom to introduce miracles at critical points in history. In a world which normally runs according to predictable scientific laws, a miracle is a startling reality that causes us to realize how much we still need the Creator for taking care of unfinished business – both through Providence and through the Redemption of Christ and the new Creation. The reality of miracles demonstrates how open the world is to God's hand, the fact that everything still responds to the King when he commands it, as his eternal plan unfolds.

The Means of Creation – Command

One of the most obvious things of the Creation account is the fact that God *commanded* each step of the process. The phrase "Let there be …" is not a wish or desire, but an authoritative intent that such a thing *shall be*, by decree. The miracles were the act of carrying out God's *command*.

Other passages in the Bible also spell out the fact that God used commands when he created the universe:

> *For he spoke, and it came to be; he commanded, and it stood firm.* (Psalm 33:9)
>
> *Let them praise the name of the LORD,*
> *for he commanded and they were created.*
> *He set them in place for ever and ever;*
> *he gave a decree that will never pass away.* (Psalm 148:5-6)
>
> *When he gave the sea its boundary so the waters would not overstep his command, and when he marked out the foundations of the earth …* (Proverbs 8:29)
>
> *By faith we understand that the universe was formed at God's command, so that what is seen was not made out of what was visible.* (Hebrews 11:3)

God is King of all

The entire Bible makes it very plain that God is the Sovereign Lord. Though too many people refuse to give God the credit for being the Ruler of Heaven and earth, it's nevertheless true and every account of him in the Bible demonstrates that.

For example, he commanded Adam and Eve to obey him about what to eat and what not to eat, and punished them when they disobeyed. He killed the entire earth's population except for Noah and his family without asking permission of anyone – because they had sinned against him, and he had the right to their lives. He destroyed Sodom and Gomorrah for rebelling against his moral Law. He demanded that Pharaoh let the Israelites go and punished the entire Egyptian nation when Pharaoh refused. He gave the Israelites his Law that set up an extensive system of government, and expected their obedience. He installed David as king over the nation and expected him to follow the Law as he ruled Israel. He punished the Israelites for their unfaithfulness by destroying Jerusalem and sending them into Exile. He used pagan nations at will and disposed of them at will.

In Jesus we again see the Lord, this time come into the flesh: one who commanded men, demons, sickness, the elements, and death itself. When Peter wanted to step out on the water, Jesus commanded – "Come!" (Matthew 14:29) – and Peter found that he *could* walk on water. Jesus commanded a man's ears to be opened. (Mark 7:34) Jesus commanded the leper to be healed – "Be clean!" (Luke 5:13) – and the leprosy left him. At no point did Jesus ever let down his authority before men, because he was and always will be the Master of all the earth. In fact, we can't be saved unless he is the Master, because we are at the mercy of forces that will not let us go until they are commanded to do so. Remember the Gadarene demoniac who was helplessly bound by the evil spirits which lived in him: only when Jesus commanded them to leave was the poor man set free. (Matthew 8:28-34)

God also showed his authority when he gave the Law to the Israelites. Only someone who could look into the bottom of the human heart could rule over men to that extent! He gave them rules not only for how to treat each other, but how to approach him – in repentance, humility and faith. When they didn't, he punished them. It's clear from his dealings with Israel that he's used to giving orders and expecting strict obedience in return.

A King created the world

We could go on looking at passages that show God as King, but any open-minded reader of the Bible will see for himself that God does things with authority; that's his nature. Now let's take this concept back to the Creation event. Knowing what we do about the Lord of Heaven and earth from the rest of the Bible, what do the commands in Genesis teach us about Creation?

- ***The Word of God is the foundation of the world.*** God spoke first, then the world came to be. This is always the order of things in God's world. His Word forms the foundation of all his works because it expresses his will, his intentions, his purposes; it outlines the way he wants things to exist and operate; it serves as the standard against which all things must measure up; it will form the basis for Judgment Day when God determines the worth and effectiveness of all things at the end of time. When the king speaks, his word is always his will for his kingdom and must be executed. In God's case we call this the "oracles" of the Lord.

- ***The origin of all things is outside the universe.*** No one can say that God is the world and the world is God! God's command came *before* anything else existed; it was the First Cause, and will always be the power which creates and upholds the universe. It stands outside time and space; it caused time and space and gave scientific laws their form and expression.

- ***Everything was made according to the will of God.*** Since he commanded things to exist, we have to assume that these weren't the ordinary words or wishes of an ordinary person. God is the Master, the Lord, the King; when he commands, things happen exactly as he wishes them to happen. When man commands, he hopes (or expects) others to carry out his wishes. But in God's case, he himself fulfills his own word. As the old saying goes, if you want something done right, you must do it yourself. So he carried out his own commands so that the result would perfectly fit his expectations.

Note that after he commanded each part of Creation to exist, he looked at it and pronounced it "good." He found it pleasing to him because it was exactly as he wanted it to be. It fit his purposes; he knew that it would serve his eternal plans to be made thus. Whatever God does, he does to perfection and excellence, and the results must please *him*.

- ***The world is his Kingdom.*** Perhaps the most striking truth to come out of the Genesis account is that we are a part of a Kingdom, made to serve God with all of our being. If he brought us into existence with a command, this means that the rest of our lives will (at least it ought to, by design!) consist of *obeying this King*.

The Creative command reveals an overall plan, a goal, a purpose for the universe. We may not know the entire plan until it unwinds through the rest of history, but we are, nevertheless, a part of something bigger than our own personal lives and interests. The plan, if you haven't seen it yet, was to build a universal Kingdom with God at its head. So it shouldn't be any surprise to you that in God's kingdom there are such things as responsibility, accountability, Law, guilt and punishment, right and wrong, reward, justice, community and relationships, and obedience. A Kingdom needs things like these to run smoothly. God's original command created this kind of world in which *obedience to the King in all forms* is our primary concern in life.

- ***There has to be a Judgment Day.*** One must know God in order to appreciate the way he does things. He is holy, righteous, and good. He himself doesn't do anything unjust. He creates things to please himself, to fulfill his wishes – but also to make a harmonious and complex whole that will effectively glorify his Name, his wisdom and power. We should expect to find, in his Creation, everything that will bring about all these desirable results.

But human history hasn't proceeded according to the original pattern. Through no fault of his own, God has had to deal with a race of rebels. Man has attempted to ruin God's plans and his creation. If it were up to us, things would *not* go in the direction that God had planned from the beginning.

But God's wisdom is bigger than our rebellion, and he had already laid plans – before Creation – to undo the effects of our wickedness before it happened. Not only does he constantly frustrate the plans of sinners – the wicked can't win, he'll see to that! – he plans to demand a full accounting from us on the Last Day. On that day, a day in which he will bring our works to an end and fully reveal his works, he will finally reveal himself as the King and Judge that he claims to be. All works of sin will be destroyed, all sinners punished, all the righteous rewarded, the old heavens and earth destroyed and new ones set up eternally in their place. Everything that we have done "while in the body" (2 Corinthians 5:10) will be judged, destroyed, rectified, or accepted – according to the will of the King who has power and authority to do so. Then, if man has not yet been convinced of it, he will realize that God was serious when he commanded us to obey him in *all things*.

The Creative command

Note that God's command is not the same as one of our commands. When we order someone to do something, we issue the order and then can only hope that they do it. We also expect them to obey us because we know that they have the ability to do what we say. When God commands, however, it's a different situation. What he says to do, usually, is *impossible* for his subject to perform. The thing or person that he commands is unable to do what he expects of them. The reason for that is this: what God desires is more than this world can do; his standards and powers are much higher than ours, so we have no hope of doing something that would please him.

He is building an *eternal* kingdom, and bringing about *spiritual* perfection on earth – and both of these things are impossible in earthly terms and capabilities. We use whatever materials are at hand when we do our own work, but God has to provide his own materials for his special work among us, because none of ours will suit his purposes. How can you use stones and cement, or even silver and gold, to build a house for God that will hold him? Solomon knew this when he built the Temple; he knew that only God's Name can dwell there:

> But will God really dwell on earth with men? The heavens, even the highest heavens, cannot contain you. How much less this temple I have built! (2 Chronicles 6:18)

When God issues a command, therefore, he has to provide his own power and materials to make sure the job gets done to his satisfaction. We call this his *creative command*:

> As the rain and the snow
> come down from heaven,
> and do not return to it
> without watering the earth
> and making it bud and flourish,
> so that it yields seed for the sower and bread for the eater,
> *so is my word that goes out from my mouth:*
> *It will not return to me empty,*
> *but will accomplish what I desire*
> *and achieve the purpose for which I sent it.* (Isaiah 55:10-11)

Since God knows that what he wants from us is beyond our ability to do, he intends to do it himself – even as he issues the command to us. In other words, he sends the power to obey him along with the command. Jesus demonstrated this principle in an amazing miracle:

> Jesus said in a loud voice, "Lazarus, come out!" The dead man came out, his hands and feet wrapped with strips of linen, and a cloth around his face. (John 11:43-44)

The man couldn't do it himself; so Jesus empowered him to do it. And, even though Jesus knew the man couldn't do it, yet he commanded him. That command reveals the deep relationship of Master and subject, between Creator and Creation, built into the world from the beginning.

If God knows very well that we can't obey his commands, and he intends to do it himself anyway, why does he bother to make it a command? Why didn't he just wave his hand over the abyss of nothingness and create a universe without bothering with commands?

We can turn to Psalm 33 for the answer. Here is the passage again:

> Let all the earth *fear* the LORD;
>   let all the people of the world *revere* him.
> For he spoke, and it came to be;
>   he commanded, and it stood firm.
>   (Psalm 33:8-9)

Notice that all the earth is told to *fear* the Lord and all the people *revere* him. The word "for" tells us the reason: because he *commanded* the earth into existence. In other words, he used commands to create the world because he wanted a **kingdom**, a world that would forever fear and serve him. The means that he used determined what the outcome would look like. *We were made to be* *servants of God and nothing else.* That's what the command of creation teaches us.

This explains the assumption, every time we read about God relating to men, that he's the Master and they simply *must* do what he wants upon penalty of punishment. All the world was *made* to obey God.

The Commands of Creation

The basic relationship of King-servant that God established at the beginning with the entire universe explains many things about our lives and the way the world works:

> • ***This is a kingdom.*** There are many aspects about a kingdom, things that we modern readers may not be familiar with until we think about it. *First*, obviously there is a king. His word is law. He is the center of the kingdom around whom the people rally in loyalty and pledge their support. *Second*, he forms the government by which the people regulate their lives. They follow his laws, his sentences, his justice. This system of government holds the kingdom together in peace and harmony. *Third*, he provides economic stability and makes it possible for the people to work and prosper. *Fourth*, he provides protection from their enemies, sometimes gathering an army and leading it into battle to defend their homes.
>
> God is like this in all these ways. When he made the world through command, he assumed the title of King over all the earth – along with all the responsibilities that come with that position. He is a good and caring King. For example, he makes sure that each of his creatures get something to eat every day:
>
>> Your kingdom is an everlasting kingdom,
>>   and your dominion endures through all generations.

> The LORD is faithful to all his promises
>   and loving toward all he has made.
> The LORD upholds all those who fall
>   and lifts up all who are bowed down.
> The eyes of all look to you,
>   and you give them their food at the proper time.
> You open your hand
>   and satisfy the desires of every living thing.
> (Psalm 145:13-16)

His justice is proverbial. His wisdom guides and governs the entire earth. He defends and protects his people from their enemies. (Psalm 23:3-5)

But the other side of the coin is that we are bound to obey him according to the Law that he set down for us. He gave us a conscience along with our minds, so that we feel the sting of disobedience when we don't do what we *know* he wants us to do. His moral government is impossible to escape completely, even in the most depraved of civilizations.

- **We will never be other than what he made us.** It's not surprising that God built a certain amount of flexibility into his creation. Evolutionists have long pointed out that creatures do change somewhat to fit into their surrounding environment (though scientists have yet to prove that creatures change from one distinct "kind" to another!). We can appreciate God's wisdom of forethought that he would make the world able to change and conform to changing physical circumstances.

There is only a certain amount of change possible, however, and that's because of the command of Creation. When God commanded the trees to exist, bear fruit, and generate more trees after their kind, *he meant it*. No tree has ever done anything other than carry out that command. None of us creatures are free to be what God doesn't want us to be.

Not only that, we *can't* be other than what he commanded us to be. If we try to change, we will more than likely pervert and ruin ourselves in the process. You can see examples of this when scientists tinker around making different kinds of animals by experimenting with their genes (they often end up with ugly monsters!), or by making hybrid garden plants that promise to overproduce but can't go on to reproduce themselves. Such tinkering strays from the original design, and that will rarely be beneficial or as efficient in the long run – only God's original, perfect designs work well in all respects.

- ***To change what God made is to destroy it.*** The last point leads to this one. If we try to "improve" on what God commanded to exist, and make it do what it wasn't supposed to do, we will ruin it. For some unknown reason, though God certainly has the power to stop us if he wanted to, he will let us twist and turn things to suit ourselves even when it means ruining things. And the worst mistake we ever made was to do that very thing to our own spiritual nature.

We were made to obey him, and to glorify him in our actions on earth. When we turned away from that calling, we turned away from what we were designed to do, and that could only result in death. Our purpose is not to live for ourselves but for God. No wonder, then, as a result of our daily fixation on ourselves, that we carelessly murder our fellow men in many creative ways, that God doesn't get the glory he deserves, and that we fail at everything we do when we don't depend on our Creator, who is the only source of all good things.

We also see the results of our rebellion in the world that we constantly twist and ruin to suit our own fancy. Instead of working on and taking care of the earth as God's stewards (Genesis 2:15), we changed it according to our own design – we created a new world in which sinners can ignore God's moral requirements and get away with it. Daily we invent ways to avoid depending on the Lord for our needs. It's no wonder that, as we face problems with our environment and struggle to survive against disease, death, and the lack of material necessities, we build up a civilization full of machinery and chemicals and atomic waste and city expansion, destroy whole forests, wipe out hundreds of species of animals and plants, and pollute our farmland and water sources with agricultural chemicals and waste materials. We made the world that we want, but we are ruining the earth and ourselves in the long run. The world was not made for such mindless destruction.

- ***We are not free agents.*** When God made man, he gave him a direct order:

> Be fruitful and increase in number; fill the earth and subdue it. Rule over the fish of the sea and the birds of the air and over every living creature that moves on the ground. (Genesis 1:28)

This fits into the general picture of a well-balanced, prosperous kingdom that we have already looked at. Man was God's vice-regent who would make such a kingdom a reality on earth. This would require dedication, wisdom, skill, motivation, and responsibility. This would only work, however, if the vice-regent would get all his orders from the King of kings – man has to find out *from God* how to rule God's world. It's not surprising that man would not be permitted to do things his own way; he was only free to obey God and do things God's way – to build God's earth and maintain the order that God intended.

- ***Sin is a disaster in the system.*** Adam decided that instead of following God's command, he would act according to his own will. He used his own senses and judgment to determine what was right and wrong. He turned his back on his high calling and accepted the deceitful promises held out to him by the Devil. Instead of depending on God's provision and God's command, he sought counsel in his own heart and depended on his own efforts for provision.

In a world that was so finely balanced, so perfect, so capable of fulfilling all of God's expectations, the least disturbance to the system would throw everything out of joint. So when the vice-regent himself rebelled, the whole world fell into ruin! It was a disaster, a deep-rooted catastrophe that, on the surface, couldn't possibly be fixed. It was directly contrary to everything that God had in mind for it.

Sin is never a small issue with God. We can only truly understand it when we remember that the world is God's Kingdom. Sin has ruined the entire structure of that Kingdom. And once we realize how catastrophic sin is to God's world, we will begin to realize the need for a drastic and effective solution to sin. Punishment is not out of order here; it's not cruel and unusual for God to punish sinners. If we don't understand his method of solving the problem of sin (in other words, someone has to die for it!), it's because we don't yet realize the enormity of our crime against God and his world.

- ***We are responsible to him.*** A command implies responsibility. In man's case, the responsibility that God laid upon him reflects the specific type of work that he has been given to do. Although it's not easy to determine exactly what Adam's responsibility actually was, on Judgment Day there will be a reckoning, there *must* be a reckoning, of accounts. Then God will make it very clear to us what it was that he called us to do.

And it will also be very clear at that time whether we actually measured up to his expectations. Right now the confusion of life, and our mistaken opinions of ourselves, make us think that we're a real asset in God's Kingdom! But all the confusion will be swept away on Judgment Day, in order to reveal whether we have built the foundation of God's dwelling using "gold, silver, costly stones" or "wood, hay or straw." (1 Corinthians 3:12)

We can expect God to apply a very penetrating analysis to our work on Judgment Day: **first**, we will then see the depth of our calling, the wide scope of activity that God expected us to work on. He gave each of us far more to do than we are usually willing to admit. **Second**, we will then see the degree that we *could* have met his expectations – indeed, what we *should* have done, apart from all excuses and the confusion of circumstances. **Third**, we will also see that his demands of us were perfectly reasonable. He never gave us more than we could do. Considering the abilities and opportunities that we've had, he has every right to expect a certain success rate from us. **Finally**, in light of these revelations, we will also be forced to admit that his punishment of the wicked, and the rewards to the righteous, are fair and just – considering what they are and have done.

> As the weeds are pulled up and burned in the fire, so it will be at the end of the age. The Son of Man will send out his angels, and they will weed out of his kingdom everything that causes sin and all who do evil. They will throw them into the

fiery furnace, where there will be weeping and gnashing of teeth. Then the righteous will shine like the sun in the kingdom of their Father. He who has ears, let him hear. (Matthew 13:37-43)

When God separates the wicked and the righteous like this, he's only doing what a good king would do to preserve order and justice in his Kingdom.

"Set in place"

One natural thing to consider when we think about the King is *what* he commands his creatures to do. There are constraints built into each created thing, so that it will be what God wants it to be, and it will fit into the whole network of the universe in a way that fulfills God's purpose for it.

> Where were you when I laid the earth's foundation?
> > Tell me, if you understand.
> Who marked off its dimensions? Surely you know!
> > Who stretched a measuring line across it?
> On what were its footings set,
> > or who laid its cornerstone
> while the morning stars sang together
> > and all the angels shouted for joy?
> Who shut up the sea behind doors
> > when it burst forth from the womb,
> when I made the clouds its garment
> > and wrapped it in thick darkness,
> when I fixed limits for it
> > and set its doors and bars in place,
> when I said, 'This far you may come and no farther;
> > here is where your proud waves halt'? (Job 38:4-11)

This entire section of Job 38-41 describes the purposes of God in the way he designed each part of Creation. Each creature has its set function, a place in the whole scheme of things. Each fulfills its purpose in the world system. The Master made each creature to fulfill its role, and therefore they can't change what they were made to do in God's Kingdom. Evolutionists admit that the creatures on earth depend on each other for survival (many times in amazing ways!), but they teach that the blind force of "chance" or natural selection did it instead of the King setting up a balanced Kingdom.

One practical side to this Biblical concept is a good example of how Scriptural truth can and must guide the scientist in how to pursue his/her field. The Bible says that the Lord made the earth to be inhabited:

> For this is what the LORD says — he who created the heavens, he is God; he who fashioned and made the earth, he founded it; he did not create it to be empty, but *formed it to be inhabited.* (Isaiah 45:18)

In other words, the purpose of the universe is to be a place where *creatures* will live, and especially as a background and foundation for the works of man and God's works among man. Most scientists think this is ridiculous, because they see scales of existence in the universe much greater and much smaller than man's immediate level. They have discovered powerful forces at work that we don't ordinarily depend on and use in everyday life – like relativity and quantum mechanics. And because they are impressed with these forces, they tend to interpret all other scales solely in terms of their favorite principle.[28]

For example, at the galactic scale we see relativistic principles at work that led scientists in this century to set aside the old Newtonian physics. And on the atomic scale scientists deal with quantum physics, again leading us to believe that the old physical model of the atom is no longer sufficient to describe reality. Scientists are confused, therefore, about which model really constitutes life. Particle physicists, for

---

[28] See Weinburg, ibid., in his chapter "Two cheers for Reductionism," where he argues that particle physics is the basis for all other fields of research. "Our present concentration on elementary particles is based on a tactical judgment – that at *this* moment in the history of science this is the way to make progress toward the final theory." P. 62.

example, try to marry both ends — the atomic forces with the cosmic scale — and define reality with a unified theory that will embrace this entire range. Other scientists see the entire universe as a living thing, and the creatures on earth are only sub-units, so to speak, of the greater whole. It has even been asked whether DNA is the center of existence, and the multiplicity of life is only DNA perpetuating itself, seeking optimum configurations.[29] So scientists are struggling to find the level of existence at which there is ultimate meaning, for which all other components of the universe are only supporting structures.

The problem is a matter of perspective, however. If the universe was made to be inhabited, then *man* is at the center of activity for the universe. And the extraordinary forces that we find at either end of the scale of reality aren't the norm, but evidences of some of the overall necessary structures that support what man has to be and do in the world. We are, incidentally, about half-way on the universal scale of size.[30] And it's not unknown even in atheistic science that man seems to be (because of the amazing way that the ends serve the middle) the product which the universe struggled to create — otherwise known as the anthropic principle. We can express all of this on a scale, as in Figure 3.[31]

---

[29] Richard Dawkins, cited in Robin Marantz Henig's work, *A Dancing Matrix*, Vintage Books, 1993, 77.

[30] For a dramatic visual demonstration of man's size midway in the universe, see the book *Powers of Ten: About the Relative Size of Things in the Universe*, Philip and Phylis Morrison and the Office of Charles and Ray Eames, Scientific American Library, 1994.

[31] Another useful median in common life is visible light, which at 10^{14} hertz is about midway on the electromagnetic spectrum. At the very least, it demonstrates again that God created the foundations of our universe across ranges, or levels, the entire range of which makes possible a *mid-range* in which we find *our* common experiences of life possible.

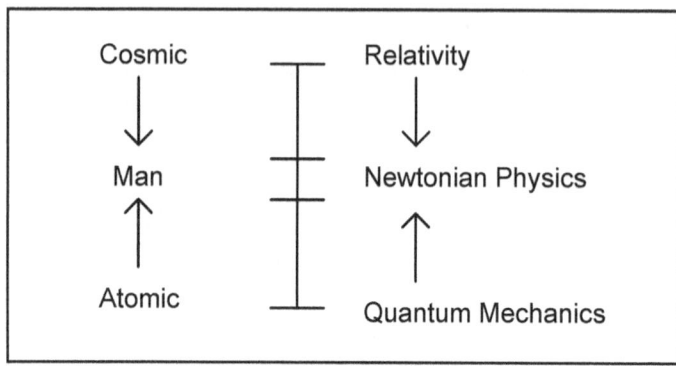

Figure 3

Another way in which we can view the universe is a canvas upon which God brought several fundamental principles to focus, producing a world in which men can live. When we examine the cosmic scale and see relativity at work, for example, we are actually looking at *one* of the principles that make up the world. But that's actually the outer edge of the picture where it's less focused on man, and therefore can be misleading when one attempts to draw conclusions from its principles about the true nature of the world. And the strange world of quantum physics has also confused people about the world we live in, as if those particular principles are normative of everyday life. Instead, it's at the *focus* of all the principles that we find the center stage of the universe, not at its outer fringes (though scientists can show us how to take advantage of those principles in interesting ways). We can picture this as in Figure 4.

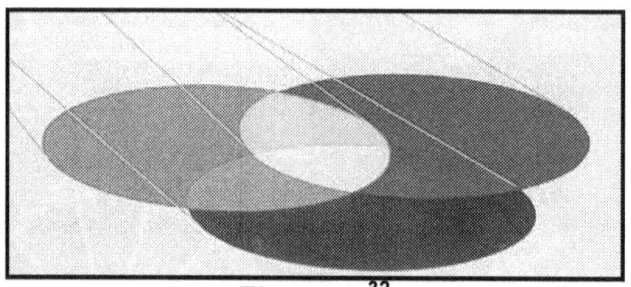

Figure 4 [32]

---

[32] Color illustration by George V. Kelvin for article "Color," *The World Book Encyclopedia*, Vol. 4; Field Enterprises Educational Corporation, 1964; 659.

The colors green, red and blue form white light at their convergence. In the same way, the separate principles discovered in various scientific fields converge to describe a world which we use to our daily advantage.

Seeing things *this* way should direct the research of scientists who want to understand the makeup of the universe. In other words, instead of pointing out the inadequacies of Newtonian physics to explain a world in which relativity and quantum mechanics operate (as if ultimate meaning lies *there*), it would be more realistic, for example, to investigate how relativity and quantum mechanics make a Newtonian world possible. Therefore, as is proper, Theology can and should guide the work of science when it comes to discovering meaning and purpose in the world.

Evolution knows nothing of a King

Once we understand how important the commands of Creation were, we instantly get an enormous picture of the universe. Scientists think that their view is already huge, with more information and laws to study than man has time for. But now we can see that every created thing stands before a King and serves his purposes. Suddenly we are faced with many more issues in life than we expected. Now, not only can we discover the physical laws governing all things, but we must move on and discover the laws and duties governing our relationship to our Maker.

Evolution can't make a world like that. According to the theory of evolution, creatures gradually change physically from one form to another. It's completely blind to purpose, to God's overruling hand bringing about a Kingdom that pleases him spiritually. In a world of evolution, nothing serves a purpose – because there's no King making things to suit himself. But if there is a King – and we see him all through Biblical history, working his will over sinner and saint alike – then he specially designed each creature to serve him. Evolution has no place in this world view.

Finally, Creation by command shows us a world that responds immediately to God's Word – not over eons of time. Evolution needs those long periods, because gradually changing matter and energy can't achieve its goals except through time. God, however, *commands* things into existence and doesn't wish to wait around for the results. That's why he often does the thing himself – he knows that we'd be forever trying to carry out his command! The entire Bible shows us this kind of God: he expects his creation to obey him, now. Man takes his time when he works, but God's miracles were always immediate.

The Pattern of Creation – Wisdom and Understanding

A good engineer doesn't begin building something without plans. He will first do research, make drawings, build prototypes and test them, and revise his drawings. There is a lot of work that goes into the project long before the actual end product is built. This is so that he can be sure the product will be safe, reliable, and useful to the user.

God approached his Creation with no less preparation, you can be sure of that. So much depends on his work that we can expect to find an infinite skill there, and a wisdom beyond our understanding. The world has to work so perfectly for so long, and achieve not only physical goals but also spiritual goals, that we shouldn't be surprised to find God taking great care in its construction.

Probably the first and greatest thing that impresses us about Creation is this fact: it's so complex at whatever level we want to look at. It seems that there is no end to things that we can learn from the world around us. Yet in all its bewildering complexity, it works so well as a whole that we are continually amazed at this engineering marvel. Scientists especially appreciate the way nature works together so well, though they don't usually admit that God's wisdom is behind the perfection they see!

The Bible gives credit where credit is due. It tells us that God made the world, and he did it by using his infinite wisdom – it's no wonder that it's so huge, complex, and yet so efficient and perfect in its operations:

> By wisdom the Lord laid the earth's foundations, by understanding he set the heavens in place. (Proverbs 3:19)

It's an eloquent testimony to God's superior intellect that, in our generation equipped with powerful scientific instruments and a knowledge greater than any other generation in history, we are only beginning to discover how little we still know of his Creation.

A huge universe

But there is even more to the universe than what our physical senses tell us. As huge as the universe is, there are realities and worlds that we know almost nothing about, but they are just as real nonetheless. The Bible gives us little glimpses of just how big God's Creation really is. For example, this passage reveals spiritual worlds, spiritual creatures, and spiritual battles that are raging all around and above our heads:

> For our struggle is not against flesh and blood, but against the rulers, against the authorities, against the powers of this dark world and against the spiritual forces of evil in the heavenly realms. (Ephesians 6:12)

The apostle Paul once visited that greater world – and came back amazed and dumbfounded about what he saw there:

> I know a man in Christ who fourteen years ago was caught up to the third heaven. Whether it was in the body or out of the body I do not know — God knows. And I know that this man — whether in the body or apart from the body I do not know, but God knows — was caught up to paradise. He heard inexpressible things, things that man is not permitted to tell. (2 Corinthians 12:2-4)

When Daniel the prophet was praying, he wondered why an answer was so long in coming. Eventually the archangel Gabriel brought an answer and an explanation for the delay:

> The prince of the Persian kingdom resisted me twenty one days. Then Michael, one of the chief princes, came

to help me, because I was detained there with the king of Persia. (Daniel 10:13)

These and other glimpses give us an idea of something huge: a vast system with Heaven and Hell on either end, and earth in the middle, upon which are fought and decided eternal issues. In this physical world, we stand on a stage, a platform, where the drama of the relationship between God and man are acted out.

We can use science to understand, in a primitive way at least, how the physical world operates. But as soon as we move away from the physical into the spiritual world we immediately come face to face with deep mystery. God rarely shows us what he is doing there, nor does he show us much of the structure of things at that level. The most we can often hope to understand about the spiritual world are the effects that it has upon the physical.

For example, Jesus said that a man does what is in his heart: he's a murderer in heart first, before he ever sets his hand against another person.

> You have heard that it was said to the people long ago, 'Do not murder, and anyone who murders will be subject to judgment.' But I tell you that anyone who is angry with his brother will be subject to judgment. Again, anyone who says to his brother, 'Raca,' is answerable to the Sanhedrin. But anyone who says, 'You fool!' will be in danger of the fire of hell. (Matthew 5:21-22)

This means that the spiritual world is the place where all actions originate; it is the seat of life.

The physical universe is playing out a special script written for it by God before the beginning of Creation. This script, for some good reasons, remains hidden to man. One reason is so that man will play his own part willingly, not knowing that greater things hang in the balance – a knowledge that would undoubtedly affect his decisions.

For example, it's common knowledge that if we knew what was in our future, we would certainly act differently than we do!

> I have seen the burden God has laid on men. He has made everything beautiful in its time. He has also set eternity in the hearts of men; yet they cannot fathom what God has done from beginning to end. (Ecclesiastes 3:10-11)

Of course matter and energy have no meaning or purpose in themselves; they only have meaning when we see the bigger picture that they are part of – the purpose that God has for them, the role they play in the eternal drama of God's will. Man shouldn't be so foolish, however, to ignore the bigger picture just because he can't see it with his physical eyes! The physical and spiritual worlds are connected with threads that we can't see. Those connections were designed purposely to glorify God; the physical universe, in God's hands, turns into a powerful tool to achieve his spiritual ends. And in this we see God's profound wisdom behind Creation – he uses the physical world to test, reveal, condemn, reward, comfort, guide, frustrate, endanger, and protect the soul of man. The mystery of his Creation, the principle that many people miss the point of, is that his spiritual Kingdom grows *by means of* his physical Kingdom. That's what we want to look at now – by looking at the three levels of Creation.

The physical level

God displayed his profound wisdom in *how* he created the world that we live in. In order to have a complete and self-sufficient system, God had to design it with certain things in mind:

> ***First***, all the resources that every creature needs must be readily available and suitable to fulfill those needs. There is always plenty of food to eat, air to breathe, water to drink, protection from natural dangers, mates for reproduction, parents who nurture and train the young – there is a never-ending supply of all good things for all creatures.

Second, every animate and inanimate part of creation must fit into the jigsaw of existence. There is nothing superfluous; every part is necessary to the success of the entire system. For example, the food chain demonstrates the fact that every level of life depends on the level below it, and is itself necessary for the level above it. Some of the relationships between levels of creatures are extraordinary – like whales, the biggest life forms, depending on plankton, one of the smallest life forms in the ocean.

Third, there must be redundancy and shock-resistance built into the system. Though it's a closed system, the world and all its creatures have to be able to absorb setbacks and allow modifications to fit a variety of changing circumstances. Moths can change colors, for example, when circumstances demand it, so that predators can't see them very well. It's natural to assume that a wise God would have made creatures able to change in some degree, to better fit in with changing circumstances. If they couldn't, there would be immediate and global extinctions of whole species going on all the time in our changing world.

Fourth, the system has to work for as long as the Lord has need of it. It can't quit on its own, because God has long range plans for it. It's the necessary foundation for the more important spiritual work that he has in mind. For example, we live in communities that provide us with basic physical services such as water, electricity, telephone, etc. But these are just low-level services that make it possible to do more important things – like raise families, work at our jobs, community service, and so on. In the same way, our physical world only serves our low-level needs, to help us live on a spiritual level and accomplish more important work there. Jesus taught this principle:

> So do not worry, saying, 'What shall we eat?' or 'What shall we drink?' or 'What shall we wear?' For the pagans run after all these things, and your heavenly

Father knows that you need them. But seek first his kingdom and his righteousness, and all these things will be given to you as well. (Matthew 6:31-33)

Fifth, the system must always be completely dependent on its Creator. Every detail must have meaning and purpose for *him* (or it will be unnecessary in his world, by definition); all of it will be called to account for how well it has served its intended purpose (that is, on Judgment Day); nothing is outside his will and knowledge (or it would not have been *his* creation); and it's continually and completely open to his hand (for example, he sometimes chooses to set aside the physical laws temporarily for the sake of a miracle). The profound overall dependence of creation upon its Maker can be seen in the following passage:

These all look to you to give them their food at the proper time. When you give it to them, they gather it up; when you open your hand, they are satisfied with good things. When you hide your face, they are terrified; when you take away their breath, they die and return to the dust. When you send your Spirit, they are created, and you renew the face of the earth. (Psalm 104:27-30)

These are the aspects of his creation that reveal God's wisdom — in the *way* he made the world, not just in *what* he did. It's not our purpose here to explore the depth of this wisdom – in other words, how clearly each part of the world fits together and operates – especially since science can easily discover its complexity and beauty for us.

One additional aspect of the wisdom of God is the fact that he purposely designed the material world to have *no meaning or purpose in itself*. It doesn't hold the secret, on the surface, for our existence here; we can't answer the question "why am I here?" only by looking at the physical world. This is the theme of the book of Ecclesiastes:

"Meaningless! Meaningless!"
says the Teacher.

> "Utterly meaningless!
> Everything is meaningless."
> What does man gain from all his labor
> at which he toils under the sun?
> Generations come and generations go,
> but the earth remains forever.
> The sun rises and the sun sets,
> and hurries back to where it rises.
> The wind blows to the south
> and turns to the north;
> round and round it goes,
> ever returning on its course.
> All streams flow into the sea,
> yet the sea is never full.
> To the place the streams come from,
> there they return again.
> All things are wearisome,
> more than one can say.
> The eye never has enough of seeing,
> nor the ear its fill of hearing.
> What has been will be again,
> what has been done will be done again;
> there is nothing new under the sun.
> Is there anything of which one can say,
> "Look! This is something new"?
> It was here already, long ago;
> it was here before our time. (Ecclesiastes 1:2,4-10)

It happens all the time, however, that if a person can't see God and doesn't understand the real purpose and meaning of life, he will turn to the world for satisfaction, though as the writer observes, such a life will be meaningless. The world wasn't designed to satisfy the heart of man, nor can he fulfill his calling as a servant of God by living only on the physical plane. We must look to a higher spiritual level for purpose and meaning in God's creation.

The moral level

Man is a preeminent part of God's world, as Genesis informs us:

> Let us make man in our image, in our likeness, and let them rule over the fish of the sea and the birds of the air, over the livestock, over all the earth, and over all the creatures that move along the ground. (Genesis 1:26)

Whereas inanimate objects and animals operate by God's design unknowingly, man alone has the ability to *know* his created purpose, and consciously carry out God's will to glorify God.

When God announced that his creation was "good", he meant that the creation *below man* pleases him by its structure, instinct and design, and *man himself* pleases him by obedience to his Word. We operate in obedience to his Law, or by **morality**. God will judge man by his moral performance, since that's our distinguishing characteristic and calling: "God made mankind upright." (Ecclesiastes 7:29) Our mental and spiritual abilities include duty and responsibility, toward God and man and the rest of the world. It was built into us, this ability to know and respond to God's commands:

> Indeed, when Gentiles, who do not have the law, do by nature things required by the law, they are a law for themselves, even though they do not have the law, since they show that the requirements of the law are written on their hearts, their consciences also bearing witness, and their thoughts now accusing, now even defending them. (Romans 2:14-15)

In God's creation, nothing will remain hidden or in question; he must have all glory, so it must be *made plain* whether his creation, and his purposes through it, were a success. It's extremely important to him that all the universe knows. Since man's heart is by nature a secret thing ("For who among men knows the thoughts of a man except the man's spirit within him?" – 1 Corinthians 2:11), therefore God, in wisdom, made the world in such a way as to reveal the true state of our hearts. The circumstances of our lives will serve as a test to show whether we are indeed morally acceptable according to our original calling.

Science can't show us this profound aspect of God's wisdom. Scientists don't have the ability to uncover the moral nature of man or God's Kingdom; rather, we become aware of it through God's revelation – his Word. It's there that we read that God expects righteousness from man; in the Bible, which is the "blueprint" of the spiritual Kingdom of God, we learn about what is good and bad, the punishment of the wicked and the reward of the righteous.

The heart of man is too often caught up with the issues of daily life: we are generally unaware that greater spiritual issues hang in the balance, things that depend on a correct course of action. We make a living, we go to school, we raise our families, we relate to friends and neighbors, little thinking about the eternal consequences of our actions. But our actions have profound eternal consequences, whether we know it or not! Just in how we treat our neighbor we can see that there are such things as justice, goodness, love and concern, indignation and hatred against sin, and so on.

We aren't always unaware of the moral side of life, however, because there is one aspect of our nature that provides at least some guidelines in moral issues – the conscience. Our heart is usually a fair indicator that we are either in conformity to God's Law or outside of it. Even the heathen, who don't know the Law that God gave Israel at Mt. Sinai, have *some* natural understanding of what is right and wrong in God's eyes. (Romans 2:14-15) There is such a thing as right and wrong all over the world, in every culture.

Because the heart is so important to our course of action in life – it's the seat of all our actions – the Scripture emphasizes the importance of protecting the heart from any influence that would "sear" or harden the conscience against what it knows to be true:

> Above all else, guard your heart, for it is the wellspring of life. (Proverbs 4:23)

God made the world with such skill that, in the very act of living out our daily lives, we show what we are inside. God tests us (Ecclesiastes 3:18); he does it through the "times and seasons" of life (Ecclesiastes 3:1-8). And as we are caught up with the circumstances of life (which, again, he determined beforehand what they should be — Acts 17:25-26), we display what is in our hearts like a neon sign: we are either inclined toward evil, or toward glorifying God by obedience to his Law. We will prove what we really are by whichever one we end up doing. It's through our *actions,* and how we respond to events that God sets up around us, that the true state of our hearts becomes known:

> But the things that come out of the mouth come from the heart, and these make a man 'unclean.' For out of the heart come evil thoughts, murder, adultery, sexual immorality, theft, false testimony, slander. (Matthew 15:18-19)

The fact that God (and other people) can so easily discern our hearts was not a chance occurrence; it was by design, as a thermometer is designed to reveal the temperature. God made the world and us in a way that shows what we really are inside. Jesus referred to this principle in his analogy of a tree:

> By their fruit you will recognize them. Do people pick grapes from thornbushes, or figs from thistles? Likewise every good tree bears good fruit, but a bad tree bears bad fruit. A good tree cannot bear bad fruit, and a bad tree cannot bear good fruit. (Matthew 7:16-18)

Jesus relies on this principle, and encourages us to do the same, because of his knowledge of how God made our hearts and how our circumstances were designed specifically to reveal our hearts. In fact, it is so axiomatic and inevitable in God's world that our actions are windows into our true spiritual state, that Jesus once counseled us to take measures to eliminate the opportunity to express our immoral tendencies — by cutting off the *instruments* of action. (Matthew 5:29-

30) In other words, don't let what is in your heart find outward expression in sin.

Again, we must emphasize that God had a purpose in designing our world like this: it's easy to tell what we are (at least if we use God's standards of right and wrong). Neither we nor God are ever in doubt about whether we honor God with our lives, since it will be plain to see by the way we live. If this weren't true, we would no doubt presume on his good will, thinking that we could fool God about what our hearts are like. But because of his wisdom in this matter, there is no question as to where we stand:

> Do not be deceived: God cannot be mocked. A man reaps what he sows. The one who sows to please his sinful nature, from that nature will reap destruction; the one who sows to please the Spirit, from the Spirit will reap eternal life. (Galatians 6:7-8)

The spiritual level

God, for his own reasons, made us to be physical *and* spiritual creatures. And there are also two other aspects to our nature: we have *needs* for which there must be ample supply, and we *express* ourselves in ways appropriate to our nature. We have already seen how God made the world to provide for our physical needs, and how daily circumstances reveal what we are inside, morally speaking. But we have yet to look at the spiritual side of our nature, the way that God both fulfills our spiritual needs and judges the state of our souls.

It's beyond the scope of our study here to outline the great spiritual works that God performed from the beginning of the world. They include the calling of Abraham and the establishing of the community of faith, the setting up of the Temple and sacrificial systems through the Mosaic Law, the founding of the kingdom through David and his successors, the ministry of the prophets, the incarnation and ministry of Jesus Christ, and the explosive growth of the Christian Church. These and many more events show a carefully planned system designed to address our spiritual needs.

We must realize, above all else, that our spiritual needs can't be met through physical means; false religions err the most on this point. In their ignorance they *cannot* find, and due to their wickedness they *will not* rely on, anything other than created things to ease their wounded consciences. So they make gods out of stone or wood, or in our day out of money and politics and atom bombs. Their gods reflect aspects of physical creation — forces and elements of this world — in which the worshiper puts his hope. "They exchanged the truth of God for a lie, and worshipped and served created things rather than the Creator." (Romans 1:25)

True religion, however, finds God not *in* the world that he made (in other words, God isn't the world itself or the powers of nature), but *apart from*, yet *by means of*, this world. This isn't easy to understand unless we rise above the world and look at spiritual realities. Remember that the Israelites were forbidden to worship any created thing, or even make an idol to represent God. The reason for this is that nothing in this world is like God, and God is far above anything that we can imagine.

We can see this clearly in his works on earth, but only if the Spirit opens our eyes and hearts to this spiritual reality. For example, the Israelites learned to follow God's guidance in the desert through the pillar of cloud by day, and the pillar of fire by night. But at no time were they permitted to mistake this physical manifestation of the guiding hand of God to be God himself. God can't be represented by any physical reality. (Exodus 20:4-6)

This aspect of God's wisdom – that he is spiritual, and must be understood through spiritual means, even though we operate in a physical world ourselves – is the most profound and the least accessible to the unaided human mind:

> We have not received the spirit of the world but the Spirit who is from God, that we may understand what God has freely given us. This is what we speak, not in words taught us by human wisdom but in words taught

by the Spirit, expressing spiritual truths in spiritual
words. The man without the Spirit does not accept the
things that come from the Spirit of God, for they are
foolishness to him, and he cannot understand them,
because they are spiritually discerned. (1 Corinthians
2:12-14)

For example, the most important of God's works is also the most mysterious — the coming of the Lord Jesus Christ, and all that he did for us. Most saw him as just a man, a humble servant, a pretender who had no earthly claim to the spiritual realities he spoke of. Yet in God's wisdom those realities *are* in Christ, behind the physical exterior, and whoever wants salvation and the treasures of Heaven will find them in him. Peter, because God the Father opened his eyes, was enabled to see the spiritual Messiah in the man Jesus. (Matthew 16:13-20)

It's that mystery — the physical level itself being of no spiritual use, yet it supports a spiritual reality that we *can* benefit from — that Paul brings to our attention when he worships God for his wisdom.

... and to make plain to everyone the administration of this
mystery, which for ages past was kept hidden in God, who
created all things. His intent was that now, through the
church, the manifold wisdom of God should be made
known to the rulers and authorities in the heavenly realms.
(Ephesians 3:9-10)

Notice that he connects the mystery of the Gospel with Creation: the physical Creation itself is of no direct benefit to man spiritually (thus salvation *must* be on a different plane), yet it proves to be the vehicle of the salvation process. Not until God reveals the hidden spiritual agenda to us will we be able to see that the world is bigger than just the physical level.

Now to him who is able to establish you by my gospel
and the proclamation of Jesus Christ, according to the
revelation of the mystery *hidden for long ages past*, but

now revealed and made known through the prophetic writings by the command of the eternal God, so that all nations might believe and obey him — to the only wise God be glory forever through Jesus Christ! Amen. (Romans 16:25-27)

Which will it be?

Once again we are faced with an either/or situation. A world made by evolution would have no meaning or purpose, no wisdom behind how it's made, no levels of existence in which creatures play out eternal agendas. An evolutionary world just exists, changes, dies – that's all. The trouble is that this theory doesn't fit the facts of our daily lives.

But if God made the world by his wisdom, then there will always be moral and spiritual events going on that prove there is a spiritual world guiding the events of the physical universe. For example, when we can easily tell the spiritual state of a person's heart by the kinds of things he does, this is a more certain proof of God's hand in Creation than any "missing link" – or lack of one –that scientists can discover in physical nature.

The Proof of Creation – Eyewitness

The Bible is *not* a scientific textbook, and both sides in the Creation debate know this. It's obvious that the Bible itself doesn't approach the subject from a scientific viewpoint. That's a framework that we moderns try to fit over the story, and it doesn't work. The entire Bible is actually a *legal* document, not a scientific treatise. It's a collection of affidavits — sworn statements — by eyewitnesses who testified to what they saw and heard.

Genesis 1-3 is an eyewitness account from the only One who could have reported the event accurately, considering the manner in which it was performed. Furthermore, while miracle was the most important *characteristic* of Creation, the concept of the witness is the fundamental *defense* of Creation. First, however, we need to look at how important the role of the witness was throughout the history of the works of God.

The reality of God

If, in all of our actions and thoughts, studying and seeking for truth, we limit our scope to what Ecclesiastes calls "everything under the sun," then we will never find God. *That* is the great mystery that has eluded the mind of man since the beginning of time. If there *is* a God, then we are suddenly faced with enormous implications for our lives. So people everywhere, in all times and places, have searched for the answer to this mystery of God.

The Bible claims to have the answer to this question: its unique contribution is the concept of the *witness*. It provides us with eyewitnesses to the real God: they testify that they have seen him and his works. *They were there* on the scene when God revealed himself; and there was no doubt in their minds that it was the true God that they experienced. So the witnesses who testify in the Bible are dealing, fundamentally, with **the reality of God** — something that we all have to come to terms with. For example, here are some well-known passages concerning the witnesses of the Bible:

> John *testifies* concerning him. (John 1:15)

> I tell you the truth, we speak of *what we know*, and we *testify* to what we have seen, but still you people do not accept our testimony. (John 3:11)

> But you will receive power when the Holy Spirit comes on you; and you will be my *witnesses* in Jerusalem, and in all Judea and Samaria, and to the ends of the earth. (Acts 1:8)

> Therefore, since we are surrounded by such a great cloud of *witnesses*, let us throw off everything that hinders and the sin that so easily entangles, and let us run with perseverance the race marked out for us. (Hebrews 12:1)

> That which was from the beginning, which *we have heard*, which *we have seen with our eyes*, which *we have looked at* and *our hands have touched* — this we *proclaim* concerning the Word of life. The life appeared; *we have seen it* and testify to it, and we *proclaim* to you the eternal life, which was with the Father and *has appeared to us*. We *proclaim* to you what *we have seen and heard*, so that you also may have fellowship with us. And *our fellowship is with the Father and with his Son, Jesus Christ*. We write this to make our joy complete. (1 John 1:1-4)

This is just a sampling, some of the better known passages. Actually the entire Bible testifies to the reality of God, in many ways. For example, God created the world, he made it for our benefit, he demands and gets glory, he guides the history of men and nations, he condemns sinners and rewards the righteous, he decides when and where people will live (Acts 17:26), he created a vast spiritual structure for our salvation and he has planned an eternity of unimaginable life for his people, making this world only an introduction by comparison. And for all these truths about God, we have testimony from reliable witnesses.

We, of course, have seen little or none of this work of God; for us, the entire business is a matter for faith. Do we have anything, though, that will be a solid foundation for our faith? That's the business of the Bible: to provide testimony of eyewitnesses from history who verified that what we believe about God, as it is written in the Bible, is all true and quite real, and we are *expected* to believe their testimony. Since these spiritual realities have tremendous implications for us, the Bible sets forth these for us as well.

Witnesses of the miracles

One of the areas that the Bible spends a great deal of time on is the subject of miracles; but, of course, the modern man's mind rebels against the idea and denies the possibility of miracles in a materialistic universe. But it's too easy to deny the stories in the Bible. We can't say that, just because they happened over 2000 years ago and therefore *we* didn't see them, they didn't occur! There are other ways of determining whether something is true, as we shall see shortly. Furthermore, if a miracle bypasses the laws that science relies upon, then hiding behind science in the face of a recorded miracle is just blind obstinacy, as well as intellectual dishonesty.

One fact that puts modern unbelievers in a particularly difficult position is this: there were eyewitnesses present when the miracles happened. We have their testimony in the Bible.

- ***God wisely provided witnesses.*** If it were not for the witnesses who were present, we would never believe the stories in the Bible. The miracles were too fantastic. We are not dealing with ordinary events here, but extraordinary ones.

The very nature of a miracle requires not understanding but *faith*. It's impossible; such things can't happen in a world that runs according to natural laws. But God didn't use natural laws when he did the miracle! He skipped the laws, he ignored the raw materials, and did it directly — it was a jump from nothing to solid results.

> By faith we understand that the universe was formed at God's command, so that what is seen was not made out of what was visible. (Hebrews 11:3)

God isn't laying this information out for scientists to inspect; there is nothing here they can understand. Nor does he ask us to "approve" his works when we can finally understand them — we never will. Nor does our unbelief disprove his miracles; the fact that we are mystified about how he might have done something only points to our limitations as creatures, and our inability to think in any other way than according to natural laws.

There are many ways to determine the truth of a historical event. Physical evidence is one; but evidence is only the leftover material *after* the event, and can usually be interpreted in many ways. A witness, however, was there on the scene, whether he testifies in man's court or God's court. He saw what happened. His testimony is invaluable to help us know the truth of a matter. In fact, a witness is more important than physical evidence, because he stood in our place — we were present at the event *through him*. We use his eyes, his mind, and his senses, to witness the event. He is as dependable as the rest of us. A court of law believes in his inherent ability to tell the facts as well as *we* could if we were there ourselves. To doubt that is to doubt common human abilities.

God's witnesses are unique among all witnesses: they testified that, by God's hand, the *impossible* happened.

God is no fool, and he knows that most of us aren't going to believe that those miracles actually happened. So he wisely made sure that there were witnesses present when he did his miracles.

It wasn't accidental that they were there; if that were true, then God himself might take issue with some of them for misinterpreting what they thought they saw when they had no business putting themselves forward as his supposed experts. Or they might have been unqualified as witnesses and given us false impressions about what happened. Instead, God hand-picked his witnesses — and stands behind their testimony. "He was not seen by all the people, but by witnesses *whom God had already chosen* — by us who ate and drank with him after he rose from the dead." (Acts 10:41) The Bible's witnesses are God-approved and certified as reliable and trustworthy. We *can* know the truth through them.

- ***The witnesses were no fools.*** People today like to think that the people of ancient times were little children in comparison with us. We consider ourselves so intelligent with our modern technology that we don't trust anybody else's opinion on things — especially in those areas where our science claims greater expertise. So we don't believe the miracle accounts. We accuse the "witnesses" of being scientifically naïve and mistaking natural events as miracles, when actually those events, we claim, have a perfectly reasonable explanation.

But whoever believes that ancient civilizations were immature and intellectually backward needs to read some more accurate history. They were very intelligent and capable people who devised some remarkably modern solutions to solve their problems. The *needs* of man remain the same through the ages because man's nature remains the same — including his intellectual prowess. We can easily see an example for this when people in undeveloped nations in our own times quickly adapt to modern technology.

All this is to say that the witnesses of God weren't stupid or gullible. When the disciples watched Peter step out of the boat and walk on water, they knew very well that they were witnessing a miracle of God, an impossibility in this natural world. Not even modern man could claim to duplicate such a feat! All the miracles that they reported to us are of such a nature that they either happened or they didn't happen. There is no room for interpretation, or natural explanations, nor were they deceived. Our scientists are just as helpless as they were when it comes to understanding what happened.

We aren't stupid either. We are dealing with miracles here, and with honest, sane people who claim to have seen the impossible happen. We have no honest recourse but to take their claim seriously. We would be offended ourselves if future generations were so arrogant that they would reject out of hand what *we* know to be true. We also offend these witnesses of the past when we arrogantly claim that miracles don't happen when they, in fact, knew that the miracles they saw *did* happen. Has our science so blinded us to the truth? When we act like that, the ancients would have had reason to doubt *our* intelligence!

- ***Their testimony is legally compelling.*** In a courtroom the witness plays an important role in a legal case. Since hardly anybody tells the truth when they are accused of a crime that they may be punished for, we need the testimony of *someone else who was there on the scene* who can either agree with the defendant or accuse him of committing the crime. The witness saw what actually happened. Whatever he says about the event becomes legal evidence that the court uses to acquit or convict the defendant.

There's another reason that witnesses are important: the members of the jury, who decide the case, *were not* there at the scene. They no doubt would like to have been there to see for themselves what really happened, but they weren't. They are therefore legally *obligated* to accept the testimony of the eyewitness in place of their being present at the scene. The witness becomes, in effect, their representative, their eyes, and literally their only means of knowing the truth. All this is a fact in our legal system — in any just legal system in the world, for that matter.

This is why the testimony of the eyewitnesses of the Bible becomes so critical for us. We who listen to the accounts of the miracles weren't there when they happened. We would love to see for ourselves whether Jesus really did what the witnesses said he did, but we will never have that privilege. What God has provided for us, therefore, are eyewitnesses who claim to have seen these things happen.

There were thousands, and in some instances millions, of eyewitnesses to the miracles of God recorded in the Bible. God didn't do his works in an obscure corner; he purposely did them in front of many people and then had their testimony recorded for our benefit so that we would believe that these things really happened. The apostle Paul echoes this care that God took to do his work in front of many witnesses:

> For what I received I passed on to you as of first importance: that Christ died for our sins according to the Scriptures, that he was buried, that he was raised on the third day according to the Scriptures,

and that he appeared to Peter, and then to the Twelve. After that, he appeared to more than five hundred of the brothers at the same time, most of whom are still living, though some have fallen asleep. Then he appeared to James, then to all the apostles, and last of all he appeared to me also, as to one abnormally born. (1 Corinthians 15:3-8)

It's astonishing how many sources we have for the miracles of God. The Israelites, for example, saw God perform awesome wonders in the desert when he delivered them out of Egypt and led them to the Promised Land. There were millions of witnesses who saw those miracles.

We even have "hostile witnesses" who can testify to God's miracles. In a court case it's sometimes possible for one side to use the testimony of a witness from the other side — called a "hostile witness." The Bible is full of testimony from hostile witnesses. Perhaps the most famous examples are the Pharisees in Jesus' day. They were no friends of Christ, they had no intention of doing anything to help him or his followers, yet they *saw* Christ do miracle after miracle and were forced to admit that they really did happen. (John 11:47-48) Their testimony is especially damaging to the case of modern skeptics who refuse to believe in Christ's miracles.

We are not free to dismiss the testimony of eyewitnesses just because we don't like the sound of it! Their testimony is legally binding. In order to challenge an eyewitness account, we have to produce our own witnesses to contradict the first witness's account. In other words, the burden of proof is on us, not on the witness. We have to prove him wrong to the satisfaction of the court, and as we know from accepted legal practice, that means producing our own witnesses.

Personal opinions don't overthrow the testimony of an eyewitness.

- ***Most of the Bible is testimony.*** The Bible is a record of the works of God, and the revelation of the true nature of God. And when it comes to anything that has to do with the true God, man is naturally a skeptic. He tends to not believe the truth about God, for many reasons. For one thing, if this God is real, then we have to do something about our sin, which is an offense to this holy God and will be the cause of our condemnation if we don't do something about it right away. Another reason is that this God requires all glory, and demands that we set aside our own glory and depend on him for everything. These and other reasons make it difficult to accept anything we hear about God.

In order to convince us, then, of the truth about God, the Lord gave us the Bible as a collection of testimonies concerning himself and his works. Not only do we have descriptions of the true God there, we have eyewitness accounts from reliable people that *this God* is real, that he really did what the witnesses said he did. Noah can testify, because of what he saw God do, that God is holy and can't tolerate a world of sinners. Abraham can testify, because of what God did for him, that God is a covenant-keeping God who intends to bless his people. Joseph can testify that God works his own plans out through the affairs of men and nations. David can testify that God rules his people in righteousness and defeats his enemies. Solomon can testify that God lives among his people and forgives their sin. Each account is an eyewitness account of the reality of Israel's God.

We must realize that this isn't a history of natural events in our world. These people saw and heard *God*, which is the very point in question in our day. We have hardly ever seen such things in our lives; we tend to doubt that there is a God. In fact, the Bible makes this a point of our faith: true faith believes in the reality of God. "And without faith it is impossible to please God, because anyone who comes to him *must believe that he exists* and that he rewards those who earnestly seek him." (Hebrews 11:6) How can we know that God exists? How can we know that there is such a God, and that he wasn't someone's imagination? By the testimony of eyewitnesses who saw him in action in this world.

No one can go back in time now and sit at Jesus' feet; we can only believe what his witnesses tell us about him. The disciples, however, had the privilege of witnessing his acts firsthand. In fact, they sometimes demanded visible proof before they would believe in him — which he gave them!

> Now Thomas (called Didymus), one of the Twelve, was not with the disciples when Jesus came. So the other disciples told him, "We have seen the Lord!" But he said to them, "Unless I see the nail marks in his hands and put my finger where the nails were, and put my hand into his side, I will not believe it." A week later his disciples were in the house again, and Thomas was with them. Though the doors were locked, Jesus came and stood among them and said, "Peace be with you!" Then he said to Thomas, "Put your finger here; see my hands. Reach out your hand and put it into my side. Stop doubting and believe." Thomas said to him, "My Lord and my God!" (John 20:24-28)

But, as Christ said, the rest of us must rely on the testimony of the apostles for our faith:

> Because you have seen me, you have believed; blessed are those who have not seen and yet have believed. (John 20:29)

A faithful witness

Because the testimony of eyewitnesses is so important for deciding a case, it's a serious offense for a witness to give false testimony. This is known as perjury, and there are heavy penalties for such crimes against the court. After all, someone's life, freedom and reputation depend on the testimony of witnesses. *It has to be true.* In the Law of Moses we read about a sobering legal procedure concerning witnesses who testify against the accused. If the accused man is found guilty, the witnesses who testified against him must be the first to lay hands on him: "The hands of the witnesses must be the first in putting him to death." (Deuteronomy 17:7) For this reason, the court will not accept false testimony, and if it has reason to think that a witness is lying then the entire case could be overturned along with punishing the false witness.

> There are six things the LORD hates, seven that are detestable to him ... a false witness who pours out lies. (Proverbs 6:16,19)
>
> A truthful witness gives honest testimony, but a false witness tells lies. (Proverbs 12:17)
>
> A truthful witness does not deceive, but a false witness pours out lies. (Proverbs 14:5)
>
> A truthful witness saves lives, but a false witness is deceitful. (Proverbs 14:25)
>
> A false witness will not go unpunished, and he who pours out lies will not go free. (Proverbs 19:5)
>
> A false witness will not go unpunished, and he who pours out lies will perish. (Proverbs 19:9)

> A corrupt witness mocks at justice, and the mouth of the wicked gulps down evil. (Proverbs 19:28)
>
> A false witness will perish, and whoever listens to him will be destroyed forever. (Proverbs 21:28)

If this is what God thinks of false witnesses, we can be sure that he intends to select faithful witnesses when it comes to testifying about himself. *The witnesses of God and his miracles gave the most trustworthy testimony ever given in the history of man.* This is the truth; it has to be, because every one of the witnesses of the Bible are under oath in God's court to tell the truth or be guilty of perjury against God himself. We can, therefore, rely completely on their testimony; our eternal salvation depends on it.

If someone successfully proves that the witness is lying, then suddenly the court brings its legal powers to bear upon the witness himself:

> The judges must make a thorough investigation, and if the witness proves to be a liar, giving false testimony against his brother, then do to him as he intended to do to his brother. You must purge the evil from among you. The rest of the people will hear of this and be afraid, and never again will such an evil thing be done among you. (Deuteronomy 19:18-20)

This shows the heavy responsibility laid on witnesses, and the supreme importance placed on their testimony. It must be accurate, true, and dependable.

Doubting a witness

So if someone challenges the witness, he has a big job on his hands. If he provides physical evidence to disprove the witness, the evidence has to be overwhelmingly convincing to the court. This might in fact work if the witness can't claim to have seen the event clearly, having made no mistakes. If he only heard a rumor or saw what evidence was left after the event was over, then more convincing evidence could prove his testimony wrong. But if the witness saw the event in its entirety and can claim to know exactly what happened, then it's unlikely that any evidence offered contrary to his testimony will have much weight in court. Physical evidence has questionable value because it's usually open to so much interpretation — either side could easily use it to support its own argument.

This means, then, that to discount the testimony of a witness, the only option left is to call him a liar. Either the thing happened, or it didn't. If it didn't and the eyewitness claims that it did, then he is, simply put, a liar. And since the eyewitness is sworn to tell the truth, to call him a liar is a serious charge to make. One must have very convincing proof in hand if he, wanting to accuse the witness of being a liar, doesn't want to incur the wrath of the court himself.

In order to disprove the stories of miracles in the Bible, we would have to call thousands of eyewitnesses liars. That would be the height of ignorance, arrogance and stupidity on our part. They were there; we weren't. They saw it happen. Of course it was impossible, but that's why God had eyewitnesses on hand — we wouldn't believe such things if people didn't tell us that they saw them with their own eyes! It's not an argument against their testimony to say that we don't believe it. In God's court, the eyewitnesses have priority and carry the case. If we don't believe them, then we must show proof to God why they are *lying*. And it's also no argument that they weren't scientifically astute enough to tell when a "miracle" was just a natural event. They aren't claiming scientific proficiency; they are claiming that God did this miracle *apart from natural means*, which is the very point in question. Our challenge, to be plain, is to prove that *God didn't do it this way!* Since we can't imagine any way of working except through natural means, we have no hope of disproving the miracle. We are cornered into believing the witness.

The Eyewitness of Creation

Now that we've established the Biblical strategy of using witnesses to testify to the reality of God and his miracles, let's turn back to Genesis where we will find the very same strategy used on the first great miracle. The Creation account in Genesis is very simple if we read it just the way it is. It says that there was a time when only God existed and the world was "formless and empty" (Genesis 1:2); it says that God commanded each step of Creation; it says that things came immediately into existence at God's command, out of nothing; it says that the whole affair took six days; it says that God called it "very good." (Genesis 1:31) Give the story to a child to read, and this is what he will see — a plain, simple account. For that matter, it's what the rest of the Bible sees there too.

An adult, however, reacts to this account with disbelief. We can't accept the stupendous miracles that would have had to occur for this story to be true. We know that such things are impossible. So our verdict is — there has to be a more reasonable explanation for the beginning of the universe than this series of miracles. We like to look to science for an explanation, because science deals in the possible, in physical laws, in solid principles. And modern science has many ingenious answers for the origin of the world and life that satisfy many people — none of which include the concept of miracles.

As it reads, however, the Creation passage is an account of the biggest physical miracle that ever happened in the existence of the universe. If we accept it for what it says, then God made the world through a miracle. What does that mean?

> **First**, it means that he bypassed all the steps that we would have thought necessary to make a world. He didn't use natural laws, which makes sense because those laws weren't yet in existence — they came into being only with the rest of the universe. He didn't work through eons to develop parts of the world. He didn't use any existing materials, because there were none. A miracle happens when God does something immediately, *apart* from natural means.

Second, science therefore *cannot* help us understand how the world began. This is true for unbelievers as well as Creationists. Science describes events in terms of natural laws. Scientists can only work with events which they can analyze and duplicate, and they need to know the methods used to produce those events. But just as we can never understand how Jesus turned water into wine, we can never understand how God commanded trees into existence. Miracle is the *same kind* of thing no matter where we encounter it in the Bible. We can never understand how such vast cosmic realities came into existence in just six days. This is not a scientific event! It's a miraculous event, and any attempt to understand it scientifically will actually diminish the truth of what happened.

Third, the concept of miracles is just too much for us to grasp. Of course the miracle is astonishing! It sounds so far-fetched that our immediate reaction is disbelief. Even the smaller miracles recorded later in the Bible would be easier to believe than this "mother of all miracles" (to use a current but appropriate expression). *That* is why we want to find a more reasonable explanation of Creation — the Bible's account is so far out of our reckoning that we feel we must find something more reasonable to keep our intellectual respectability. But the *reason* for looking elsewhere — which is that we can't accept the staggering nature of the miracle involved — should indicate that there is a spiritual problem involved; it's dishonest to ignore plain testimony just because we don't like the sound of it.

Fourth, the miracle of Creation is the groundwork for all the works of the Lord in the rest of history. We see in this miracle the beginning of all the rest of God's miracles. God demonstrated not only his ability but his *tendency* to do what he wants through miracle, not through natural means. We ourselves work with the world he gave us, which means that science can provide us with the tools to achieve our goals. But God works around those laws to do what he wants; he doesn't use the steps that we have to struggle with. We see this fact all through the Bible. Both the physical creation and the new spiritual creation are results of *miracles*, because created things, as we have seen, can't give him the spiritual element that he wants for his purposes.

Fifth, when God performed the miracle of Creation, we ought to expect, since he was so careful in other instances to do the same, that he provided an eyewitness of the event — he knew we would never believe it otherwise. And he did: there *was* an eyewitness of the miracle of Creation.

> Now the earth was formless and empty, darkness was over the surface of the deep, and the Spirit of God was hovering over the waters. (Genesis 1:2)

God knew that generations of men wouldn't believe the account of how he made the world. He also knew that man would amass great amounts of knowledge and think himself able to challenge the wisdom of the Almighty, denying the truth about God. So, as a "preemptive strike" against the empty wisdom of men in future ages, God made sure that there was a witness at the greatest of all physical miracles: the Holy Spirit.

His choice of a witness was strategic. The Spirit is the greatest of all witnesses; he is called "the Spirit of truth." (John 14:17) The Spirit was the most reliable witness that God could have chosen for several reasons:

- ***Only the Spirit can tell us what really happened.***
Since we are dealing with the miraculous in the Creation

event, we need someone who can faithfully report on the actual event and how it unfolded. If a scientist were there, even though equipped with the most sophisticated of instruments, he could never have understood what he saw. When God makes something huge like the universe out of *nothing*, and does it instantly, we just can't fathom what kind of power and wisdom is at work.

But the Spirit perceived the actual process: God's command, God's will, creation's obedience, existence out of nothing, the physical world made for spiritual purposes, God's blessing. These are miracles and spiritual concepts. There was actually a tremendous amount of spiritual activity going on at Creation, but the Genesis account only gives us a basic overview of the bare miracles involved — we have to look elsewhere in the Bible for a fuller explanation of what God accomplished and set up there at the beginning. Nobody could have possibly understood this kind of event except the Spirit of God.

- *He tells the truth.* No one can accuse the Spirit of telling a lie, or of not being scientifically astute. Man is desperately ignorant in comparison, and in the dark about God and his works, until the Spirit enlightens his mind and enables him to see the truth. The Spirit is literally our link to the truth. "But when he, the Spirit of truth, comes, he will guide you into all truth." (John 16:13) "And it is the Spirit who testifies, because the Spirit is the truth." (1 John 5:6) Truth is the way *God* looks at things, since he is the Creator and Judge of all things. But we certainly can't know the mind of God unless the Spirit reveals it to us — which he does:

> The Spirit searches all things, even the deep things of God. For who among men knows the thoughts of a man except the man's spirit within him? In the same way no one knows the

thoughts of God except the Spirit of God. (1 Corinthians 2:10-11)

Until the Spirit teaches us, we can't know the truth about God and his works. That's why Jesus told Nicodemus, an expert in the Law of God, "I tell you the truth, no one can see the kingdom of God unless he is born again ... I tell you the truth, no one can enter the kingdom of God unless he is born of water and the Spirit." (John 3:3,5)

- *He is the expert witness.* The Spirit was always called to testify when men needed to hear the truth about God. We find him present at many critical junctures in Biblical history, even in those situations when *men* were witnesses of God — they were enabled to see and know the presence of God *through the work of the Spirit*. Their ability to witness depended completely on the Spirit testifying to them of the reality of God.

We find this repeatedly in the Scriptures. David was filled with the Spirit and saw spiritual realities, which prompted all of his worship that is written in the Psalms. The prophets saw, through the revelation of the Spirit, the realities of Heaven and the coming kingdom of God. The apostles were filled with the Spirit and enabled to witness about Christ to the nations. John was filled with the Spirit when he received the revelation of Christ on Patmos. The Spirit has always been behind the testimony of human witnesses.

Therefore, to doubt the testimony of the Spirit is the greatest of sins. He is the fundamental source of all true knowledge of God. Jesus foretells disaster to the person who would call the Spirit a liar:

I tell you the truth, all the sins and blasphemies of men will be forgiven them [*even, as we find in*

> *the parallel passage of Luke 12:10, sins against Christ himself*]. But whoever blasphemes against the Holy Spirit will never be forgiven; he is guilty of an eternal sin. (Mark 3:28-29)

The Spirit didn't tell us the truth about Creation just to open himself to our foolish accusations against him — like being ignorant of scientific principles. Because the miracle of Creation is so important to our understanding of God, and God demands that we trust him in this, the Spirit himself testifies to the method of Creation; he will trust no man to interpret this important spiritual event. This isn't a matter for trifling with the Almighty Creator. He purposely set up this situation in this way: we either believe his chosen witness, or we are in *legal* trouble with the Judge of Heaven and Earth.

But, modern skeptics will say, it was a long jump in time between the Creation of the world and the recording of it in the book of Genesis. Even if it were true that the Spirit was there as an eyewitness, how can we be sure that these words in Genesis — written by a man — faithfully represent the mind of the Spirit?

For that objection we find our answer in 2 Peter. Genesis is part of the "Law of Moses." (Luke 24:44) Whether Moses wrote the entire book, or (what's more likely) acted as editor of previously existing material passed on to him from the patriarchs which he included in his Law that he then passed on to Israel, the point is the same. The Scripture very plainly tells us what kind of man Moses was:

> Since then, no prophet has risen in Israel like Moses, whom the LORD knew face to face, who did all those miraculous signs and wonders the LORD sent him to do in Egypt — to Pharaoh and to all his officials and to his whole land. For no one has ever shown the mighty power or performed the awesome deeds that Moses did in the sight of all Israel. (Deuteronomy 34:10-12)

> When a prophet of the LORD is among you, I reveal myself to him in visions, I speak to him in dreams. But this is not true of my servant Moses; he is faithful in all my house. With him I speak face to face, clearly and not in riddles; he sees the form of the LORD. Why then were you not afraid to speak against my servant Moses? (Numbers 12:6-8)

That last sentence is a relevant one in light of the modern controversy about Genesis. Those who spoke against Moses found themselves immediately in trouble with the Lord, because Moses *spoke the Word of the Lord*, by the power of the Spirit. To doubt him was to doubt God himself. It was a serious offense with a serious penalty, as his own brother and sister found out!

It's important to establish Moses as a **prophet**, in connection with Creation, because Peter tells us *how* the prophets knew what to say in their prophecies:

> Above all, you must understand that no prophecy of Scripture came about by the prophet's own interpretation. For prophecy never had its origin in the will of man, but men spoke from God *as they were carried along by the Holy Spirit.* (2 Peter 1:20-21)

Moses, as the greatest of the prophets, spoke what the Holy Spirit told him to say — *not* his own version of the story. In other words, Moses received the truth about Creation from the only eyewitness who was present — and reported the very words of that eyewitness to us, faithfully and accurately, as every prophet was bound to do. And, even if Moses had previously written records available to him (which may have been the case), as a prophet he would certainly be led by the Spirit to select and record only that which was the truth. Moses wasn't there at Creation, of course, so he could only depend on what the Spirit told him about it. But we have already seen that the Spirit is always careful to tell us the truth about things, not myths or interpretations or springboards for our scientific conjectures. It was a cooperative venture between Spirit and prophet to bring us the record of an event which none of us saw, yet it's something that we all need to know about.

Dare we call the Spirit a liar?

Now we have come to the heart of the problem. At the risk of belaboring the issue, we have carefully taken up each point so that there is no mistaking what's at stake. Modern unbelievers purposely avoid talking about what they are, in fact, doing when they deny the Genesis account of Creation. We want to be very plain about this and pinpoint exactly what they are doing.

The only thing left to decide, therefore, is this: is the account of Creation in Genesis true or not? As we have just seen, this is the same thing as saying — Is the Spirit of God telling the truth *or is he lying*? When someone claims to be a witness, he is legally liable for what he says; ignorance or lack of scientific sophistication is not the issue. Someone's reputation (God's) is at stake, and a witness doesn't step up and take the stand lightly. And the event itself is of such a nature that either the thing happened as the witness claims or it didn't happen. There are only two options available for us: either it's the truth or it's a bald lie.

It staggers the imagination to think that a human being, a sinner from birth, ignorant of so much truth, who can only know what his senses tell him and what has been told him by other ignorant humans, and who was born only yesterday compared to the ancient event of Creation, would dare to call the Almighty God a *liar* about his own work. Yet that's exactly what's at issue here:

> Anyone who does not believe God has made him out to be *a liar*, because he has not believed the testimony God has given about his Son. (1 John 5:10)

When God himself (and that's who the Holy Spirit is) gives the testimony, our only safe recourse is to believe him. But people call him a liar all the time about the vast and convincing testimony that he has provided about Jesus Christ, as this passage shows. It's no wonder, then, that they also accuse him of lying about the origin of the world in his personal testimony recorded in Genesis.

This means that the issue of Creation is *not* a scientific one. God doesn't give us scientific details about what happened; he provides a legal witness to the event and *demands* that we believe what the Spirit tells us. We, as the members of the jury, so to speak, have only one option legally: to accept the testimony of the one who was there, since we weren't there. We are legally and morally obligated to accept his testimony! The simplest believer can know what happened at the beginning of the world; he doesn't need to be a scientist because it wouldn't help in any case.

Furthermore, any additional scientific investigation of the event would have to be on the assumption, already established, that the Genesis account is literally true. A believing scientist doesn't accept the Genesis account because of his own research, but by the authoritative statement of Scripture. He knows already that his studies of physical evidence will neither contradict the account, nor will it explain its miraculous nature. This appears to be blind prejudice to the unbelieving world, but actually it rests on better authority — the testimony of the Spirit — than does evolution which can provide no witnesses for its claims.

Modern unbelievers don't take the trouble to provide witnesses against God — because there are none. Rocks can be made to say anything one wishes. Physical evidence can be used by both sides in a courtroom, since it's always open to interpretation. No clever or devious use of physical evidence will sway the judge in favor against the clear testimony of the only eyewitness. Legally, the eyewitness carries the weight of the argument in court and decides the case.

Evolutionists, then, are calling God a liar when God says that he created the world through miracle. They say it more politely than this, of course — they say that the story is symbolic, that it's open to interpretation, that it's a charming myth and ancient folk literature. But the essence of what they are saying is that *they do not believe this testimony as it stands*. They do this in spite of the fact that God's creative work is always through miracles, that countless witnesses stand ready to testify to the reality of miracles, and that we can never know the truth of the matter unless we believe those whom God has sent to reveal this truth to us.

> And it is the Spirit who testifies, because the Spirit is the truth. For there are three that testify: the Spirit, the water and the blood; and the three are in agreement. We accept man's testimony, *but God's testimony is greater because it is the testimony of God*, which he has given about his Son. (1 John 5:6-9)

The Genesis account of Creation is actually a test of our faith in the truthfulness of the Spirit. If we can't believe the sworn testimony of the Spirit about the first work of God in the world, then naturally we won't believe any of the testimonies that follow concerning the rest of his works. If we call God a liar about the greatest of his physical miracles, then we are hardly in a position to understand the greatest of his spiritual miracles — the redemption brought about by the Lord Jesus Christ. As this passage from 1 John shows, it's the same witness who testifies of both miracles.

Finally, for the determined doubter who questions why we should take the Spirit's testimony as the truth, we have only the challenge from Christ:

> If anyone chooses to do God's will, he will find out whether my teaching comes from God or whether I speak on my own. (John 7:17)

In other words, we can't know for certain that what God says is true until we accept it wholeheartedly as *truth from God*. The testimony of the eyewitness requires no proof; but when we finally accept what really is the truth, then we will experience the peace and assurance that comes with knowing the truth.

The Agent of Creation – The Spirit of God

The Spirit was involved in Creation in another important way – which we can appreciate more if we first turn to the rest of the Bible and watch him at work there. For a long time now, there has been a great deal of confusion about the Holy Spirit and what exactly he does among us. Different churches and denominations have their different theories. But if we look carefully at the Bible, from the beginning to the end, we can begin to see a pattern of the Spirit's work, a pattern that we can then apply back to the Creation event.

The special work of the Spirit

Usually we think of the Spirit in terms of sanctification — that is, making us free from sin, or holy. "But you were washed, you were sanctified, you were justified in the name of the Lord Jesus Christ and by the Spirit of our God." (1 Corinthians 6:11) "To God's elect ... who have been chosen according to the foreknowledge of God the Father, by the sanctifying work of the Spirit, for obedience to Jesus Christ and sprinkling by his blood." (1 Peter 1:1-2)

But that's not the *primary* work of the Spirit according to the Bible. In a total of over 80 different passages that talk about what the Spirit does, I found only five places where it refers to his work of cleansing from sin, and some of those are marginal. In reality, about half of the passages teach that the Spirit *reveals* the things of God, and the other half talk about the Spirit's *empowering* work.

We've already looked at the revealing work of the Spirit. When he revealed to Moses the true account of what happened, he wasn't only a witness of the event but he went on to reveal the mystery so that Moses could understand it. And the fact that Moses recorded the truth in his books, so that the rest of the people of God would know the truth, was because of the Spirit who will always reveal the mysteries of God to his people. Remember what Peter said about the prophet being "carried along by the Holy Spirit" as he brings God's message to us. (2 Peter 1:21)

The second thing that the Spirit does is to give power, and that's what we're interested in here. "But you will receive power when the Holy Spirit comes on you; and you will be my witnesses in Jerusalem and in all Judea and Samaria, and to the ends of the earth." (Acts 1:8)

The kind of power that this verse is talking about isn't any power that we are familiar with. Simon made that mistake when he saw the apostles working miracles and tried to buy the power of the Spirit from them. (Acts 8:9-24) The power that the Spirit gives is a new thing, something that this world doesn't know anything about.

The first time that we find the empowering work of the Spirit in the Bible is in the Genesis Creation account.

> In the beginning God created the Heavens and the earth. Now the earth was formless and empty, darkness was over the surface of the deep, and the Spirit of God was hovering over the waters (Genesis 1:1-2)

What exactly was there at the beginning, the building blocks that God used to make the world, we don't know; we do know that it was "without form" and "without substance" (as the Hebrew words mean), which are the two necessary characteristics of matter as we know it. In other words, the Spirit brought non-existence into existence; he gave life and substance to what used to be nothing. The earth and plants and animals and man all exist because the Spirit gave us the ability to exist. Without him we would return to nothingness.

That's what happened to the world when the Spirit moved in the beginning. What happens in men's souls now? Here is where we need the Spirit most of all, because we are all dead to the world of God from our birth. (Ephesians 2:1-3) Even if we see God (the first job of the Spirit), and even if we *know* the truth about God and his world, we still can't do anything about it. God requires obedience from us — but we can't obey him because we are so bound up in our sin, and without power to obey his commands. He requires faith from us — but we can't believe in him because we are so confused, wandering in this dark world, and we can't understand what he's talking about. He calls us to live in *his* world, but we can't get out of our world. At the very least we are to "love the Lord your God with all our heart and with all your soul and with all your mind," (Matthew 22:37) but unfortunately we aren't interested — there are other things that we love more.

When the Spirit works on the heart, however, that person wakes up to God's world, like opening one's eyes on a bright morning. "Wake up, O sleeper, rise from the dead, and Christ will shine on you." (Ephesians 5:14) He can see things now that he hasn't seen before. Even this dark world that we live in gets a new light: the Spirit shines on our lives, on circumstances, on other people, like a spotlight, and shows us things that we couldn't see before.

The Spirit not only wakes us up to the world of God, he makes us *able* to live in God's world. "Flesh and blood cannot inherit the Kingdom of God" (1 Corinthians 15:50), simply because the conditions there would kill us. The air is different, the food is different, the light is different (I'm using symbols of the realities, you understand; "air" and "food" and "light" in Heaven are spiritual things, whereas we think of our physical world when we hear those words.) Paul said that before we can hope to rise into Heaven, some things about us have to change:

> So it will be with the resurrection of the dead. The body that is sown is perishable, it is raised imperishable; it is sown in dishonor, it is raised in glory; it is sown in weakness, it is raised in power; it is sown a natural body, it is raised a spiritual body. (1 Corinthians 15:42-44)

In order to live before God and not die, we have to change completely. Our natures as they are now can neither survive before God's glory, nor can we understand or appreciate what we would see there. Our physical senses weren't made to be aware of the things of God. Unless, of course, the Spirit gives life to our souls — our souls *were* made to be aware of God. That's why the Bible talks about having "eyes to see" and "ears to hear." The Spirit makes us alive spiritually (which Jesus called, appropriately, being "born again" — John 3:3) so that our spiritual senses can start picking up on the things of God. In order to pick up the signals from a radio station, you have to first turn the radio on. In the same way, before anybody can hope to know God, their souls must be made alive first.

The Spirit makes it possible for us to obey God's commands; without him we could never do them. (Ezekiel 36:26-27) The Law is spiritual, Paul says (Romans 7:14), and the Spirit shows us what God means by his Law and how he will make us conform to its requirements. The Spirit of God blew over the bones in Israel and made them alive again. (Ezekiel 37:1-14) The Lord will build his Kingdom "not by might nor by power, but by my Spirit" (Zechariah 4:6); because of this, his Kingdom will be eternal and it will consist of things that will satisfy both him and us. Jesus drove out demons by the Spirit of God. (Matthew 12:28) Jesus said that, when someone has the Spirit in him, it will be a spring of water welling up inside to eternal life. (John 4:14) "The Spirit gives life, the flesh counts for nothing" (John 6:63) — and Jesus' words were Spirit because they give us spiritual life, the awareness of God and ability to live for God. Peter, the disciple whom the Jews had last seen denying the Lord, stood up at Pentecost full of the Spirit and preached the eternal Gospel to the Jews — with thousands of conversions as a result. (Acts 2) The Holy Spirit gives joy to God's people. (Romans 14:17) It's because of the Spirit's work that we have faith in Christ — a faith that comprehends the breadth and depth of Christ's person and work. (Ephesians 2:8; 3:16) The Spirit washes and renews us so that we become heirs of God's promises. (Titus 3:5)

The Spirit's power for serious work

When God has serious work to do in his Kingdom, he always does it through the Holy Spirit. This is because the Spirit's power is irresistible: nothing can stand before it, nothing remains unchanged when the Spirit touches it. The Spirit can do impossible things with the material world, because he uses a power from outside the world – the power of the Creator himself. And what's more important, the Spirit can change the human heart from a rock to a heart of flesh, and change a sinner into a saint. Nothing on earth can do such a thing. Surely the power of the Spirit is beyond our reckoning!

Jesus' ministry displayed the power of the Spirit from the time when the Spirit descended on him. He quoted, at the beginning of his ministry, the prophecy of Isaiah that would account for his amazing works:

> The Spirit of the Lord is on me,
> because he has anointed me
> to preach good news to the poor.
> He has sent me to proclaim freedom for the prisoners
> and recovery of sight for the blind,
> to release the oppressed,
> to proclaim the year of the Lord's favor.
> (Luke 4:18-19)

He drove out demons, for example, "by the Spirit of God." (Matthew 12:28) He did impossible things, things that only the Creator could do, because the same power was within him as was present at the beginning of the world.

The Apostles, filled with the Spirit, went on to do the same kinds of miraculous things that Jesus did. Peter preached a sermon to thousands of Jews, and thousands of them believed the Gospel and were saved. (Acts 2) The Spirit worked through Peter and John to heal the cripple at the gate of the Temple. (Acts 3:1-10) The Spirit gave Paul healing powers, so much so that people only had to touch pieces of cloth from him in order to be healed. (Acts 19:11-12)

We've already seen one critical reason that the Spirit must provide the power for a miracle: when God commands his subjects, they generally can't do the thing he commands. So the Spirit must give that creature the power and ability they need to obey God's command. Again, as we see in the ministry of Christ and the apostles, the command came first and then the thing was done — obviously the Divine power was present to finish the work of creation to God's satisfaction. For example, when Jesus visited a synagogue, he met a man who had a withered hand – a cripple who no doubt thought he would always be a cripple throughout life. But Jesus, instead of simply touching him and effecting a cure, took the same approach that the Creator did at the beginning of the world: he *commanded* a cure.

> He looked around at them all, and then said to the man, "Stretch out your hand." He did so, and his hand was completely restored. (Luke 6:10)

On another occasion he met a man lying on a mat beside the Pool of Siloam, helpless to move until Jesus commanded him to get up. (John 5:1-9) He also told the paralytic, who was lowered through the roof, to "get up, take your mat and go home." (Mark 2:11) In each instance he told them to do the impossible; he obviously intended to provide the power himself, the strength that they would need to obey his command.

The Apostles also relied on the power of the Spirit, with the same miraculous results. When they met the cripple at the Temple gate, they commanded him to do what he couldn't do on his own:

> Then Peter said, "Silver or gold I do not have, but what I have I give you. In the name of Jesus Christ of Nazareth, walk." Taking him by the right hand, he helped him up, and instantly the man's feet and ankles became strong. He jumped to his feet and began to walk. (Acts 3:6-7)

The Old Testament also witnesses to the empowering work of the Spirit. For example, the prophet Ezekiel witnessed the dry bones coming to life as God "breathed" (the words "spirit" and "breath" come from the same Hebrew word) on them. As he goes on to say, this represents what the Spirit will do with all of God's people:

> Then you, my people, will know that I am the LORD, when I open your graves and bring you up from them. I will put my Spirit in you and you will live, and I will settle you in your own land. Then you will know that I

the LORD have spoken, and I have done it, declares the
LORD. (Ezekiel 37:13-14)

The power of Creation

Now if we take this principle back to Creation, we can understand why the Spirit was present: he was going to give the universe the *power of existence*, the capacity of pleasing God with its design and structure, the ability to "obey" God's command to be a part of a "good" world. Without the Spirit, matter and energy could never exist, let alone measure up to God's design specifications. With the Spirit, however, trees and rocks and animals and especially man find that they can do exactly what they were made to do. This idea directly contradicts the basic idea of evolution, which teaches that the ability to evolve is naturally inside a creature – that it can happen without God's help.

The Spirit also upholds Creation, which means that he gives it the means to *continue* to operate in the presence of God according to its original design. Take the Spirit away, and all matter and energy in the universe would cease to exist. Several passages teach us about the ongoing work of the Spirit in our world, a power that makes it possible for all things to exist:

> Do not cast me from your presence or take your Holy
> Spirit from me. (Psalm 51:11)

> If it were his intention and he withdrew his Spirit and
> breath, all mankind would perish together and man
> would return to the dust. (Job 34:14-15)

In another Psalm we read of the Spirit creating and supporting all life, and the removal of God's presence means death:

> These all look to you
> to give them their food at the proper time.
> When you give it to them,
> they gather it up;

> when you open your hand,
> they are satisfied with good things.
> When you hide your face,
> they are terrified;
> when you take away their breath,
> they die and return to the dust.
> When you send your Spirit,
> they are created,
> and you renew the face of the earth.
> (Psalm 104:27-30)

There is an even more important role of the Spirit in God's world, and that's to support life itself. The Bible calls the Spirit, "the Spirit of life." (Romans 8:2)

> The Spirit of God has made me; the breath of the Almighty gives me life. (Job 33:4)

> The Spirit gives life; the flesh counts for nothing. The words I have spoken to you are spirit and they are life. (John 6:63)

> And if the Spirit of him who raised Jesus from the dead is living in you, he who raised Christ from the dead will also give life to your mortal bodies through his Spirit, who lives in you. (Romans 8:11)

> ... the last Adam, a life-giving spirit. (1 Corinthians 15:45)

> He has made us competent as ministers of a new covenant — not of the letter but of the Spirit; for the letter kills, but the Spirit gives life. (2 Corinthians 3:6)

> ... the one who sows to please the Spirit, from the Spirit will reap eternal life. (Galatians 6:8)

Life, if we can give a tentative definition, is the ability to experience. Any organism, from the smallest amoebae to man who is the most complex creature of all, in some way experiences its environment and responds to what it experiences. Creatures of earth have different kinds of senses in order to pick up on such things as light, sound, smells, movement, and time and space.

It's the same way in the spiritual world of God, though creatures there have different senses in order to pick up on its spiritual environment. But immediately we have a problem: due to sin, a human being is dead to that spiritual world, and can't sense what is going on there. A dead soul knows nothing about God by direct experience, only by hearsay. But when the soul is made alive – raised from the dead into spiritual life by the Spirit – he experiences God directly, which is what eternal life is. Eternal life, Jesus said, is to " know you, the only true God, and Jesus Christ, whom you have sent." (John 17:3) The only possible way that man, as a sinner, spiritually dead because of wickedness, could ever know God is if the Spirit wakes up his soul and infuses life into him, thereby opening his eyes to the presence and reality of God. (John 3:5)

The Spirit of Creation

It should be an easy matter to take this concept back to the Creation event, even though we aren't told in Genesis what exactly the Spirit did in the course of events. We *are* told that he was there — "And the Spirit of God was hovering over the waters" (Genesis 1:2) — and therefore we can assume that he did what he has *always* done throughout our history. **First**, the Spirit made it possible for the physical creation to exist exactly as God commanded it to (he empowered it to exist according to the specifications of the Word of God). **Second**, he gave life to the creatures that God made.

Furthermore, we should remember that the work done in the ministry of Christ and the Apostles was *miraculous* and not according to natural principles of the world. The Spirit's power is extraordinary; it's the power of God himself, and it forces the world to conform to God's command contrary to its natural tendencies.

Whenever the Spirit had work to do on earth, he used irresistible powers that this world couldn't stop. Not only that, the things that God wanted to do were clearly impossible, and that's why he used the Spirit to do it – like bringing in big guns when little pistols are useless against the enemy. God obviously doesn't rely on evolution to do his creative work; he doesn't now, he didn't in Christ's day, and so therefore he didn't at the beginning of the world. Evolution can't produce the kind of world he's interested in.

The Joy of Creation – Blessing

In the Creation account it says specifically that God "blessed" two different groups: the fish of the sea and the birds of the air (Genesis 1:22), and man and woman (Genesis 1:28). What does it mean to be "blessed?" If we look carefully, it seems that to be "blessed" means to "be fruitful and increase in number." It was, in other words, God's way of making sure that they would always reproduce and never fail to have descendants.

> God blessed them and said, "Be fruitful and increase in number and fill the water in the seas, and let the birds increase on the earth." (Genesis 1:22)

> God blessed them and said to them, "Be fruitful and increase in number; fill the earth and subdue it. Rule over the fish of the sea and the birds of the air and over every other living creature that moves on the ground." (Genesis 1:28)

To be "blessed" also means to be happy – the result of enjoying what God has given us in life, and staying in the road that he leads us. Psalm 1, for example, says that a man will be blessed – or happy, as the word there can be translated – if he both stays away from sinners and meditates on God's Law.

The blessing of life

That act of blessing in Genesis was obviously a creative act. When God gave the command to "be fruitful," he also gave the power or ability to become fruitful. Immediately after that command, the animal and human creatures proliferated and "filled the earth." There is something mysterious and instinctive, compelling, satisfying, and rewarding in the process of begetting, bearing, and nurturing young. That command to fill the earth was so powerful that, for as long as the earth has stood, there have always been creatures living on it. We are desperate, in fact, to survive and to create more of us. Someone once called it the "lust for life."

God's blessing also insures that, for as long as the earth lasts, there will always be generations of living things. If God had not added this element of insured continuity to the process of life, it would have ended not long after it started. As it is, it can't stop – not without doing violence to our very makeup. The sexual drive is unquestionably one of the most powerful instincts built into the nature of all creatures. We can't turn it off. And that undying instinct is due to the original command, still ringing down through the millennia, never to end until the world itself comes to an end. By God's decree there will always be living creatures.

God wisely built the element of pleasure into obedience. For example, it was no accident that what he *told* us to do – to be fruitful – is the very thing that we *want* to do. Sex is one of the most intense forms of physical pleasure. We enjoy doing what God made us to do; we were designed that way, and his blessing of fruitfulness was intended to fill our lives with pleasure as we carry out his instructions. (This is assuming, however, that we do it according to *his* instructions – sexual sin is so destructive of individuals, families and nations because it ignores God's overall purpose for our lives for the sake of pleasure alone. In other words, you can't break the rules and do something just because it feels good – you're going to destroy something or someone in the process.)

But the pleasure of sex isn't the only enjoyment that a creature has in God's world. God gave us other physical blessings: abundant food, warmth and shelter, family, companion-ship, protective care. All these things together make a harmonious whole, in which we enjoy life. All these things are from God's hand, who takes care of his creatures and gives them things that they need as well as enjoy:

> The LORD is faithful to all his promises
> and loving toward all he has made.
> The LORD upholds all those who fall

>   and lifts up all who are bowed down.
> The eyes of all look to you,
>   and you give them their food at the proper time.
> You open your hand
>   and satisfy the desires of every living thing ...
>
> He fulfills the desires of those who fear him;
>   he hears their cry and saves them.
> The LORD watches over all who love him,
>   but all the wicked he will destroy.
>   (Psalm 145:13-16,19-20)

Walking in God's way

But blessing runs deeper than simple physical pleasures. In other passages in the Bible we find that we are blessed – happy, rewarded, and satisfied – when we walk in the way that God appoints for us. This idea actually reflects the root of the Hebrew word used. The root letters behind the word "blessed" means "to go straight, go on, advance".

Psalm 1 speaks of *the way* that a happy man walks in, and the results of living the "straight and narrow" walk:

> Blessed is the man
> who does not walk in the counsel of the wicked
> or stand in the way of sinners
> or sit in the seat of mockers.
> But his delight is in the law of the LORD,
> and on his law he meditates day and night.
> He is like a tree planted by streams of water,
> which yields its fruit in season
> and whose leaf does not wither.
> Whatever he does prospers.
>
> Not so the wicked!
> They are like chaff
> that the wind blows away.

> Therefore the wicked will not stand in the judgment,
> nor sinners in the assembly of the righteous.
>
> For the LORD watches over the way of the righteous,
> but the way of the wicked will perish.

The point is to stay out of the path of sinners, whose lifestyle *veers away* from what God intended for man, and to walk in God's ordained path instead. The reason is simple: the way of wickedness is no end of trouble, misery, hardship, pain, suffering, guilt, broken relationships, hatred, jealousy, failure, loss and death. There is no life, no joy, no peace in living in wickedness. Their life is a continual hedge of thorns. (Proverbs 22:15) The only thing that sinners have to look forward to on God's earth is destruction and death. There is so much trouble in living in sin simply because the world wasn't made to accommodate sinners! It's like rowing upstream: you can do it, but by the time you get there, you will wish you hadn't and you won't have anything for your troubles. God in his wisdom made the world like that for sinners.

On the other hand, righteousness (God's kind – not the crazy opinions that people often have about what is right and wrong) leads to life, peace, joy, blessings, success and harmony. God made the world to *work with* the righteous, to help them along, to "yield fruit" for them as they obey God. As they honor him, he honors them with long life and happiness:

> Taste and see that the Lord is good;
>   blessed is the man who takes refuge in him.
> Fear the Lord, you his saints,
>   for those who fear him lack nothing.
> The lions may grow weak and hungry,
>   but those who seek the Lord lack no good thing.
>   (Psalm 34:8-10)

This idea of following "straight paths" is a continual theme that runs throughout the Bible. For example, David prays that the Lord might "lead me, O LORD, in your righteousness because of my enemies

– make straight your way before me." (Psalm 5:8) – a request he repeats in Psalm 27:11. Whoever acknowledges God will find their paths being made straight. (Proverbs 3:6; 4:11) We are counseled to "Let your eyes look straight ahead, fix your gaze directly before you." (Proverbs 4:25) Righteousness makes the way straight for us, whereas the wicked are brought down by their wickedness. (Proverbs 11:5) "A man of understanding keeps a straight course." (Proverbs 15:21)

Jesus also referred to the roads that sinners and the righteous take:

> Enter through the narrow gate. For wide is the gate and broad is the road that leads to destruction, and many enter through it. But small is the gate and narrow the road that leads to life, and only a few find it. (Matthew 7:13-14)

Happiness in righteousness

There's a parallel here between the moral and the physical sides to Creation. Just as created things do best – they are happy and succeed – when they follow the instincts for survival and reproduction that God first built into their natures, man enjoys life the most when he follows strictly the instructions that God gave him at Creation.

Man was made to be the ruler of the earth, the creature who represents God's authority and wisdom as he rules God's world in God's name. In order to do his job well, man needs to know and follow God's will – because he must execute that will over the earth. He has the mind to know God's will, the heart to desire it, and the intelligence to execute it in the earth in physical terms. His happiness, therefore, depends on more than physical pleasures, more than the animals were given. He has to curb his natural passions in light of what he knows of God's purposes and plans for him and, through his agency, for the rest of the world.

In order to prepare man for this higher role, "God made mankind upright." (Ecclesiastes 7:29) In other words, he made man "in the image of God" – holy, pure, a judge and lawgiver, a fair and just ruler, a caring and loving father, sensitive to and zealous for the truth. If man had *continued in the way* that God first made for him, the earth would still be a paradise. The reason is simple: when the king does his duty, the kingdom – and, therefore, the king himself – is happy and prosperous. Things work. Plans succeed. Everything proceeds exactly as the Creator first intended it.

Unhappiness in unrighteousness

But the sin of Adam and Eve ruined the plan. "God made mankind upright, but men have gone in search of many schemes." (Ecclesiastes 7:29) Those other "schemes" are the kind of life that man wants, apart from what God commanded him to do. For example, instead of obeying God's original command to avoid the fruit of the Tree of the Knowledge of Good and Evil, Adam and Eve began making their own decisions – they wanted what they thought they could get by eating it.

> When the woman saw that the fruit of the tree was good for food and pleasing to the eye, and also desirable for gaining wisdom, she took some and ate it. She also gave some to her husband, who was with her, and he ate it. Then the eyes of both of them were opened, and they realized they were naked; so they sewed fig leaves together and made coverings for themselves. (Genesis 3:6-7)

When this happened, man charted out a course for himself apart from God's ways, in a different direction from the one that God intended for man to go in. The outcome was predictable, since only when we walk in his ways are we "blessed" – or happy and successful. Sin, which is "lawlessness" (1 John 3:4) – that is, straying *away* from God's way – results not in happiness but misery and death:

> When you were slaves to sin, you were free from the control of righteousness. What benefit did you reap at

that time from the things you are now ashamed of? Those things result in death! (Romans 6:20-21)

The important thing to remember is that this is *by design.* "God cannot be mocked. A man reaps what he sows. The one who sows to please his sinful nature, from that nature will reap destruction." (Galatians 6:7-8) The pronouncement of death to Adam was as much a prediction as it was a curse. People who live by the flesh instead of by God's command will find "thorns and snares" frustrating them (Proverbs 22:5), and misery and death all along the way.

We can use one powerful example to illustrate the moral nature of the world. The reason that sexual immorality is wrong is because it is *destructive* – on many levels – of the happiness and peace of the basic family. Long-reaching emotional, spiritual, and physical damage is done with seemingly an "innocent" act of immorality. And the consequences can far exceed our fears: David, for instance, paid dearly for his adultery with Bathsheba, with results not only immediate in the loss of trust from his people and the loss of his child, but with the far-reaching trouble that he had for years with his own sons.

We were made to obey God; therein is the secret of our happiness. We are "blessed" only when we take the straight road that he laid out for us. Any other road can't succeed. This is hard for a willful sinner to admit, but it's easy to see when we examine the failures in our society. What lies behind the suffering, misery, death, disease, brokenness, war, and destruction that fills our world? Inevitably we will find godlessness, willfulness, rebellion, sin of all kinds and forms, ignorance of God's truth, the worship of false gods, and dishonor to the glory and name of the only true God. The way of the wicked will *always* lead to death, because only one way leads to life in God's Creation. It was designed that way from the beginning.

In a poignant passage in the prophet Hosea, God describes the world that man has made. Not only is man himself suffering the consequences of charting his own course in life, but the very creatures that were made man's subjects in Genesis 1:26, the creatures that man was assigned to take care of, are also suffering because of their ruler's wickedness:

> There is no faithfulness, no love,
> no acknowledgment of God in the land.
> There is only cursing,
> lying and murder,
> stealing and adultery;
> they break all bounds,
> and bloodshed follows bloodshed.
> Because of this the land mourns,
> and all who live in it waste away;
> *the beasts of the field and the birds of the air*
> *and the fish of the sea are dying.*
> (Hosea 4:1-3)

Blessing means responsibility

So we are living in a moral universe, not just a physical one. *There are physical consequences from our moral actions.* In other words, when we sin, both we and the world suffer. When we do what is right, everyone prospers. That truth in itself demonstrates that a purely scientific viewpoint of the world is not only shortsighted, it can be criminal if done purposely. We can't shirk our obvious responsibilities before God. The Bible never permits us to view our place in the world apart from our responsibility before God; and the curse of death forces that truth upon us constantly.

One more thing. You can probably see that, in order to have a world in which there is responsibility along with pleasure, Someone has to make it that way. Simple evolution can't make a world like that. According to evolution, things just happen – pleasure is just icing on the cake, if and when it happens. And there's no such thing as responsibility, because to the evolutionist there is no God to be responsible to. But according to the Bible, pleasure is built into the system as part of the command of Creation. And so is responsibility: we will enjoy life the most in God's world if we do things God's way.

The Builder of Creation – Christ

Every kingdom has a king, and you can usually tell what the king is like by looking at how his kingdom runs – he spreads his influence all through the kingdom. If things are running smoothly and everyone is happy, then the king knows what he's doing and he's a good king. But if things are in a bad state, and there's a lot of discontent among the subjects, then the king isn't doing his job. The king is in the position to affect the well-being of all his subjects; from his throne he can touch the lives of everyone in the realm. He has powers that no one else has; he has responsibilities that nobody else can claim.

We have already seen that the universe was made, the Scriptures tell us, by God's command, for God's purposes, and it's headed for Judgment Day where it will be examined closely to see if it conforms to God's eternal will. All we lack to finish this picture is the King himself, the One who sits on the throne over the world and directs its affairs. The Bible very clearly shows us Christ in this position; he is called "the ruler of God's creation." (Revelation 3:14)

The King of kings

In our day it's hard to picture what a kingdom must be like, because we are used to equality and public rule. We usually have a negative picture of a kingdom: we imagine a self-indulgent tyrant who has no concern for his subjects, who only lives to tax his people into poverty for the sake of his own comforts and enjoyments.

But there have been good kings in history. As a matter of fact, the only earthly government that God has ever put his approval on is the kingdom in David's day: David was even called "a man after God's own heart." So, what would life be like in the ideal kingdom?

First, the king would naturally have the well-being of his subjects on his heart. **Second**, the king would make sure that everyone can make a living, and that their business efforts would be profitable. **Third**, the king would make sure that everyone has the basics of life: food, clothing, shelter. **Fourth**, the king would set up a system of law and order, giving out justice to the wicked and the righteous alike. **Fifth**, the king would do whatever necessary to protect his people from their enemies. **Sixth**, the king would lead his people to God in true worship.

Christ not only *is* the King of the universe, he acts like it, according to this list of duties of a good king. Although he's been active as King since the beginning of Creation, let's limit our study here to just the Gospel accounts.

As he lived and worked among men on earth, he demonstrated kingly qualities that are easy to see. For example, he cared about his people constantly – providing for them, praying for them, teaching them, protecting them – his love for his people was the thing that motivated all his efforts on their behalf. It was for them that he came to earth. His highest sacrifice on the cross was only for them!

We can also pick out examples of the King taking care of his own. He fed them when they had nothing to eat; he protected them from the "wolves in sheep's clothing" – the Pharisees; he paid their taxes for them; he helped them find fish; he taught them the truth about God and poured out the Spirit on them so they could see God; he laid the law down and demanded that his subjects obey him. If we have our eyes open, we can easily see that his entire ministry was actually the work of the King working on behalf of his subjects.

He still takes care of his people. He continues to send the Spirit to them so that they can know God, so that they can come before God in Heaven and present their requests in person. He sends them food and other necessities of life. He protects them now from greater spiritual dangers. He teaches them through his Word, by means of the Spirit. He rules by means of his spiritual government, complete with laws and administrators under him who care for us in his Name. Since he is still King over the world, he hasn't grown lax in his duties or cold in his care for us. He is constantly overseeing his vast kingdom and making sure things run smoothly according to his will.

Made through Christ

But Christ's connection with the universe is even more important than his political role as King. The world was actually made *through* him; it exists day by day because of his direct, constant action upon it. In other words, he himself made the world in the beginning; it's his special creation, the work of his hands. And he made it in such a way that it depends completely on his daily care for it. Without his constant attention to its affairs, the world would cease to exist.

From the very beginning, Christ has maintained a rigid hold on the universe that it can't escape. In fact, that explains why the universe is still running exactly according to God's original plans. Christ rules over the universe with intimate knowledge of every detail, with full responsibility for its progress, with full power to direct everything according to his will. Earthly kings can't possibly attend to every detail of their kingdom, nor can they directly affect every circumstance in the life of each subject in the kingdom. Christ, however, can and does work at that level throughout his kingdom. He determines when and where people will live (Acts 17:26), he gives them the food they eat every day, he leads them daily through circumstances of his own choosing. Through his wisdom and power he maintains complete control.

When Christ became King

Hebrews tells us the unique relationship that Christ has with the Father:

> In the past God spoke to our forefathers through the prophets at many times and in various ways, but in these last days he has spoken to us by his Son, whom he appointed heir of all things, and

> through whom he made the universe. The Son is the radiance of God's glory and the exact representation of his being, sustaining all things by his powerful Word. (Hebrews 1:1-3)

First, the way that God makes himself known to his creatures is by means of Christ. Since none of us can see God directly, we instead look at Christ to learn about God. He is the manifestation of God, the fullness of God in the flesh, the way we learn about God. In him we learn the character of God. By his actions we understand the works of God. He's an accommodation to our limitations, so to speak, since unless God revealed himself in this way to us we would never know God.

> ... God, the blessed and only Ruler, the King of kings and Lord of lords, who alone is immortal and who lives in unapproachable light, whom no one has seen or can see. (1 Timothy 6:15-16)

So, since God himself is unapproachable Christ is the special way that God has provided for us to know him: we *can* approach Jesus, hear him speak, touch him, and know through him that God exists:

> That which was from the beginning, which we have heard, which we have seen with our eyes, which we have looked at and our hands have touched — this we proclaim concerning the Word of life. The life appeared; we have seen it and testify to it, and we proclaim to you the eternal life, which was with the Father and has appeared to us. We proclaim to you what we have seen and heard, so that you also may have fellowship with us. (1 John 1:1-3)

Second, God made the universe *through Christ*. This was to be Christ's Kingdom, and *he* will be its absolute ruler. We can better understand this if we think about a new market that a business wants to get into. The board of the company will assign a certain department head to lead the new project: it will be up to him to hire new employees, buy the supplies needed, set up the production line, set the schedule, take care of the finances, and make regular progress reports back to the board. In short, he's responsible to make a profit – using the resources of the company, with the board's blessing, acting in the name and authority of the board but doing the work himself.

In Psalm 2 we read about this same kind of business transaction when God turned over this new Kingdom of Creation to the Son, for him to manage and build up:

> Why do the nations conspire
> and the peoples plot in vain?
> The kings of the earth take their stand
> and the rulers gather together
> against the LORD
> and against his Anointed One.
> "Let us break their chains," they say,
> "and throw off their fetters."
>
> The One enthroned in heaven laughs;
> the Lord scoffs at them.
> Then he rebukes them in his anger
> and terrifies them in his wrath, saying,
> "I have installed my King
> on Zion, my holy hill."
> I will proclaim the decree of the LORD:
> He said to me, "You are my Son;
> today I have become your Father.
> Ask of me, and I will make the nations your inheritance,
> the ends of the earth your possession.
> You will rule them with an iron scepter;
> you will dash them to pieces like pottery."

> Therefore, you kings, be wise;
> be warned, you rulers of the earth.
> Serve the LORD with fear
> and rejoice with trembling.
> Kiss the Son, lest he be angry
> and you be destroyed in your way,
> for his wrath can flare up in a moment.
> Blessed are all who take refuge in him. (Psalm 2)

Notice the degree of control that the Son has over his Kingdom: even rebellion by the kings is useless, because he intends to rule all with an iron scepter. This is *his* world now.

Third, God made Christ the heir of all things. It all belongs to him to do as he pleases. He especially proves his ownership in what he is *able* to do with it. Ownership isn't just a matter of possession for him, as it is for us; all the world lays bare under his hand, under his scrutiny, and he uses it to serve his purposes. He speaks and it obeys, instantly, and does whatever he demands of it. For instance, a dog will obey its master but it will ignore a stranger. In the same way, the universe responds immediately to Christ's word of power. He wields *miraculous* power over his kingdom. Since every part of the universe can't resist his commands, it's clear who is the Master and who is the subject; he proves his authority by his power.

Fourth, Christ sustains the universe through his Word. The same Word that created the universe supports it and keeps it going day by day. The power of that Word is illustrated in the fact that, unknown to them, and in spite of their disobedient hearts, people and nations nevertheless end up doing exactly what he wants from them all through history. "For he must reign until he has put all his enemies under his feet." (1 Corinthians 15:25) His Word is that of a King; he commands, and his subjects *must* obey. But what he is making out of all this is a well-balanced kingdom: in the end, when it's all over, he will be pleased with the results and he will then turn it all over to the Father.

The point in Hebrews 1:1-3 is that, from the very beginning, Christ has been the head of the universe; God relates to his Creation at all times and in every way through the powerful and effective administration of Christ.

Other Scriptural testimony teaches the same truth.

> In the beginning was the Word, and the Word was with God, and the Word was God. He was with God in the beginning. *Through him* all things were made; without him nothing was made that has been made ... He was in the world, and though the world was made *through him*, the world did not recognize him. (John 1:1-3, 10)

> ... yet for us there is but one God, the Father, from whom all things came and for whom we live; and there is but one Lord, Jesus Christ, *through whom all things came* and *through whom we live*. (1 Corinthians 8:6)

> For *by him* all things were created: things in heaven and on earth, visible and invisible, whether thrones or powers or rulers or authorities; all things were created *by him* and *for him*. He is before all things, and *in him* all things hold together. (Colossians 1:16-17)

But even the Old Testament only gave hints about this King, so that when Paul writes about him he calls Jesus the "mystery of God." It wasn't made plain that Jesus himself was the Master until he came in the flesh "to his own" – when he came into his Kingdom in the same outward form as his subjects.

> He was in the world, and though the world was made through him, the world did not recognize him. He came

to that which was his own, but his own did not receive him. (John 1:10-11)

Christ the Creator

Over time, especially after the resurrection when they finally understood the true nature of Christ, the Apostles saw *the Creator* in Jesus. They wrote their Gospels reminiscing about the *kind* of work that Christ did among them – a work that no one except the King could do.

- Only the **Creator** of the world could do miracles. The kinds of things that Jesus did reflected not only the same kind of work that happened at Creation, but in the same *way* that it was done. For example, he created enough bread and fish to feed thousands of people immediately – out of *nothing*. The original loaves and fishes that he had were only a pitifully meager starting point that represents how useless the world's contribution is to God's purposes; there just wasn't a natural explanation for how he did such a thing. And he brought the dead back to life with a *command* – remember the original Commands of Creation in which something that couldn't obey God found power in his Word to obey his wish? He *cursed* the fig tree, and *blessed* the food he used to feed the crowds, both acts in which his Word had power in itself to either kill or proliferate – again, the same kind of work that God did in the beginning.

- Only the **King**, through whom the world was made, could speak with such authority and wisdom. The people were astonished at his teaching, because he spoke with an authority that ordinary teachers didn't have:

    When Jesus had finished saying these things, the crowds were amazed at his teaching, because he taught as one who had authority, and not as their teachers of the law. (Matthew 7:28-29)

That authority had power and conviction to it; his words stab the conscience, so that we know we are in the presence of the One to whom we must give account of ourselves. We belong to him; that's why he has the right to speak to us as he does, and why we know that we must do as *he* says, no matter what others may tell us.

- Only the **Lawgiver** could rightfully expect such complete obedience from men. Our obedience isn't allowed to be superficial because Christ's realm, and the depth to which he reaches in our hearts, isn't superficial. An ordinary ruler can only hope to make our outward actions conform to his laws; but Christ, who rules all of Creation with infinite precision, requires obedience from the heart. His Sermon on the Mount is an excellent analysis of how far-reaching his realm is over men. "Surely you desire truth in the inner parts; you teach me wisdom in the inmost place." (Psalm 51:6)

The Creator leads the way

There are two areas where it's necessary that Christ be the Creator. **First**, he has to have such power and authority over the first Creation that he can destroy sin and its effects. "The reason the Son of God appeared was to destroy the devil's work." (1 John 3:8) And that's exactly what we see in his ministry, as he tackled sin and its destruction head on. He has the authority to name sin and rebuke it; he undoes the effects of sin – misery, destruction and death; and he lays the ax at the root of sin so that it can't continue to destroy his people. For such work he needs absolute power and authority, as he claimed several times:

All authority in Heaven and on earth has been given to me. (Matthew 28:18)

But take heart! I have overcome the world. (John 16:33)

Second, and this is the amazing part, *he himself* will lead the first Creation through death and resurrection into the second Creation. The first Creation is doomed to destruction, because of the sin and death that entered the world at the beginning. We need a new model, a new world, and a new nature because the old nature is no good anymore. That model is Christ: we know what we *will* be by looking at what he is *now* after his resurrection.

The world itself, as well as the sons of God, wait for the day when the old Creation will be shaken out (Hebrews 12:26-27) and we will be made new – in the image of the Son of God who rose from the dead as a spiritual man:

> The creation waits in eager expectation for the sons of God to be revealed. For the creation was subjected to frustration, not by its own choice, but by the will of the one who subjected it, in hope that the creation itself will be liberated from its bondage to decay and brought into the glorious freedom of the children of God. We know that the whole creation has been groaning as in the pains of childbirth right up to the present time. Not only so, but we ourselves, who have the firstfruits of the Spirit, groan inwardly as we wait eagerly for our adoption as sons, the redemption of our bodies. For in this hope we were saved. (Romans 8:19-24)

> For since death came through a man, the resurrection of the dead comes also through a man. For as in Adam all die, so in Christ all will be made alive. But each in his own turn: Christ, the firstfruits; then, when he comes, those who belong to him. (1 Corinthians 15:21-23)

And in what Paul calls a mystery, Christ represents in his own body the passage of the first Creation to the second Creation. The first physical kingdom will change into a new spiritual kingdom; the King himself puts his physical body to death (the first Creation must be put aside) and then leads his subjects into a new life. That new life is what we will be like, if we join ourselves to him. So, he became one with us physically so that we could become one with him spiritually.

> Since the children have flesh and blood, he too shared in their humanity so that by his death he might destroy him who holds the power of death — that is, the devil — and free those who all their lives were held in slavery by their fear of death.(Hebrews 2:14-15)

> So will it be with the resurrection of the dead. The body that is sown is perishable, it is raised imperishable; it is sown in dishonor, it is raised in glory; it is sown in weakness, it is raised in power; it is sown a natural body, it is raised a spiritual body. If there is a natural body, there is also a spiritual body. So it is written: "The first man Adam became a living being"; the last Adam, a life-giving spirit. The spiritual did not come first, but the natural, and after that the spiritual. The first man was of the dust of the earth, the second man from Heaven. As was the earthly man, so are those who are of the earth; and as is the man from Heaven, so also are those who are of Heaven. And just as we have borne the likeness of the earthly man, so shall we bear the likeness of the man from Heaven. (1 Corinthians 15:42-49)

Finally, we know that his resurrection into a new Creation was planned *before* the first physical Creation. Obviously God had all this planned out from the very beginning. Therefore Creation was the first step to an overall plan which included Christ's physical life, death, resurrection, and our union with him to form a Second Creation.

> He was chosen before the creation of the world, but was revealed in these last times for your sake. (1 Peter 1:20)

> … the Lamb that was slain from the creation of the world. (Revelation 13:8)

To summarize, the world was made *through Christ* because, **first**, it must be totally under his control. **Second**, he intends to destroy it completely, because as it stands – under the effects of sin and death – it can't continue on into eternity in God's plans, nor can it contribute anything of value to a new, eternal, spiritual kingdom. **Third**, when the time is ripe (and in himself he already took the first step) he will do away with the physical creation that we are familiar with and replace it with a perfect spiritual Kingdom. The universe then is a kingdom in which Christ is working out his own agenda, from beginning to end.

The Goal of Creation – God's Glory

God is of such a nature that, when we are in his presence, he totally overwhelms us with himself. We suddenly realize how huge he is, how important he is to us. We can see that everything in the universe is in his hands and depends on him completely for even the smallest things. It's that realization that we get, when we look at him, that makes up his glory. As Paul says it, "For from him and through him and to him are all things. To him be the glory forever! Amen." (Romans 11:36) Everything else in creation is as nothing compared to God, and we know it. This is what the Bible means by his glory.

What does Glory mean?

The word "glory" in the Bible is derived from the Hebrew word "to be heavy" – a description often used of gold, for obvious reasons. Anybody who finds himself in God's presence *feels* the presence of God in a real way, like feeling the ominous buildup of a storm. It was this massive presence that overwhelmed the builders of the Temple in Solomon's day:

> When Solomon finished praying, fire came down from heaven and consumed the burnt offering and the sacrifices, and the glory of the LORD filled the temple. The priests could not enter the temple of the LORD because the glory of the LORD filled it. When all the Israelites saw the fire coming down and the glory of the LORD above the temple, they knelt on the pavement with their faces to the ground, and they worshipped and gave thanks to the LORD. (2 Chronicles 7:1-3)

Glory also means this: who gets the *credit*? In other words, who was responsible for what happened? In this sense, God deserves all glory, since he is ultimately responsible for everything in our world – except sin, for which man is responsible. God made all things, he provides for all things, he judges all things, he guides and directs all things, and in the end will replace everything with a new heaven and earth of a new design that will fully glorify him as a wise and caring Creator.

When it comes to giving God the credit he deserves, however, the entire world is guilty of slighting him and denying him glory. Sinful man would rather give glory to another god, or to himself, rather than to the true God. For example, did today's newspaper mention the fact that God gave everyone their food today? Did it give him credit for guiding the affairs of governments and businesses around the world? Did it mention that he took the lives of millions and brought them before his Judgment Throne? No, the newspaper never mentions any of this, even though it's quite true. Who gets the credit instead? We give credit to Mother Nature, to fortune and luck, to evolution, to science and its laws, and also a healthy dose of credit to ourselves – as if we can do quite nicely without God's help. But God is involved in everyone's life, so much so that we can't move without his knowledge and authority and help; yet hardly anybody even mentions his name as the supreme King of the universe.

Jealous for his glory

This fact alone has cast a pall of impending disaster over the world, since God is *jealous* for glory. When he so richly deserves glory, and we stubbornly deny him that glory, there must be trouble.

> I am the LORD; that is my name!
> I will not give my glory to another
> or my praise to idols. (Isaiah 42:8)

> For my own sake, for my own sake, I do this.
> How can I let myself be defamed?
> I will not yield my glory to another. (Isaiah 48:11)

Idolatry is this sin of giving credit that ought to go to the true God to other gods that are *not* what we say they are. The punishment to idolaters is severe. God alone must be worshipped, he alone must be trusted, he alone must be obeyed.

In fact, God does things purposely in a way that gets him more glory. He does things that other gods can't do, in ways that they don't even dare to promise to do. For example, Elijah, who knew the ways of God and the importance of God's glory, challenged the prophets of Baal: let the true God come down and set fire to the sacrifice on the altar. And then in order to show how magnificently God can do the impossible, he poured water on the sacrifice to frustrate their hopes in the false god and to present the true God with an opportunity to display his power. (1 Kings 18:16-40) All of God's miracles, throughout the Bible, left no doubt in the minds of those who witnessed them as to who was really at work. As Pharaoh's magicians had to admit, in the face of impossible miracles, "This is the finger of God." (Exodus 8:19)

Only when we grasp how important God's glory is to him will we begin to understand why he made the world in the *way* he did. He doesn't do things in a way that would leave doubt in our minds as to who was actually responsible for them. Rather, he will do something totally impossible in order to convince us that *he* did it and nobody else was involved. So, when God created the world, he certainly would not have used methods that would lead us to believe that he had no vital and direct part in Creation! He would have done it in such a way that we are forced to admit that only the God of the Bible could do this.

Evolution or miracle?

Evolution is the opposite of miracle. Evolutionists insist that the organism itself has within itself everything it needs to move on to the next step in its development. There is nothing mysterious in evolution. According to its theory, an organism's progress is predictable (that is, if we knew all the circumstances involved); it's all in the makeup of the thing. A miracle, on the other hand, is an outside influence: the organism doesn't have the power or design for the next step. It only becomes something if God reaches down and makes it that way. By using a miracle, God creates *out of nothing* a completed organism or galaxy.

The Goal of Creation: God's Glory

If the world evolved through billions of years, and life evolved from simple forms to its present state of complexity, then there is nothing in the picture that demands the presence or activity of the God of the Bible. The whole thing can be explained away with a fertile scientific imagination. Even Theistic Evolutionists actually contribute nothing to the cause of Creation when they insist on God's guiding hand as evolution makes a world. Evolution, by definition, is a natural process that can be easily understood and described (given enough time and scientific expertise), and it's only natural to expect that the evolutionary process would have taken billions of years to unfold.

If, however, God created the universe by miracle, by command, by bringing completed worlds and animals out of nothing, immediately – then we know that we are dealing with a God who does the impossible. He doesn't need any process or scientific law or material already in existence to make a world. His very act of using a miracle shows a King at work, demanding obedience from the entire universe, the Judge who creates at will and who destroys at will. There is nothing at all natural going on in *this* picture.

Now if God is jealous for his glory, if he wants to make sure that we form an accurate understanding of who he is and how he does things, he won't use methods that will mislead us about him, or make us think that some other force may have been at work instead. He is going to do things in a way that will make the message plain. So, miracles glorify him; evolution does not. Since he insists on getting glory, he's going to use methods that will get him that glory – that is, he's going to be a miracle-worker. Creation by command gives him the credit he deserves.

The Glory of God in Creation

The Creation account shows off what this God can do, and the results of his creation shout his glory:

> The heavens declare the glory of God;
> the skies proclaim the work of his hands.

> Day after day they pour forth speech;
> night after night they display knowledge.
> There is no speech or language
> where their voice is not heard.
> Their voice goes out into all the earth,
> their words to the ends of the world.
> (Psalm 19:1-4)

It's not so much *what* is happening in the universe *now* (the answer to which science gives us some help), but *how* the universe first got here, that so glorifies God. Scientists know something of how things work in the universe, and we all take advantage of that knowledge to make life more comfortable. Nobody has to believe that there is a God in order to build or use a TV, for example.

But unbelieving scientists are offended at the idea that God made the world by miracle. They would rather believe that it all happened quite naturally. They would be shocked, however, if they learned, through some means, that their theories of how it all came into being were wrong – that instead of a long, steady, progressive evolution from the Big Bang to complex nature, God commanded existence out of nothing, immediately, straight into its present complex state. That would contradict their theories and put them at a loss to explain anything about origins. That idea puts the spotlight on God who works miracles, who is King, who is Judge over the universe – and takes the spotlight away from natural causes and the self-sufficiency of matter and energy.

This is, in fact, exactly what the Genesis account is designed to do. It glorifies God by pointing out the *miraculous* nature of the event. Only God could have done the impossible: to create in six days, to create out of nothing, to create by command, to create purpose into the physical world's design. Only a God who split apart seas, raised the dead, healed the blind, and sent down bread from Heaven would have made the world in the way that Genesis describes. This method alone brings him glory; any other means of creation, no matter how reasonable and rational it seem to us, takes away from *this* God's glory.

If God made the world in this particular way, through miracle, then it accomplishes several of his purposes:

> **First**, it proves that the world is more than just a physical reality. If the universe were only made of matter and energy, of atoms and galaxies, then evolution would be the natural explanation for how it all came together. Shake a bowl-full of atoms long enough and you may come up with all sorts of combinations. In fact, that's *all* you would have to do to come up with something; it doesn't take a miracle to shake atoms together. But if God made the world by miracle, then obviously there is something going on under the surface that we don't see – something more than atoms and galaxies. The world can't exist without him. It can't have meaning or purpose without him. Nor does it have within itself whatever it takes to please him. You see, the *way* he made the world tells us a lot about what life will be like in his specially-made world. We ultimately must deal with *him*, and what he first had in mind, in order to grasp the point of the universe's existence.
>
> **Second**, it shows that he can unmake it in exactly the same way that he made it. Whatever God puts together, he can take apart – and by means of the same catastrophic, immediate method.
>
>> First of all, you must understand that in the last days scoffers will come, scoffing and following their own evil desires. They will say, "Where is this 'coming' he promised? Ever since our fathers died, everything goes on as it has since the beginning of creation." But they deliberately forget that long ago by God's Word the heavens existed and the earth was formed out of water and by water. By these waters also the world of that time was deluged and destroyed. *By the same Word* the present heavens and earth are

> reserved for fire, being kept for the day of judgment and destruction of ungodly men. (2 Peter 3:3-7)

Third, it instills fear in us – at least for those who believe the account. As Peter tells us, there is an obvious conclusion for those who read the Genesis account: this God can do whatever he likes with us!

> Since everything will be destroyed in this way, what kind of people ought you to be? You ought to live holy and godly lives as you look forward to the day of God and speed its coming. That day will bring about the destruction of the heavens by fire, and the elements will melt in the heat. But in keeping with his promise we are looking forward to a new heaven and a new earth, the home of righteousness. (2 Peter 3:11-13)

The purpose of glory

This kind of Creation makes us ask the question, "What kind of God do we have here?" The disciples were struck with the same amazement when Jesus rebuked the winds and waves:

> The men were amazed and asked, "What kind of man is this? Even the winds and the waves obey him!" (Matthew 8:27)

The Scripture always uses plain and no-nonsense ways to glorify God. First it focuses our attention on him, as the primary actor in history. Next it very plainly teaches us that he is the real mover in the world: he's the source of all good things, he's the source of all wisdom, he's the Law and standard that we must live up to, he's the Judge of all our actions, he's the power that we need to do our own works. There's never any question, after reading the Bible, who is running the universe and how he runs things.

The entire Bible plainly shows us a God who does miracles, who commands his subjects and expects their complete obedience – even if that means doing it for them. It shows us his unique ways of doing things, ways that produce results contrary to all expectations. He works through his Spirit, because that power overwhelms all earthly powers. His works are things that only he can do – no other god can claim to do the kinds of things that God does. Wherever we turn, we are presented with a God who routinely does the impossible for the purpose of drawing all attention to himself. He alone must get glory, and the Bible sees to it that he does.

So we shouldn't be surprised, when reading the Genesis account, that the Bible is doing the same thing there. It's showing us very plainly what kind of God we are dealing with: he's a God who works by way of miracles, he's the King who commands and provides the power to obey. By making the universe this particular way he shows how different he is from other gods – for example, evolution. Only when we believe Genesis, as it stands, will we truly glorify the God of the Bible.

Only by learning about, and turning to, *this* God who works in *this* way will we be ready for the next step in our salvation. We will find that he works in the same ways no matter what he does for us.

The Test of Creation – Judgment Day

We saw that, ultimately, God seeks glory in all that he does. And the universe is a particularly effective platform for getting him glory. This was no accident: just as a master craftsman will make his own tool chest in a way that will show off his skills to his customers, the Lord made the universe in such a way that it's hard to miss the point of his wisdom and power. Only the Almighty could have done such a thing in such a way.

Not only can we see how capable and wise he is in making the physical world, it's truly awesome to see how he could interweave the lives of men and nations in such a way as to perfectly fulfill his spiritual purposes too. We are often dumbfounded when we try to imagine how God will derive glory out of the complicated, entangled disaster that we have made of things. And how could he possibly be in control over the seemingly random and rebellious acts of human beings who are determined to do the *opposite* of his will? For example, look at the massive scale of destruction of the devil, the darkness and deceit of the world system – this doesn't give us much hope that God is really the Master of all the earth.

Nevertheless he *is* in complete control, there will be no surprises for him, and everything will turn out in the end exactly as he planned – which will bring him everlasting glory when he shows all of us how he could do such a thing. Somehow he will straighten everything out: the wicked will get exactly what they deserve, and the righteous will get what they deserve, and nobody will be treated the least bit unfairly. It's going to take an infinite wisdom to do that.

The Last Day will be one of the most crucial events in God's timetable for the world. It's then that he will unveil the secrets behind the control and power that he exerted over the entire world all through history. There before his Judgment Seat we will hear the explanation for everything that has happened; there we will see the mysteries uncovered, and then we will all know what's going on just as he now knows. This is the idea of Judgment Day.

What does Judgment mean?

The concept of judgment is often misunderstood. People often confuse it with the act of passing a sentence on a convicted criminal. But there's something much more important that has to happen before the court reaches that stage of passing out the sentence.

You probably noticed that, when accused of a crime, most people rarely tell the truth about themselves. Usually the defendant will plead "not guilty"; if we simply accepted the bare statement of the defendant, we would let most if not all of the criminals in our justice system go free! Everyone has a "good" excuse for what happened, nobody is responsible (or so they claim), and it's always someone else's fault. So we have to have a better way of coming to some sort of decision than believing the accused.

So, we have a judge. He listens to the arguments for the prosecution and for the defense, he listens to the witnesses, he examines the evidence, and then pronounces his impersonal judgment on the case. In a court setting, the judge is the person who determines the answer to the question: *what really happened?* When he's satisfied that he has heard everything, he then gives a ruling: *this*, in my judgment, is what really happened. His assessment is what the court officially records to be the truth, and any subsequent actions of the court will be based on his assessment. For example, if the man is guilty, the police will take him off to prison and be perfectly in the right for doing so – the judge declared him guilty, so nobody can legally argue about what the authorities proceed to do with him.

God is a Judge

The Bible tells us plainly that God is the Judge over all the earth. The reason is this: the Lord is capable, in a way that no human judge can hope to copy, of discerning the true state of a person's heart. "Man looks at the outward appearance, but the Lord looks at the heart."

(1 Samuel 16:7) Jesus, it was said, "did not need man's testimony about man, for he knew what was in a man." (John 2:25)

Because God is the ultimate Judge – because he always knows what's going on in his world (he *has* to know as he performs his work as King over his Creation), Judgment Day was a foregone conclusion from the first day of Creation. He made all things with that day in mind; it was over the horizon at the first dawn. We can see the first traces of his judgment in his pronouncement about what he had made:

> God saw all that he had made, and it was very good.
> (Genesis 1:31)

The point is that his world must measure up, it must meet his expectations, or it's no good to him. Either it brings him glory by being and doing what he told it to do, or he will do away with it as worthless to him. Therefore everything stands under his constant scrutiny; he has been judging it from the very beginning.

From that day until now, the Lord has the world continuously under examination. When Adam and Eve – the first criminals – tried to hide from God in their sin and shame, he immediately went to work uncovering what really happened, and only after the facts were laid out in the open did he issue his judgment and condemnation. Also, in Genesis 6 we read that –

> The LORD saw how great man's wickedness on the earth
> had become, and that every inclination of the thoughts
> of his heart was only evil all the time. (Genesis 6:5)

Again, throughout the history of Israel, God was about the business of judging their hearts and actions. Since they usually tried to cover up their sin, he first had to expose it to full view so that we could see what was really there; *then* he issued his sentence based on the facts. When the truth is known, then God issues his verdict and he receives glory based on the facts he uncovers. Much of the work of the prophets centered around exposing the secret sins of the Israelites to public view.

Jesus often uncovered the hearts of men. The Pharisees, the woman at the well, Peter's heart, Nathanael, the rich young ruler, Paul the persecutor – all these people tried to hide their hearts from God, but Jesus easily stripped away the veil and exposed what they really were.

Judgment started at Creation

We mustn't miss the importance of the connection between the Judge and the Creator. The One who *made* all things, has the power and authority to *judge* all things. He alone "knows how we are formed." (Psalm 103:14) The Designer knows best whether his Creation meets the specifications.

But not only *can* he judge us, not only does he have the ability to uncover our hearts, he fully *intends* to expose what we are. The Lord didn't make the world simply to exist, but to be a showcase for himself and his abilities, a platform to reveal who he is and how he works through us, and a kingdom in which all his subjects obey him willingly and completely. We are foolish if we think we will escape his notice. He promised us many times that he's watching us and is planning to uncover what we are before the entire world:

> No one lights a lamp and hides it in a jar or puts it under a bed. Instead, he puts it on a stand, so that those who come in can see the light. For there is nothing hidden that will not be disclosed, and nothing concealed that will not be known or brought out into the open. Therefore consider carefully how you listen. (Luke 8:16-18)

So, he will always be testing us to see if we measure up to his standards.

This brings out an interesting characteristic of God's Creation. Since we are always to be under his judgment to see if we meet his specifications, God designed the world in such a way as to easily reveal the true state of our hearts. Whether we know it or not (and usually we don't) we show the world *by our actions* what we really are inside. This wasn't by accident but by design of the Creator. The process of judgment has already started, from the beginning of the world. Just by living, we show God and everyone what we are. We already saw that this shows an amazing wisdom behind the way that God made the world, and how we so easily and yet unknowingly reveal what we really are. Judgment Day will be only the final wrap-up of the process that started in the Garden of Eden.

Jesus revealed this aspect of Creation's design in several passages:

> By their fruit you will recognize them. Do people pick grapes from thornbushes, or figs from thistles? Likewise every good tree bears good fruit, but a bad tree bears bad fruit. A good tree cannot bear bad fruit, and a bad tree cannot bear good fruit. Every tree that does not bear good fruit is cut down and thrown into the fire. Thus, by their fruit you will recognize them. (Matthew 7:16-20)

> You brood of vipers, how can you who are evil say anything good? For out of the overflow of the heart the mouth speaks. The good man brings good things out of the good stored up in him, and the evil man brings evil things out of the evil stored up in him. But I tell you that men will have to give account on the day of judgment for every careless word they have spoken. For by your words you will be acquitted, and by your words you will be condemned. (Matthew 12:34-37)

> But the things that come out of the mouth come from the heart, and these make a man 'unclean.' For out of the heart come evil thoughts, murder, adultery, sexual immorality, theft, false testimony, slander. (Matthew 15:18-19)

> The good man brings good things out of the good stored up in his heart, and the evil man brings evil things out of the evil stored up in his heart. For out of the overflow of his heart his mouth speaks. (Luke 6:45)

In other words, right at Creation the Judge made us in such a way that we *will* tell the truth in our actions even if we lie with our mouths. What profound wisdom behind the design of Creation – the Judge is always at work in us.

> His eyes are on the ways of men; he sees their every step. There is no dark place, no deep shadow, where evildoers can hide. God has no need to examine men further, that they should come before him for judgment. Without inquiry he shatters the mighty and sets up others in their place. Because he takes note of their deeds, he overthrows them in the night and they are crushed. (Job 34:21-25)

Judgment Day

On Judgment Day the work will be finished. Jesus Christ will then dominate all of Heaven and earth, the new Kingdom will be ready for unveiling, the old kingdom will be ripe for destruction, and eternity will begin. A new chapter in the history of the world will start. The Judge will then "open the books" and examine the entire situation before him. Since he has already designed the system to reveal its true nature on its own, it will simply be a matter of looking at each creature under Heaven and pronouncing its destiny according to its developed character. In other words, how did it turn out? Whatever fits in with the new spiritual Kingdom will be kept, and whatever doesn't fit will be destroyed.

> As the weeds are pulled up and burned in the fire, so it will be at the end of the age. The Son of Man will send out his angels, and they will weed out of his kingdom everything that causes sin and all who do evil. They will throw them into the fiery furnace, where there will

> be weeping and gnashing of teeth. Then the righteous
> will shine like the sun in the kingdom of their Father. He
> who has ears, let him hear. (Matthew 13:40-43)

If you think about it, you would realize that only by finishing in this way will God get the full glory that he deserves. If there will be no Judgment Day, there would be too many questions left hanging. We have already been asking those questions ourselves: for example, why is there evil? What was accomplished by having millions die in ignorance of Christ? What about the "innocents"? Is it really important to be so careful about how one lives? If these questions were left unanswered, God's character would be forever in doubt. People would think that he wasn't fair with us, that he was expecting more of us than we could reasonably do. But God *is* just, and he does all things *well*. Therefore, Judgment Day is going to clear his character in such a way that even the most rebellious and hard-hearted of the wicked will have to admit that God is just.

> The righteous will be glad when they are avenged, when
> they bathe their feet in the blood of the wicked. Then
> men will say, "Surely the righteous still are rewarded;
> surely there is a God who judges the earth." (Psalm
> 58:10-11)

The arrow of time

Scientists often speak of the "arrow of time" – that characteristic of the universe that makes it run only in one direction, time-wise.[33] In other words, we aren't comfortable with a world that runs backwards, like a comic film sequence played backwards to make impossible things happen. A broken jar can't put itself back together, or jump back up on the table from which it fell. Neither can the universe itself "rewind"; it must proceed forward along the time line. So far the scientists haven't discovered *why* this is true about the

---

[33] See a fuller discussion of this principle of physics in Paul Davies' chapter "The Arrow of Time", *About Time: Einstein's Unfinished Business*, Simon & Schuster, 1995, 196-218.

physical world. They have most other things about the world figured out, but the "arrow of time" is still a mystery.

It has never been a mystery, however, that the Creation is headed toward Judgment Day. That's the driving principle behind the "arrow of time." Judgment Day *must* happen, because God must get full glory for all of his works. Unless everything moves along and eventually comes to an end, there won't be any final explanation for everything that has happened in history.

There may be a physical law behind the "arrow of time" that scientists will one day discover, but the main *reason* for that inexorable march to the end (in other words, the spiritual foundation for the physical reality) is the absolute necessity for the final wrap-up of all of God's works. He must be revealed fully. It must be made plain that the entire universe and its history was the work of his hand. Along the way, throughout history and the events of men and nations, we will learn more and more about God's wisdom in how things turn out – he knows exactly what he's doing, and it's obvious that he knows how to deal with sinners. But when the universe finally reaches the *end* of its journey, that will be the signal for the greatest revelation of God. We were all designed to meet him there for judgment, and meet him we will; hence the "arrow of time." We are being dragged forward to that Throne.

Judged by our actions

Let's step back now and look at the entire Creation from the point of view of Judgment Day. By designing the universe – and us – in such a way that it would be continuously displaying its true character and usefulness to its Creator, God ordained that the very structure of the world will be moral and spiritual, not solely physical. In other words, it's true that we have bodies, and we live in time and space in a material world. But time and space are only the means for a higher purpose: they provide a "stage", so to speak, for a moral existence. God is primarily interested not in how the laws of physics work, but in whether his creatures glorify him.

Man in particular has a body which he uses either to glorify his Creator or dishonor him. We can't help it, because our mouths were made to praise *him* and our hands were made to build *his* kingdom on earth. A mouth that doesn't praise God is dead, void of spiritual life and purpose. It's only fit to be thrown away – it isn't doing what it was designed to do. Hands that don't build God's kingdom on earth are dead, spreading destruction and misery among God's creatures instead of handing out the treasures of Heaven among God's subjects. In other words, we fulfill our purpose if we use our physical bodies to build a spiritual kingdom. God intends to judge us by our actions done while *in the body*, because we were given bodies specially designed to glorify him:

> For we must all appear before the judgment seat of Christ, that each one may receive what is due him *for the things done while in the body*, whether good or bad. (2 Corinthians 5:10)

So, Judgment Day tests the worth of the original Creation. The two events are linked together, like two knots at either end of the same rope. It is one continuous story, from beginning to end. Whatever Creation started, God intends to test and finish up at the end of time.

The Window of Creation – Revelation and Faith

There are two problems that make it difficult for us to find out exactly what happened at the beginning of the universe: first, none of us were there. We like to see things for ourselves before we believe them. Since no human being was there at the Creation, we naturally wonder whether the account that we have in Genesis is really reliable; that's why many people prefer the scientific answer, since its realism and familiar principles appeal to us more than the amazing miracles that Genesis claims happened.

Second, and this is a more difficult problem, even if we would have been there, we wouldn't have been able to tell exactly what was going on. It was such a complex spiritual event that most of it would have been way beyond our abilities to follow and understand. We've already looked at the fact that a miracle is something that we can't understand; we can see the beginning, and we can see the result, but how in the world it happened is a mystery to us. The Creation would have been just as much a mystery to us if we would have watched it.

So, if we want any hope of understanding what went on, we have to look inside the "sealed box" where all the activity is going on. It's like a machine: feed the raw materials in one end, and out comes the finished product on the other end. But what happens inside the machine is a mystery – unless we manage to find a window where we can look inside.

Evolution has its own explanation for what happened in there. But they didn't look in the right window; I think they're looking out some other window. Scientists can tell you how the world works *now*, but they don't have any idea of how the world was *first made*.

God has provided that window for us: it's a combination of revelation and faith. Using these two concepts, we can easily see how

God made the world; everything we've looked at so far requires the window of revelation and faith.

Revelation

We tend to underestimate the vast distance between the Creator and his creatures. Followers of other religions can't accept the fact that the universe itself isn't God. To them, all of existence, including whatever gods one cares to believe in, are part of a continuous span between the gross physical and the purely spiritual. Everything is part of God to them – and if it is, then *they* are also part of God. (By the way, one reason they believe this is because they don't want to believe in Creation. If everything is part of God, then everything is *eternal* and therefore wasn't created. And *that* lie comes from the devil.)

Christianity, however, teaches that before the world was made, God existed alone, needing nothing but himself to exist. When he made the universe, therefore, it was *out of nothing*; he used nothing *of* himself, the universe is in no way part of himself, and it can just as easily be annihilated without any effect upon himself. This total and complete separation of identity between God and the world is basic to our Christian faith. We need to accept this truth if we really want to understand the true nature of many of his works in the world – not the least being the Incarnation of Christ.

The Creation event also depended on this separation. The world is not God. This means is that we can understand the world we are a part of, but we have no way of knowing God himself unless he comes in to us from the outside and reveals himself to us. He is not *in* the Creation, in the sense of being an integral part of its makeup; therefore we must look *outside* the universe – in a spiritual world – in order to find him. Or should I say, our only hope is if he comes in from the outside and finds us.

The meaning of the word "revelation" is to uncover, to take away the veil. What this means in respect to God is that he is *completely* hidden from our view until he himself pulls the veil away. The Scripture says that "clouds and thick darkness surround him"

(Psalm 97:2). We can't easily know God as long as we are so limited by the physical world we are a part of. It's like being in a fog: we need the strong rays of the sun (or Son, as Hebrews 1:3 tells us) to penetrate the fog and clear away the confusion. So, if we are to learn anything about God, we can only wait until he has mercy on us and reveals himself to us.

There are two ways in which we can know God, and both of them depend on his self-revelation: first, through natural theology, which is a careful analysis of God's Creation looking for the telltale signs that he really did make the world. We've already looked at this approach. And the Bible does say that the created world tells us something of his nature and the way he works –

> ... what may be known about God is plain to them, because God has made it plain to them. For since the creation of the world God's invisible qualities — his eternal power and divine nature — have been clearly seen, being understood from what has been made, so that men are without excuse. (Romans 1:19-20)

But the problem is that our sin prevents us from learning about God in nature. Natural theology is useful up to a point, but its main shortcoming is that it deals only with the physical evidence of Creation, which can be interpreted in various ways, depending on the theological persuasion of the investigator. An atheist will see design as part of the process of evolution, and modern scientists are developing sophisticated theories that can, on paper at least, explain how the world got to its present state using only math, physics and chemistry – and they willingly ignore the God in the process. Therefore, the only way that man can know the truth about God now, in a way that there can be no confusion or debate, is if God deliberately reveals himself through his Word and rips away the veil in our minds (which have been corrupted by sin and mortality) so that we *can* see him.

The Bible is the primary source and method of the revelation of God. In fact, that's the primary purpose of the Bible – *to reveal God*. We show our ignorance of its purpose when we use it for everything except that! If knowing God is, literally, eternal life (John 17:3), then we need a completely reliable source that reveals him to us so that we can live and not die. Only the Bible can do that for us.

Without revelation we are at a complete loss to know the truth about God. Notice how many theories about God have come from false religions as well as various philosophies throughout history, though they each *claim* to know the truth about God. Besides the fact that they can't all be right when no two of them agree with one other, their account of God doesn't fit the facts. They talk about a God they don't know, have never met, and he can't fulfill their most basic needs. As the prophets of Baal discovered, Baal will not – and can't – answer when there is real work to be done. (1 Kings 18:16-40)

If we expect God to send rain and sunshine and other natural processes of the world, which the Baal worshippers were careful to do, then it's easy to attribute whatever happens in the world to Baal. But when we need a miracle, an event that is contrary to the way this world works and can't possibly happen except by divine intervention, then false gods can't help us. And revelation shows us that the God of the Bible is fully capable of helping us, as well as very willing, by using impossible miracles.

We need the revelation of God in the Bible for some important reasons:

> **First**, when God shows us the truth, it's the truth *as we need to see it*. Without him guiding us in the right direction and interpreting the facts for us, we would surely get it wrong and dishonor him with our false ideas about how the world supposedly works. Look at what evolutionists have done! They look at the physical world and explain its origins with ridiculous theories of how dead matter can form galaxies and life and human beings all by itself!
>
> When governments "doctor" the truth before they reveal information to the public, it's called

"propaganda." But when God "doctors" the truth, it's because he knows unless he does, we *will* get things wrong. As the source of all wisdom, he knows *how* to tell us the truth in such a way that our finite minds will get the right impression of it. That's precisely why the Creation account is stated exactly as it is; this is the *only* way that it can be described without misleading us about the way it really happened. There is no other way to describe it and be correct.

Second, we can't know the truth unless God tells us. Human beings are intelligent creatures and capable of amazing mental activity; but spiritually we stand at the edge of an unknown reality, on the circumference of the mysterious world of God, unable to peer into the mystery there and fathom his being.

> I have seen the burden God has laid on men. He has made everything beautiful in its time. He has also set eternity in the hearts of men; yet they cannot fathom what God has done from beginning to end. (Ecclesiastes 3:10-11)

> In the same way no one knows the thoughts of God except the Spirit of God. (1 Corinthians 2:11)

The Bible reveals God to us in many ways, because God is so complex that many ways are necessary to reveal him. In each case, we are surprised at what we find out about him. The Bible corrects our false notions about him, it's a broadening out of our horizons, an enlargement of our hope in God, a new fear and humility before him, a changing of our life's direction because of him, a new love and devotion for him. We certainly learned none of this at the feet of science!

All through the Bible, God had to reveal himself to man before people got the right idea of who he is and what he does. The Spirit revealed God in Christ to the Apostles, who then went out and told the world what they saw. The prophets saw the coming of the King and warned of his pending reforms over the Israelites. Ezekiel saw the Lord leave the Temple and later return to it. We could use many more passages to demonstrate the principle that God opened the eyes of those to whom he wished to reveal himself; until he did, they had no idea that he was even present among them, much less what he was doing in particular. For example, God opened the eyes of Elisha's servant so that he could see what was going on around him:

> When the servant of the man of God got up and went out early the next morning, an army with horses and chariots had surrounded the city. "Oh, my lord, what shall we do?" the servant asked. "Don't be afraid," the prophet answered. "Those who are with us are more than those who are with them." And Elisha prayed, "O LORD, open his eyes so he may see." Then the LORD opened the servant's eyes, and he looked and saw the hills full of horses and chariots of fire all around Elisha. (2 Kings 6:15-17)

Third, revelation is necessary for one other reason: without it, appearances would deceive us. The physical world gets in the way of our understanding of God. We too often misinterpret what happens in history; we lay something at God's feet when he is in no way to blame for it, or we take credit for something when really God was working it out all along. For example, when the Babylonians overran the nation of Judah, Habakkuk thought that God had forgotten his justice – how could he let these godless men destroy his own people? But the Lord revealed to him that *he* was the one using the

Babylonians – and he showed Habakkuk what he was really doing *through* the Babylonians:

> O LORD, you have appointed them to execute judgment, O Rock, you have ordained them to punish. (Habakkuk 1:12)

Without the revelation, the circumstances didn't make sense and seemed contrary to God's ancient promises. But the revelation made it plain that these armies (unknown to themselves, of course) were doing God's work of purging iniquity from his people.

Now let's apply the principle of revelation to the Creation account. What is critical to grasp here is that *unless God shows us, we can't possibly know what really happened.* It's not a matter of training, as if we would eventually know what happened, given the time and scientific expertise; that's what evolution claims with its scientific theories. The Bible, however, is showing us what we can never discover on our own. Things happened in that event that no amount of instruments or scientific training will uncover. It was a spiritual event, performed by Someone who refuses to use any natural means to accomplish his will. There was *nothing there except him* in the beginning! No matter or energy, laws of physics, chemical formulas, *nothing.*

How does one take a picture of nothing? How can we conceptualize a spiritual event? How can we know the steps of that event, and understand what happened, unless the Creator himself shows us what he was doing and interprets it for us? How can created beings possibly know their beginning when that beginning was a miracle?

Physicists are aware of that very real limitation. They keep backing up their explanation of the evolution of the universe to the moment of the Big Bang – even to the trillionth of a second after the Big Bang; but they are at a loss to know what lies precisely *before* that beginning moment of existence. They need a revelation just as much as anybody, because their equations can't give them the answers they are looking for and they just can't handle the idea of *nothingness*. But they can't bring themselves to accept the Bible's revelation of that moment when there was nothing, and the action that God took to bring matter into existence.

The revelation of Genesis 1-3 unveils the King at work, making a kingdom of subjects, and making the Kingdom *his* way – through miracles. It shows how utterly dependent we are on him — if he can command and make a world, he can also command and destroy the world just as easily. This isn't the solid, never-ending universe that evolution claims! What Genesis shows us is information about our world that is *not* what we expected when we use science alone to examine our physical world.

The Bible shows us that same foundation and relationship between us and our Creator everywhere we read it, not only in Genesis. Notice that many times, when man and God had dealings with each other, we find the same Creation themes at work. For example, when God opened up the Red Sea so that the Israelites could cross it and escape the Egyptians, we are told plainly how that event happened. God did it by means of a *miracle* (not a natural event!), and he did it by *command*. Unless the Bible would have told us this very plainly, however, we wouldn't have accepted the story as it stands.

In order to see and understand the truth about God and Creation, we don't need to be scientific experts. The only thing we need is God's revelation: he can show this truth to anybody who has an open mind and a humble heart. Scientists feel that they are the only ones who can understand how the world was made, but they make a serious mistake. God reveals this knowledge to his children, to those who are willing to listen to him. We can and should pursue scientific research in other areas, but on the issue of Creation we will only know the truth if we use the only thing that can clearly show us what really happened: the Bible.

Faith

Faith is such a characteristic feature of God's people that we find it from beginning to end in the Bible, from Abraham the "father" of the faithful to the Church of the faithful in Christ found in Revelation. But though faith is a universal characteristic among Christians, this doesn't mean that it's something easily understood or easily had. Faith is a gift from God (Ephesians 2:8) and is beyond the natural ability of human beings, especially because of our sin.

Faith is always the way we have to approach all matters of the Spirit, because none of our physical senses can enable us to know the certainty of the world of God. This is because faith is a special spiritual skill that makes the impossible happen: it gives us a vision, an understanding, of God's world. Without faith we can't understand the truth even if we are looking straight at it!

Faith, as Hebrews tells us, is "being sure of what we hope for and certain of what we do not see." (Hebrews 11:1) What faith gives us is **the ability to see God's spiritual world**. Though our physical senses can't know God, our souls can – when the Spirit makes our dead souls alive so that we *can* see God. The Spirit reveals God – this is his job among us – so that we can see and know the truth about God. Without the Spirit we can see nothing; but because of the Spirit, a light from Heaven shines down on us and we can know God personally.

> The Spirit searches all things, even the deep things of God. For who among men knows the thoughts of a man except the man's spirit within him? In the same way no one knows the thoughts of God except the Spirit of God. We have not received the spirit of the world but the Spirit who is from God, that we may understand what God has freely given us. This is what we speak, not in words taught us by human wisdom but in words taught by the Spirit, expressing spiritual truths in spiritual words. The man without the Spirit does not accept the things that come from the Spirit of God, for they are foolishness to him, and he cannot understand them,

because they are spiritually discerned. (1 Corinthians 2:10-14)

In order to do this, the Spirit has to take us outside this physical world, beyond where our normal senses operate, and show us the spiritual world in a way that we will know for certain that such things are true. This is the root of true faith. Abraham, the "father of the faithful," first experienced this when God gave him the promise of a son:

> Abram believed the Lord, and he credited it to him as righteousness. (Genesis 15:6)

The promise was clearly incredible; he and especially his wife Sarah were too old to have a son. But something in what Abraham saw, through his faith, convinced him that God's promise would most certainly happen in spite of its impossibility:

> Against all hope, Abraham in hope believed and so became the father of many nations, just as it had been said to him, "So shall your offspring be." Without weakening in his faith, he faced the fact that his body was as good as dead — since he was about a hundred years old — and that Sarah's womb was also dead. Yet he did not waver through unbelief regarding the promise of God, but was strengthened in his faith and gave glory to God, being fully persuaded that God had power to do what he had promised. This is why "it was credited to him as righteousness." (Romans 4:18-22)

Faith – our awareness and certainty of spiritual realities – keeps us in touch with God and serves us in an important way: it makes the things of God so real that we change our lives to fit what we know, much to the surprise of those who don't see what we see! We live in God's presence, we live for God's heavenly rewards, we live in the fear of God and his commands, we don't fear the world anymore, we don't yield to temptations, we hate our spiritual enemies, we love our brothers and sisters in the Lord. None of this makes sense to an unspiritual man, but it makes perfect sense to a Christian who has seen the reality of this new world of which he is now a citizen.

Life here becomes a parallel existence, so to speak: our physical senses tell us about the physical world we live in, and our awakened spiritual senses tell us about the world of God that we live in. We become "strangers and aliens" in this world while we make our way toward the place where we know that we have our eternal citizenship. (Hebrews 11:13-16) We are actually living in two worlds, and can see both of them: our physical eyes for this world, and our spiritual eyes, or faith, for the world of God.

We find, at all the critical junctures in Biblical history, that faith was the only way to truly understand the work that God was doing. Each event required a special skill of discernment that reason or senses couldn't provide. For example, only by faith could the disciples know who Jesus really was. According to physical senses, he was only the carpenter's son; the Jews in general were completely confused about him:

> When Jesus came to the region of Caesarea Philippi, he asked his disciples, "Who do people say the Son of Man is?" They replied, "Some say John the Baptist; others say Elijah; and still others, Jeremiah or one of the prophets." "But what about you?" he asked. "Who do you say I am?" Simon Peter answered, "You are the Christ, the Son of the living God." Jesus replied, "Blessed are you, Simon son of Jonah, for this was not revealed to you by man, but by my Father in Heaven." (Matthew 16:13-17)

That special revelation that was given to Peter was light from Heaven, unveiling the real glory that was behind the outward humility of Christ. Only in that way could the disciples know the truth about him.

Faith is necessary to understand many other spiritual works recorded in the Bible: for example, David in his battle against Goliath, the truth about Christ's birth, the prophecies of the Old Testament, the forgiveness found in the Temple worship in Jerusalem. Without faith we would form a wrong interpretation of what is really going on – we will miss the fact that this is really God working, doing things in ways peculiar to himself. For example, Paul was thankful that the Thessalonians could see the true nature of his preaching:

> And we also thank God continually because, when you received the word of God, which you heard from us, you accepted it not as the word of men, *but as it actually is*, the word of God, which is at work in you who believe. (1 Thessalonians 2:13)

When we rely on faith so heavily to understand God's works, we naturally find ourselves in a predicament. It's natural for unbelievers to assume that, since faith deals with the invisible world and with what our senses can't help us understand, we Christians are dealing therefore with the non-existent and unimportant. If nobody can see God, and we have to accept the Bible's explanation that God really was involved in Creation (though nobody saw him at work!), then why do we need to believe in something we can't see? This is the charge that unbelievers will inevitably make against Christians whenever we fall back on "faith" to interpret Creation. If we deliberately point to the unseen to explain the visible, why then resort to it at all?

The reason is this: the God who is above and beyond Creation, who is in no way a part of this world, is responsible for making this world what it is. We have to look outside the system to explain the system. Evolution looks within the system, hoping that the world will explain itself (which it can't, because there are many things that can't be accounted for by using only evolution). The only explanation that works, the only truth that fully accounts for the world we live in, is that a spiritual God made it all out of nothing for his purposes. Only faith can see that, so only faith finds the truth.

Faith is the *only* way we will know God or understand his works. So, let's take this truth back to the Genesis account of Creation and apply it. Let's not continue to stumble over the incredible nature of the account and substitute a "reasonable" scientific answer. Our ability to reason depends on our senses and what we know about *this* world; but our faith reaches beyond this world to a God who says he can – and did – make the world through miracle.

Only someone who truly knows God – that is, who sees God in faith – will be convinced. Faith can easily see that a miracle-working, holy King who does his will by creative command, by means of the power of the Spirit, would not have made the world in any other way except what the Genesis account states very clearly.

The Genesis account *requires* faith. It makes no sense unless we can see the greater spiritual forces at work behind the making of the universe. We read there that God spoke and the whole universe came into being immediately. "*By faith* we understand that the universe was formed at God's command, so that what is seen was not made out of what was visible." (Hebrews 11:3) Our senses can't explain that truth, scientific instruments can't explain it to us, our reason and rational minds can't explain it – the only "instrument" capable of grasping the nature of what happened and how it happened is this *spiritual* sense of faith that God gives his people.

This is so fundamental a truth that we can claim without hesitation this fact: if someone with all the scientific training in the world were there at Creation when it happened, he would have come away from the event having no understanding of what he saw, even though he might have had all the data and recording instruments he could have wished for, and plenty of time to analyze the data. Evolution only requires mathematics, physics, chemistry, and various instruments to be understood. But the skill needed – indeed, required – to understand *this kind* of Creation recorded in Genesis is faith.

If we use anything less than faith, however, we will be completely blind to the tremendous spiritual work going on in it. Without faith the event becomes too fantastic to believe; so we fall back on what we can learn with our senses, and of course we then miss out on the hand of God working his will into his world. We will never believe in a miracle-working God without faith; we will never bend our knees in humble fear and submission to the King who commands. Without faith, "it is impossible to please God, because anyone who comes to him must believe that he exists and that he rewards those who earnestly seek him." (Hebrews 11:6)

A strictly scientific viewpoint of Creation can't please God, because there's no faith in it. Neither can a hybrid version of Creation and evolution please him because such a position substitutes rational scientific answers for the impossible miracles. What this Genesis account is designed to do is make a believer out of you, a humble servant of the King, ready and willing to receive heavenly treasures for your life on earth. At the end of time, those who approached God with faith will be rewarded.

> These have come so that your faith — of greater worth than gold, which perishes even though refined by fire — may be proved genuine and may result in praise, glory and honor when Jesus Christ is revealed. Though you have not seen him, you love him; and even though you do not see him now, you believe in him and are filled with an inexpressible and glorious joy, for you are receiving the goal of your faith, the salvation of your souls. (1 Peter 1:7-9)

There is one more truth about the Creation account that we mustn't overlook. Since the entire Bible is a book that requires faith, we would expect its introductory chapters to set the tone for what is to come. We see miracles here, we see the impossible happen, we are introduced to a unique God, who intends to do the same kinds of things for his people across all ages. We see the world spring into a state of servanthood at its very beginning; we see a power that nothing in the universe can copy. All the elements for historic Judaism and Christianity are in this story of Creation. It's as if this account is an archway spanning the entrance into the rest of God's Word: written across it, in unmistakable letters, is the message, "All who enter here must enter with *faith*."

Part Three:

How the Biblical writers used the Creation account

How the Biblical Writers Used the Creation Account

Even though the case for Creation is very clear throughout the Bible, it helps to see even more proofs that we really are on the right track. I'll have to admit that, so far in our study, we had to do some serious doctrinal research and apply it back to Genesis – but you may be wondering by now if we had the right to look at things this way.

Genesis 1-2 is quite clear: the only way we can reject its account is to call its author a liar; that's essentially what people do if they see it as symbolic only. The great doctrines of our faith that we've looked at through the Bible prove that the God of Creation is the same God at work in *all* of Biblical history. The God who made us is the God who redeems us – through miracle and command and the Spirit. He uses the same methods from beginning to end.

But we don't want to deceive ourselves. It's exhilarating to run along the mountaintop of doctrine, matching what we see in Israel's history and the history of the Church with the Creator God in Genesis. Is this right, though? Are we making too much of a good thing? People will often get excited about a pet idea in the Bible, so much so that they believe they see it *everywhere* in the Scriptures! Is there some way we can check ourselves to make sure we're on the right track here?

Fortunately there is a way; we don't have to guess or wonder about this. The Bible writers, and the saints they wrote about, are going to lead the way for us. They too had the Creation account in their Scriptures. Since they were led by the Spirit to know the truth about God, they will show us what to believe about Creation and, what is very important, *how to use* this information.

What we are going to do now, then, is look at how they handled the subject. It's very important to watch *how* they used it: they knew what the real issues were, they knew what to look for in the Creator, they knew how to make use of the facts of Creation. We have to follow their lead if we want to get the most out of the Creation account.

In fact, they show us what we have already suspected in our study: that God still uses the same methods that he used in Creation. The Creator God is still alive, working among us in the same way, because he's still working on the same plan that he started out with. He's not done yet! The Bible writers saw that plan and understood it.

Furthermore, the Biblical writers took advantage of what they saw available in their God. Here is a God who has no difficulty solving the problems that man has! We will notice, when we read their testimony, that this God answered their prayers with the same kind of power, wisdom, and methods that he used at Creation. They prayed, in other words, *to the Creator!* And they were *not* interested in a God who works through evolution, scientific principles, or any form of modern unbelief. They wanted the God who can do miracles, who speaks and makes the world conform immediately to his will. They wanted the God who did these works to answer them; they weren't satisfied with anything less.

The point is that we shouldn't be satisfied with anything less either. It's one thing to pity the people of past ages for being scientifically naïve; but when we note that they got powerful answers to their prayers, when they got their lives straightened out and their great needs met by the Creator himself, that should make us wonder if *we* are the ones getting shortchanged by our modern scientific world view. If you had a choice between waiting on science to make your life happier and fulfilled (you'll be waiting all your life, by the way!) or going in faith to the God of the Bible and getting *your* miracle, which would you rather do?

That's exactly why we have this testimony from the Bible – to encourage us to trust in this God, and to show us what he will most certainly do for us when we believe in him.

2 Kings 19:15

> Hezekiah received the letter from the messengers and read it. Then he went up to the temple of the LORD and spread it out before the LORD. And Hezekiah prayed to the LORD: "O LORD, God of Israel, enthroned between the cherubim, you alone are God over all the kingdoms of the earth. You have made heaven and earth. Give ear, O LORD, and hear; open your eyes, O LORD, and see; listen to the words Sennacherib has sent to insult the living God. It is true, O LORD, that the Assyrian kings have laid waste these nations and their lands. They have thrown their gods into the fire and destroyed them, for they were not gods but only wood and stone, fashioned by men's hands. Now, O LORD our God, deliver us from his hand, so that all kingdoms on earth may know that you alone, O LORD, are God." (2 Kings 19:14-19)

The situation was this: Sennacherib, a king in Assyria, sent his army out to lay waste to the surrounding nations, and it finally arrived at Jerusalem. He sent a threat to Hezekiah, king of Judah, to surrender immediately. His reasoning was that he had totally destroyed other nations who relied on their gods – proving that he was stronger than all those gods. So it was useless for the Jews to depend on the Lord for protection; the God of the Jews would be just as powerless to save his people as the other gods proved to be.

Hezekiah couldn't accept this. He immediately went to pray to the Lord. Notice, however, which God he calls on: *the God who made heaven and earth.* He realized that he needed the Creator for this crisis. It's true that other gods couldn't stop Sennacherib, because they were empty hopes of false religions. But Israel's God was real; he was so real that everything and everybody on earth were in his hands – he could do what he wanted with them. What Hezekiah was asking for, therefore, was the kind of power that could stop the enemy in his tracks. In other words, he was asking for a miracle from the only God who could do such a thing.

Notice what happened:

> That night the angel of the LORD went out and put to death a hundred and eighty-five thousand men in the Assyrian camp. When the people got up the next morning — there were all the dead bodies! So Sennacherib king of Assyria broke camp and withdrew. He returned to Nineveh and stayed there. (2 Kings 19:35-36)

This was an astonishing display of the Creator at work, doing what everyone thought was impossible. There was no natural explanation for that event – even disease couldn't work so fast.

What we need to learn here is that Hezekiah knew what to ask for: he wanted the *same kind* of power and wisdom that created the world, because only that kind of answer would fulfill his present needs. If he had gotten a *natural* answer – destruction of the enemy by disease, success for his soldiers, boredom on Sennacherib's part as he prolonged his siege – then it would have taken much longer to solve the problem (if ever!), which wasn't what Hezekiah needed at this moment. He needed a full-scale miracle, immediately, and he got one. Any other "solution" would have made people wonder whether God were really in charge.

So it was the Creator God who did an immediate, massive, and impossible miracle in Hezekiah's day was the Creator himself. Hezekiah showed much wisdom and insight into the ways that the Creator works when he appealed to this God.

2 Chronicles 2:12

> Praise be to the LORD, the God of Israel, who made heaven and earth! He has given King David a wise son, endowed with intelligence and discernment, who will build a temple for the LORD and a palace for himself. (2 Chronicles 2:12)

When Solomon came to the throne of Israel, he began the work of building the Temple. Such a work required materials and skilled workers that sometimes could only be found in other nations. For example, here in this passage, we find that Solomon had appealed to Hiram, king of Tyre, for craftsmen and special materials.

It's interesting to see Hiram responding to Solomon's request in this way: he makes reference to the Lord, the God of Israel, *who made heaven and earth*. There must have been a reason for his focus on the Creator! The reason is this: Solomon was about to do something that required a great deal of wisdom, more wisdom than men were ordinarily endowed with. The Temple was the resting place of God on earth and must be built exactly to God's specifications. There would be a million ways of getting it wrong if Solomon didn't have revelation from Heaven about how God wanted it done.

The surrounding nations all had their own gods, and temples to house them in. Of course they were all wrong in their false religions, because their gods weren't real. But how would man ever know the truth about the real God? How would he learn the way to approach this God – the prayers he demanded, the sacrifices, the articles in his Temple to be used for worship? All this would require insight into the true God, a wisdom that comes from eyes opened to spiritual realities.

We know in our day that the Temple was remarkably suited to represent the life and ministry of Jesus Christ. There have been many good studies done on the symbolism of different parts of the Temple worship and how they corresponded exactly to the work of Christ. This symbolism was no accident; the wisdom of God is behind it. In fact, the wisdom of the Creator is behind it: the same God who made the world in "wisdom and understanding" laid out the plans for the Temple. The Creator first made man, and then decided how this creature of flesh and blood could approach the Almighty and worship him. There is no other source for this vital information.

Solomon was in touch with the mind of the Creator when he built the Temple, and *that's* why it fulfilled its purpose so well. The

Creator knows how to use something that is physical for his own spiritual purposes. Just as he made man to be a moral creature, and to glorify him through physical acts, the physical Temple had a spiritual use and glorified the Lord. People found spiritual forgiveness there through the physical sacrifices. We can see the same methods used, both at Creation and here at the building of the Temple. The wisdom of the Creator is the key, the kind of wisdom that can design something to operate not only at the physical level but also at the spiritual level.

Nehemiah 9:6

> Blessed be your glorious name, and may it be exalted above all blessing and praise. You alone are the LORD. You made the heavens, even the highest heavens, and all their starry host, the earth and all that is on it, the seas and all that is in them. You give life to everything, and the multitudes of heaven worship you. (Nehemiah 9:6)

When the Israelites returned from Exile in Babylon, Jerusalem was still in ruins. They had to do a lot of rebuilding to restore their homes, the walls of the city, and the Temple. But it wasn't easy: they had enemies all around them who gave them no end of trouble as they tried to rebuild their lives.

Nehemiah, the military and political leader of the Jews, was zealous for the work of God. He wanted to make sure that they got it right this time: after 70 humiliating years in Babylon, he didn't want the Jews to do anything that would risk such a punishment again. So they had a great assembly of all the people, Ezra the priest read the Law through from beginning to end, and the Levites stood up to pray for the whole assembly.

This verse is the beginning of their prayer. Notice that they immediately call on the God who *made the heavens, even the highest heavens, and all their starry host, the earth and all that is on it, the seas and all that is in them.* In other words, they want the ear of the Creator. Why is that?

Read the rest of the prayer and you will find out why. The priests retold some of the history of the Israelites – when they were enslaved in Egypt, and God rescued them from Pharaoh's hand by means of *miracles*. They remembered that God fed the Israelites bread, meat and water in the middle of the desert – again through *miracles*. They remembered that God rescued them from their enemies and drove out the Canaanites from Palestine, all through *miracles*. Time and time again the Israelites rebelled against God, and he allowed them to fall into the hands of oppressive nations – but then he relented over and over and rescued them by means of *miracles*.

Is the pattern becoming plain? When the Jews found themselves in trouble, surrounded by enemies, faced with the possibility of destruction just when they had arrived home to build things up again – they called on the Creator who continually uses miracles to protect them. They knew that they needed nothing less than the power of Heaven to protect them.

They knew that the Creator does miracles, that it was the Creator who provided for their ancestors and protected them along the way. No other god works like this; no other god (or force or principle of science) *can* work like this. Also, the fact that Israel's God used miracles in their day was, to them, the natural thing for him to do. How else *would* the Creator solve their problems? He simply wouldn't use any method other than miracles, because that's how he first created the world – and the result, remember, was *very good*. He works the same way in all ages when there's a need that's impossible for the world to supply. It was all one way of working to them.

Isaiah 27:11

For this is a people without understanding; so their Maker has no compassion on them, and their Creator shows them no favor. (Isaiah 27:11)

We need the Creation account in Genesis to help explain passages like this one! It appears in this verse that Israel's God no longer has any mercy; he has forgotten his promise of love and care to them, and is ready to throw them away.

But actually that isn't the case at all. Remember that God created the world by command. He created a Kingdom, he is the King over all, and this kingdom consists of subjects who were made to do his will. Any creature that rebels against God's rule is naturally destined to suffer the legal consequences of its actions; it's a political act, a form of treason against the state.

Israel has forgotten that creative Command of Genesis; they forgot that they exist only to do his will. As a result, they have become a nation full of rebels, so much so that the other nations around them, instead of seeing God's representatives doing the work of God's Kingdom, see rebellious subjects instead! God's name is being tarnished in the world by those who ought to understand and promote his eternal purposes the best. That's why the prophet complains about their lack of understanding: they should have known, from the Genesis account, what their calling is in life: to be servants of the King.

Isaiah 40:27-31

> Why do you say, O Jacob,
>   and complain, O Israel,
> "My way is hidden from the LORD;
>   my cause is disregarded by my God"?
> Do you not know?
> Have you not heard?
> The LORD is the everlasting God,
>   the Creator of the ends of the earth.
> He will not grow tired or weary,
>   and his understanding no one can fathom.
> He gives strength to the weary
>   and increases the power of the weak.
> Even youths grow tired and weary,

> and young men stumble and fall;
> but those who hope in the Lord
> will renew their strength.
> They will soar on wings like eagles;
> they will run and not grow weary,
> they will walk and not be faint. (Isaiah 40:27-31)

Here the prophet reminds the people of something that we are all quick to forget: God doesn't get tired as we do. What he wants to do, he will do; nothing will prevent him from finishing what he starts.

Life has so many problems, and we get weary trying to make it through the daily battles. At times it all seems so hopeless and pointless – so we finally lie down and give up. Then we accuse even God of getting tired of *us* and giving up on us.

It's in that time of weariness and doubt that we need to remember the Creator. He doesn't get tired, or weary of the world or us. He is on constant watch over us. He stands ready to give us whatever we need – the strength to continue, the wisdom to know what to do next, the patience with our childish willfulness, the forgiveness for our continual sins. He never wearies of us.

Young men don't often run out of energy. The prophet uses them as an example of how awesome the power of God really is. The young men may grow weary, but God will give overwhelming power to those who trust in him – be they young or old – directly, through his Spirit, in a way that will look completely mysterious to those who look for natural answers behind miracles.

This is the God of Creation who helps us; he isn't at a loss for answers when it comes to giving us help or answers beyond our wildest dreams. He works miracles to get his people through this world to his eternal Kingdom. Notice that it's the same God who made the universe: power beyond imagination, power from outside the world, power that will overcome any problem that we encounter in the world.

Isaiah 45:7-9

> I form the light and create darkness,
>   I bring prosperity and create disaster;
>   I, the LORD, do all these things.
> "You heavens above, rain down righteousness;
>   let the clouds shower it down.
> Let the earth open wide,
>   let salvation spring up,
>   let righteousness grow with it;
>   I, the LORD, have created it.
> "Woe to him who quarrels with his Maker,
>   to him who is but a potsherd among the potsherds on the ground.
> Does the clay say to the potter,
>   'What are you making?'
> Does your work say,
>   'He has no hands'? (Isaiah 45:7-9)

There are times when we have to be reminded who is Boss! The Creator, if you remember, made a world that pleased him. This is his Kingdom, and he spoke a world into existence that would suit his purposes. He isn't interested in doing things our way.

We don't like to remember this. We would rather circumstances go *our* way, and we work to please ourselves. We are always butting heads with the Lord when it comes to fulfilling our lusts and desires. Even when we pray, we expect the Almighty to fulfill our "wish list" as if he were Santa Claus. The reason he doesn't is that we are usually asking for things that he doesn't approve of: "When you ask, you do not receive, because you ask with wrong motives, that you may spend what you get on your pleasures." (James 4:3)

Keep in mind two things, however: **first**, we can't win if we are determined to rebel against God. This is his world, and it works as he wishes. To fight God is to row upstream; we won't accomplish anything except a life full of "great frustration, affliction and anger." (Ecclesiastes 5:17)

Second, the One who made the world has exclusive rights to everything – including us. His Creative Command made *subjects*, not independent agents. We please him only if we do the work he has given us. Our duty isn't to complain, or blame him for not giving us what we want; our duty is to find out what he wants us to do and then do it.

If God wishes to put a person through a miserable life, that's completely up to him and within his rights as Creator and Master. How can we complain about it? The King knows exactly what he's doing. It could very well be that our hardships are discipline from a loving Father who is making us righteous:

> No discipline seems pleasant at the time, but painful. Later on, however, it produces a harvest of righteousness and peace for those who have been trained by it. (Hebrews 12:11)

Isaiah 51:12-13

> I, even I, am he who comforts you.
> Who are you that you fear mortal men,
>   the sons of men, who are but grass,
> that you forget the LORD your Maker,
>   who stretched out the heavens
>   and laid the foundations of the earth,
> that you live in constant terror every day
>   because of the wrath of the oppressor,
>   who is bent on destruction? (Isaiah 51:12-13)

We have many fears in life, but really it doesn't make sense to fear anything if the Creator has promised to protect us. If we know our Creator on personal terms, we should go directly to him to take care of these enemies that we have. After all, he made them too! He knows very well how to bring them to ruin.

The God who *stretched out the heavens and laid the foundations of the earth* knows how to deal with men and nations. To him, they are only a drop in the bucket. It's no wonder that Jesus recommended that we shouldn't fear those who can only destroy the body; instead we should "be afraid of the One who can destroy both soul and body in hell." (Matthew 10:28)

The apostle Paul asked, "If God is for us, who can be against us?" (Romans 8:31) God makes the majority! There is no problem, no enemy, no power on earth or in Heaven that can stand against the Almighty.

> For I am convinced that neither death nor life, neither angels nor demons, neither the present nor the future, nor any powers, neither height nor depth, nor anything else in all creation, will be able to separate us from the love of God that is in Christ Jesus our Lord. (Romans 8:38-39)

He uses methods and powers and wisdom that completely destroy the enemy, before they even have a chance to know what hit them. In fact his methods of dealing with the enemy can be downright brutal and final, when it comes to protecting those who trust in him. See Psalm 18 for an example.

Keep in mind that the prophet Isaiah is recommending the Creator as our Protector. The Creator does miracles, he uses a power that crushes the things of earth, immediately, finally. The Creator can simply command his enemies to disperse, if he wishes. All it takes is his Word to accomplish his will. All these principles are first taught to us in the Genesis Creation account; the prophet is merely applying what he learned there to this new problem. We can expect the same God to use the same methods, because we *need* those kinds of methods to deal with our problems. Nothing else will help us.

Isaiah 65:17

> Behold, I will create
>   new heavens and a new earth.
> The former things will not be remembered,
>   nor will they come to mind. (Isaiah 65:17)

This is a well-known passage that talks about God's future plans for his people. Notice several things about it: **first**, only the God who made the first world has the power and authority to destroy it and create a second one. Until he acts, the present earth will continue existing just as he first commanded it. It can't help but follow that original blueprint, since it only exists to serve his pleasure and can't escape from his purpose for it.

Second, he doesn't like the way things are going in the world. We ruined his Creation; man, the obstinate rebel who refused to follow the pattern set out for him from the beginning, changed the course of nature to suit himself, not his Master. So the Lord has to dismantle the whole business and make a new world.

That day will be just as miraculous and monumental as the first Creation. Hebrews tells us that the Lord will one day end all things in a peculiar way:

> In the beginning, O Lord, you laid the foundations of the earth, and the heavens are the work of your hands. They will perish, but you remain; they will all wear out like a garment. You will roll them up like a robe; like a garment they will be changed. (Hebrews 1:10-12)

And Peter tells us just how that will happen:

> But they deliberately forget that long ago by God's word the heavens existed and the earth was formed out of water and by water. By these waters also the world of that time was deluged and destroyed. By the same word the present heavens and earth are reserved for fire,

being kept for the day of judgment and destruction of ungodly men ... But the day of the Lord will come like a thief. The heavens will disappear with a roar; the elements will be destroyed by fire, and the earth and everything in it will be laid bare. (2 Peter 3:5-7,10)

Now this isn't what the scientists tell us! They can tell us how the world works *now*, but the beginning and the ending of the universe are miraculous events, and they don't happen at all in the way that science would have predicted. God will need a new kind of world, and evolution can't do it – it couldn't give God the kind of world he wanted in the first place, and it can't create a paradise for God's people in the future either.

Jeremiah 10:10-13

> But the LORD is the true God;
>   he is the living God, the eternal King.
> When he is angry, the earth trembles;
>   the nations cannot endure his wrath.
> Tell them this: 'These gods, who did not make the heavens and the earth, will perish from the earth and from under the heavens.'
> But God made the earth by his power;
>   he founded the world by his wisdom
>   and stretched out the heavens by his understanding.
> When he thunders, the waters in the heavens roar;
>   he makes clouds rise from the ends of the earth.
> He sends lightning with the rain
>   and brings out the wind from his storehouses.
> (Jeremiah 10:10-13)

The Lord is complaining against his people Israel. They've been following the practices of their neighbors for centuries: they form gods out of wood and stone and gold and silver, apparently never seeing how foolish that is. And so it is in our day: matter and energy aren't man's God! They are senseless, they can do nothing for man's soul.

The Lord alone, the God of Israel, *made the earth by his power; he founded the world by his wisdom and stretched out the heavens by his understanding.* Here again we see the Creator stepping forward and proclaiming his skill: he made the world, and he knows *how* he made it. It would make good sense to look to the Maker of the world when we have problems in his world.

The reason that people need God is that they have problems they can't solve on their own. They need someone who is above the world, someone with irresistible power and unfathomable wisdom. The Israelites were hoping that the gods that their neighbors told them about would help them, because each god claimed to be able to do this or that if only the worshipper would bow down to it. And another reason they were hoping in the false gods is that those gods never demanded holiness from the worshipper.

The God of Israel, however, was the God who made the world, not all those false idols. The thing is, however, is that he *does* demand holiness from us. If we want help from the real Creator to solve our problems, we must be ready to obey the *commands* of his Kingdom. That's what God's world is: his realm, a place where he rules in absolute authority. He can do anything we need; but we owe him absolute obedience in return.

Furthermore, we will find that there is no escaping this God. As long as we are in his world, all roads eventually lead to him. Some will find a God of terror at the end of their road, and wish they had never been born; others will find the hope and delight of their hearts. In both cases, however, the Lord shows off his amazing wisdom in the way he designed the system – that all roads *will*, by his decree, lead to him and to Judgment Day.

Jeremiah 32:17-23

> Ah, Sovereign LORD, *you have made the heavens and the earth by your great power and outstretched arm.* Nothing is too hard for you. You show love to thousands but bring the punishment for the fathers' sins into the laps of their children after them. O great and powerful God, whose name is the LORD Almighty, great are your purposes and mighty are your deeds. Your eyes are open to all the ways of men; you reward everyone according to his conduct and as his deeds deserve. You performed miraculous signs and wonders in Egypt and have continued them to this day, both in Israel and among all mankind, and have gained the renown that is still yours. You brought your people Israel out of Egypt with signs and wonders, by a mighty hand and an outstretched arm and with great terror. You gave them this land you had sworn to give their forefathers, a land flowing with milk and honey. They came in and took possession of it, but they did not obey you or follow your law; they did not do what you commanded them to do. So you brought all this disaster upon them. (Jeremiah 32:17-23)

Jeremiah was the prophet at work in the days immediately before Jerusalem fell to the Babylonians; he saw the people finally defeated and dragged off to Babylon in exile. He was called the "weeping prophet" because, even though he warned the people what was coming, they ignored him and continued to rebel against God.

At one point Jeremiah was told by God to buy a field for a certain price. This greatly puzzled him, because the command came just as the Babylonians were surrounding Jerusalem and threatening to destroy the city, and either kill the Israelites or drag them back into exile in Babylon. Buy a field *now*? Jeremiah asked. But then he remembered the God of Creation: the God who *made the heavens and the earth by your great power and outstretched arm.*

Notice what he connects in his mind: the Lord who "made the heavens and the earth by your great power and outstretched arm" with the God who "performed miraculous signs and wonders in Egypt and have continued them to this day, both in Israel and among all mankind, and have gained the renown that is still yours." In other words, it's the *same* God at work, using the *same* methods (miracles and commands), doing things for the *same* reason – his glory, so that men would fear him.

God first made the world – *through amazing miracles*. He later rescued the Israelites from Egypt – *through amazing miracles*. Now, in Jeremiah's time, he is about to punish his people and send them off to exile in Babylon; but one day he will relent and bring them back – *through amazing miracles*.

Notice again that he focuses on the God who works the *same* way in every instance. His work at Creation was no different from his work in Egypt, because the needs were so great in both instances that they required the impossible.

So Jeremiah took heart in the God who did these miracles, because the Israelites would desperately need that kind of power to preserve them through the Exile and restore them to their homeland later.

Acts 4:24-31

"Sovereign Lord," they said, "you made the heaven and the earth and the sea, and everything in them. You spoke by the Holy Spirit through the mouth of your servant, our father David:

> 'Why do the nations rage
> and the peoples plot in vain?
> The kings of the earth take their stand
> and the rulers gather together
> against the Lord

and against his Anointed One.'

Indeed Herod and Pontius Pilate met together with the Gentiles and the people of Israel in this city to conspire against your holy servant Jesus, whom you anointed. They did what your power and will had decided beforehand should happen. Now, Lord, consider their threats and enable your servants to speak your word with great boldness. Stretch out your hand to heal and perform miraculous signs and wonders through the name of your holy servant Jesus." (Acts 4:24-30)

When the new Church was spreading the Gospel of Christ throughout Jerusalem, Christians naturally ran into trouble with unbelievers. The Apostles began to experience persecution at the hands of the Jews for their new faith in Christ. Their response was to immediately go to God in prayer for help. It's revealing to see *which God* they called on – the God who *made the heaven and the earth and the sea, and everything in them.*

They wanted the Creator's help, and they homed in on several of his characteristics: **first**, his *power*, since they needed that kind of power to counteract the forces of darkness and persecution that were arrayed against them.

Second, they needed the *authority* of the Lord of heaven and earth – one who would command his subjects, even those who refused to obey him, to submit to him whether willing or not. Remember the Command of Creation? They knew that if this God commanded their enemies to back off, they wouldn't be able to resist his command.

Third, they specifically asked for *healings* and *miraculous signs and wonders* to support their ministry. They wanted positive proofs in their ministry that would convince people that here was the real God, the God who could do the impossible for his people. They needed a miracle-working God to go before them, and naturally the One that came to mind was the One who first created all things – *through miracles*!

Only the One who performs miracles, who regularly turns to miracles to do the impossible in the face of great need, could answer this prayer. In other words, they knew their God; they knew how to use the information in Genesis to their advantage when presenting their requests to him. They didn't disappoint him with doubts of his abilities, but asked for what he could do, and what he had already proven (at Creation) that he could do. Their prayer was answered immediately in a way that showed the hand of the Creator:

> After they prayed, the place where they were meeting was shaken. And they were all filled with the Holy Spirit and spoke the word of God boldly. (Acts 4:31)

2 Corinthians 4:6

> For God, who said, "Let light shine out of darkness," made his light shine in our hearts to give us the light of the knowledge of the glory of God in the face of Christ. (2 Corinthians 4:6)

Those of us who know Christ as Savior will all testify to the truth of this statement. For the first part of our lives, we were in spiritual darkness, unable to know God or hear his voice. Spiritual things meant nothing to us. But when we first met Christ, he was a light that shone into our dark souls; he gave us life in our souls, and opened our eyes so that we could see him as he truly is.

This event is no less a miracle than any of the others we've been looking at in Scripture. A human being is desperately wicked, a born rebel to God's Law. It requires a miracle of grace, the hand of God, the touch of the Spirit himself, to change us from sinner to saint. A Christian is literally a "new Creation" –

> So from now on we regard no one from a worldly point of view. Though we once regarded Christ in this way, we do so no longer. Therefore, if anyone is in Christ, he

is a new creation; the old has gone, the new has come!
(2 Corinthians 5:16)

The way it happens is significant, since it's the same method that the Creator used when he originally made the world. **First**, he speaks his will over the darkness, because he's the King and he wants to make something happen. Out of nothing will come a new creation. **Second**, the thing is done immediately: the darkness which couldn't produce light on its own, suddenly is filled with light in response to the Creative power. And notice that it says, *God* made the light shine in us. This is the same approach that he takes to all his creative acts.

Actually this passage sheds light on the subject in both directions. **First**, the experience of spiritual rebirth confirms how God worked at Creation: the Word, his will, the original darkness and nothingness, the creative Command, the immediate response of existence and life – it's all here, just as it tells us in Genesis. So this bears out the fact that we are looking at the works of the same God, who does things in the same way now that he did at the beginning.

Second, the physical Creation can teach us a great deal about the second, spiritual Creation in Christ. How do people come to know God? How do they escape their bondage to sin and death? What state are people in, naturally speaking? To what does God bring them in rebirth? The answers to these questions are in Genesis! When Christ came and proclaimed the Gospel, the Jews should have recognized their God, from the Old Testament and especially from the Genesis account, doing the same kinds of works in the same way he has always done them from the beginning. And when someone is born again, it's no less a miracle than the Creation was – if we define miracle as the finger of God working apart from natural means.

2 Peter 3:11-15

Since everything will be destroyed in this way, what kind of people ought you to be? You ought to live holy and godly lives as you look forward to the day of God and speed its coming. That day will bring about the destruction of the heavens by fire, and the elements will melt in the heat. But in keeping with his promise we are looking forward to a new heaven and a new earth, the home of righteousness. So then, dear friends, since you are looking forward to this, make every effort to be found spotless, blameless and at peace with him. Bear in mind that our Lord's patience means salvation. (2 Peter 3:11-15)

We already looked at Peter's testimony about how the world was made. But he goes on to connect the God who made the world with the God who will finally destroy the world. Let's follow his thinking here. He knows that God created the world through miracle, by the power of the Spirit, in a way that nobody could have imagined or understood. It was obvious to him that it was a work of six days, commanded into existence by the King who makes all things for his own purposes.

Now, when this God comes to destroy the world, how will he do it? Obviously by the same miraculous way! He's going to send a calamity that this world has never known and burn the heavens and earth with fire, melting the very elements. And he's going to do it by issuing his Word, a command, that will bring it about. No natural processes here!

Now Peter draws the application. If this is how God works, if he works by miracle, if he issues commands and the creation responds immediately with disastrous consequences, *how then should we live?* The answer is that we should *fear* this God, if this is how he works. If God works as evolution says, then we have nothing to fear but nature itself; God himself would have to abide by his own natural rules. But if God throws away the rules of nature when he has destruction to do (or creation!) then events will turn out in a tremendous speed, allowing nobody time to repent, and in such a final way that there will be no turning back to get a second chance. It will come upon us, as Jesus warned us, *suddenly*. (Mark 13:35-37) Better for us if we get ready now for that day.

More references ...

Old Testament Scriptures constantly return to the theme of Creation. Passages too numerous to mention here reveal how deep-seated was the doctrine of Creation in the national mindset of Israel. It was the Lord who made the heavens and the earth; therefore all other "gods" were only idols without power, so that it's of no use to turn to them for help. (1 Chronicles 16:26; Psalm 96:5; Isaiah 45:18) The God who made the universe certainly has the power and wisdom and resources to bless his people. (Psalm 115:15; Psalm 134:3) When we need help, we need to turn to the Creator who can do the impossible. (Psalm 121:2)

The Apostles also understood the importance of the Creation doctrine. Only the God who made the world is living; other "gods" are worthless and dead and deserve no worship. (Acts 14:15) If God made the universe, he certainly isn't forced to live in a temple made by human hands. (Acts 17:24) God made the world in the way *he wanted* to make it – and that included keeping certain things hidden from us until he was ready to reveal them to us. (Ephesians 3:9) God gives new believers a new nature – they have now the very image of the Creator himself. (Colossians 3:10) God made the world in the beginning, and he will unmake it when he is done with it. (Hebrews 1:10-12) Those who suffer persecution should commit themselves to their "faithful Creator." (1 Peter 4:19)

Are we part of the faithful?

Not only have we seen undeniable proof that the saints of the Bible believed Genesis to be literally true, we also have been presented with a challenge. The challenge is this: are we part of the people of God? The answer to that is in whether we believe the same things about God that these Biblical saints believed. If we do, we are a part of them; if not, then they stand apart from us and condemn us for our *unbelief*.

There is no point for us to pray as the saints in the Bible prayed if we don't believe that Genesis is true as it stands. They asked for what the Creation account showed them about God and the way he works; it's plain to see that they believed in the very things that modern evolutionary scientists refuse to believe in. If we don't believe it, then we have broken faith with our spiritual forefathers. We don't share their faith in *this* God, that he would do *these* kinds of things in our day. If we change the account in any way at all, by reading in evolution and cutting out the miracles and commands, then we have left the historic faith and are literally creating a new god who works in different ways from the ways that the Prophets and Apostles believed about their God. The Church consists of people who have the *same* faith in the *same* Biblical God. If we don't believe in that God, we have no right to claim spiritual descent from these spiritual giants of the faith.

Part Four:

How to present Creation

How to Present Creation

The debate about Creation is a hot issue, and usually those who argue about it fail to convince each other. Many people, of course, join the ranks of the evolutionists because they themselves don't have any strong feelings about the issue, and the scientific arguments sound good enough to them. But those who are determined to believe the Bible's account make little headway when they try to convince others of their position.

The reason they can't seem to convince others is simple: they're fighting on the wrong battlefield. Military commanders know that a sure way to lose the battle is if you let the enemy pick the battlefield. The enemy will select an area in which he has the greatest advantage – on top of a hill, across the river, commanding the highway, etc. If you fight him on *his* terms, you are almost certain to lose the fight. The idea is to pick your own location and put him in the weaker position.

Winning the debate about Creation, therefore, is all a matter of how you present the argument. Believe me, the evolutionists have carefully chosen their battlefield – they have for the last 200 years! – and Christians have often fallen into their trap. As long as you don't question their strategy, they will always win. The way they have stacked the odds, you're fighting an uphill battle which is almost impossible to win.

What you must understand is that their strategy depends a great deal on deceit. In addition to many deliberate lies and deceits *within* their argument, their overall presentation is a deceit: they say that the only way to approach the question of Creation is *their* way. In other words, only a scientist can truly discover and understand how the universe was made. That's simply not true. *If* the Bible is a lie, *if* there is no God, *if* there is only matter and energy in the universe, *if* there is no soul, *if* there is no such thing as absolute right and wrong, *if* there are no Heaven or Hell, no reward for the righteous and punishment of the wicked, *then* their statement would be correct. Do you see what evolutionists are demanding that we give up in order to just talk to them about Creation?

No, we don't have to do it their way. Science is not the only way to look at Creation; it isn't even the best way to look at it. Science is actually misleading if we use only that to study the question of origins. Science is good for our present era, in a limited practical way, because it gives us the ability to understand matter and energy and use it for our benefit. But it can't open the door of God's spiritual world to us, which is the real foundation of existence and explains the essence of things for us. And when it comes to how the universe started, science can't help us at all, if the Bible is right in saying that it was a miraculous event and not a sequence of natural causes.

The strategy that we want to develop is this: let's ground ourselves in what we know is true. Let's stake out an area of truth that we are convinced about, and fight from there. Few of us are capable of even fighting on the scientific playing field, let alone winning; we just don't have the education or expertise to challenge the scientific findings of the atheists. But we don't have to: there are certain things that we know are true, without any doubt, and those things seriously challenge the conclusions of the scientists. We have weapons that will destroy their arguments. If we learn how use these weapons, and stand our ground on what we know already to be true, we will find that the enemy will become helpless before us. More people will begin seeing the issue our way and will throw their support into our cause. The debate will begin to swing in favor of those who believe God instead of the scientists.

As we will see below, this is a war: believing God's account is our responsibility, our legal obligation. Anybody who doubts God's Word is on the wrong side of the firing line! They are outside of God's will, they have set themselves up as enemies of God. Our duty is to evangelize them, not to banter scientific jargon with them. They are in the dark, they are to be pitied, they are themselves being deceived even as they seek to deceive others. Our job is to shine the light of truth before them so that they can see there is a God and believe in him. If we fail to carry the battle to this level, we ourselves don't really understand what is going on and we will certainly never carry the day against the enemy. God has called us to fight for the sake of his Kingdom, and he expects us to do it *his* way if we hope to win and bring him glory.

So, if you want to honor God in how you present Creation to someone, and if you want to make sure that the person gets a correct view of what Creation really is, keep these things in mind:

The doctrines define Creation

I hope you saw clearly, in our discussion so far, the strategy that I've used: we *know* what we already believe about God and his works. So why not use that to interpret Genesis? The entire Bible describes God, his nature, how he works, the kinds of things he does for his people – there were millions of witnesses to these truths. Therefore, it follows that the first account in the Bible would fit right into this overall picture. It's the same God using the same method to achieve the same kind of results.

The best way to interpret the Bible is to let the Bible interpret itself. This is by far the strongest position to take when defending any part of it. Somewhere in its pages, the Bible will tell us the answer to any passage that may be giving us difficulty. Bible interpreters have always known that. The Bible is the truth from the mind of God, and it's best to let God explain to us what he meant in what he wrote.

It's by far the weakest position to isolate a passage and try to figure it out without the help of the rest of the Bible – which is exactly what people have done with the Creation account in Genesis. It's as if the God of Genesis worked through normal scientific methods, and the God of Elijah and of the Church worked through miracles. The pictures that we get of God in these two schemes don't match! The unbelievers can clearly see that we are inconsistent in our argument, as if it is God who changes tactics when we don't understand what's going on.

If our faith can't see its way through to a miracle-working God in Creation, then of course we think he can only work through scientific laws in his world. But if our faith can accept the fact that Jesus fed thousands of people from virtually nothing, then we proclaim a God who can do anything he pleases. You see? Our interpretation is guided by our faith (or lack of it!) instead of our faith being instructed by the Word. We have the Bible saying only what we believe it to say, instead of what it plainly says. God is at *our* mercy, instead of we at his.

It's time that we face honestly what we have been doing, confess our sins to the Lord, and let him instruct us for a change. Our faith must *grow*; we mustn't continue to let our lack of faith rewrite the Word of God. We already have a head start: there are parts of the Bible that we believe with all our hearts. We believe the accounts about Jesus, that he was God in the flesh, a miracle-worker, the King of kings, the Savior and Redeemer of man. We know these things and hold those doctrines precious. So let's boldly apply those same doctrines back to the Creation account and have enough faith that the Creator is the *same* God who saves us through Christ and *his* works.

It's a moral issue

Ultimately the Creation debate isn't a scientific issue; it's a moral issue. What I mean is this: we've seen that the Genesis account is the testimony of an eyewitness – the Holy Spirit. It's telling us about God, what he is like and how he does things. God's glory is at stake here, because it makes a great deal of difference in whether you believe in a God who can do miracles or a God who can't. If this is so important to God, therefore, he wouldn't be satisfied that people flip a coin when trying to decide how to read Genesis. He's going to judge us according to how we decide the matter. Either we honor him or we don't; either we give him glory for his works or we don't; either we believe him or we don't.

We aren't making a mountain out of a molehill here. There are many other examples in Scripture when God took men to task about whether they believed his Word, and about whether they were careful to give him the glory he deserved. For example, Jesus was amazed at the disciples, and rebuked them for not having faith enough to know that he can calm a storm with just a word. (Mark 4:37-41) To doubt God's abilities means that we are in legal trouble; we become traitors to the state because we have called into question the character of the King. We have challenged his testimony about himself. This can only lead to a showdown in his court.

Judgment Day won't be a forum where we can finally clear up scientific questions. Since Creation was the foundation for a moral and spiritual universe, we will be faced with our responsibilities, our duties before the King who created us by command. We will be challenged with such questions as this: did we do what we were made to do in God's world? If we haven't faced it before then, we will be forced to face the fact at Judgment Day that God created us in a special way, through special methods, to be obedient subjects. He will demand a spiritual accounting of us then. Scientific data will be completely out of place in that tense and terrifying scene.

So, when discussing Creation even with unbelievers, the main point that you must keep bringing them to is this overriding issue of the goal of Creation, and how the methods that God used to create the world were especially fitting to meet that goal. All creatures are obligated to glorify their Creator, for the very qualities that makes him their King and Master. To deny those qualities is to insult him.

Scientists, as well as anybody else, have to be told that they are offending God in the way they are doing science. We sin against our Maker in *all* things, science included. Don't mistake me: we can do good science, and we can use science to help improve our lives in many ways. But science is just like any other human endeavor: we can and will pervert it, when it suits us, and use it to rebel against God's dominion over us. Scientists are *sinners* just like the rest of us. Many of them have used their skills to dishonor God, and they have to be *told* that if they are to know the truth.

That's the thrust of the argument. Do that, and you will prove that you understand the point of Genesis. This is the way the Bible presents Creation, and you will do well to take the same approach. If you avoid the moral issue (and many will, because it seems so offensive to put the argument like that) you will lose the argument, dishonor your God, and prove that you really don't understand the Bible's explanation of Creation.

Stay away from scientific arguments

Unless you are a skilled scientist yourself, it's no use to play their game their way and insure your defeat. They're good at what they do. If you take up their challenge and present Creation as a scientific issue, you will never prove that God is the Creator in the way the Bible presents him.

Creationists often take this approach: they argue the science of Creation, as if God would certainly have made his universe along accepted scientific principles, and hope by that that the unbelievers will be convinced. For example, the Flood geologists often go to great lengths to prove the Flood by means of known scientific principles, as if they desperately want the Bible to be a science textbook that explains perfectly reasonable physical events that any scientist, whether he/she is a believer or not, would have to accept on a purely scientific basis. One explanation, for instance, of how the Flood could have occurred is that a passing asteroid came so near the earth that it upset the continental plates (which just happened to be poised for a catastrophe!) and started the Flood.

Now my point is this: whether scientific Creationists can explain such things in a way to satisfy the scientific community is their business. *You and I can't.* As soon as we try to argue with science, we will be immediately put in our place by scientists who know far more about their fields than we do. They know enough mathematics to make our heads spin; they can "prove" anything they like on paper, and how would we know whether they were wrong or not? The chemists know the intricacies of DNA and the processes of life; the physicists know the mysterious world of the atom and the great forces of the cosmos.

How can we argue against such expertise that has proven itself over and over with scientific discoveries and a powerful array of working products? If we try, we will be mercilessly exposed as ignorant laymen who don't know what we're talking about.

The encouraging thing is that we don't have to be scientists to understand Creation. What the scientists haven't told you about, what they are deceiving you about, is that *they* don't know what happened at the beginning either!

Here's a little secret about the way scientists work that perhaps you didn't know. When they try to figure out what might have happened at the Beginning, they base almost everything they have to say about it on one principle: **uniformity**. In other words, since nobody was there at the beginning, the *only* way we can know how it started is to look at how things are running *now*. And obviously the world is presently operating by means of scientific laws, through time, step by step. Then they reason backwards and assume (you see, they make assumptions too!) that things have *always* been the way they are now – working by those same principles. In other words, they "discover" the past only by looking at the present.

We, however, have an Eyewitness. There *was* someone there at the beginning, and what happened then was catastrophic and not at all according to scientific principles. The world may run now according to those principles, but it certainly didn't start out that way – nor will it end that way, according to the Creator's plans (which we can read in the Bible). So scientists are also reduced to the "layman's" level when the subject of Creation comes up: only those who are experts in God's spiritual works and ways will truly understand what happened.

Therefore, don't fall prey to the misconception that scientists always know what they are talking about. In our contemporary society, people tend to hold up scientists as "high priests" through whom we can understand ultimate truth; as if only through science will we know truth. So everyone thinks that the greatest minds, the geniuses in mathematics and physics and chemistry have the greatest chance to grasp the real meaning of life. *This is a lie.* God has *revealed* to us in his Word what he did to make our world, and the geniuses missed it – they continue to miss it, even when told. God purposely revealed these deep mysteries to his children alone; only believers can know the mind of God. And notice that they don't need a scientific background to grasp the point!

> I praise you, Father, Lord of heaven and earth, because you have hidden these things from the wise and learned, and revealed them to little children. Yes, Father, for this was your good pleasure. (Matthew 11:25-26)

> We do, however, speak a message of wisdom among the mature, but not the wisdom of this age or of the rulers of this age, who are coming to nothing. No, we speak of God's secret wisdom, a wisdom that has been hidden and that God destined for our glory before time began. None of the rulers of this age understood it, for if they had, they would not have crucified the Lord of glory. (1 Corinthians 2:6-8)

The big issues clear up the little issues

Don't get stuck on the little issues. That's poor strategy when you're trying to convince someone of the truth of Genesis. If you let them run you around in circles on little points, you won't have the chance to bring in the really big guns that would easily convince them.

What I'm thinking of primarily is the issue about the days of Genesis 1. There has been so much debate about whether those days were 24 hours in length or long eras of time, that inevitably the Creation debate swings back to that argument time and time again. Everyone thinks by now that the entire Creation issue depends completely on how we interpret the days of Genesis.

It doesn't. Creation focuses on God, and *how he works*. We first have to learn about *him* in order to understand how he made the world. If you can prove that God works through miracles, then the question of whether they were normal days will naturally follow –

anything other than a literal day wouldn't be a miracle! The point to prove is that God is a miracle-working God, not whether the day was 24 hours. If we look at only the days of Creation, we will get nowhere. Focus instead on God. We can easily prove that God does his creative work through miracles – the proof is all through the Bible. From *that* proof we can then answer the question of the days.

There are other issues that you can get bogged down in. For example, many people try their best to explain how evening and morning could possibly exist *before* the sun, moon and stars were created. They also try to explain how plants could grow *before* the sun was created. Their answers to these dilemmas, of course, are always "scientific" and therefore absurd; they don't convince the scientists, and they aren't being fair to the text.

For some reason, people haven't yet considered another possibility: that it happened exactly as Genesis says, not in a way that science would understand, by means of the wisdom and power of a God who knows how to do what he wants even when we can't follow it. In other words, there are aspects to Creation that we will never understand that, if we knew about them, would perfectly explain such impossible details. If we were God the problem would clear up immediately in our minds; but we aren't, so they may always be a mystery to us. There are some things about the works of God that will never be clear to us.

It's often the case that we don't know all the answers to a problem. There's nothing wrong with that; the scientists don't know all the answers to their problems either! What we have to focus on is what we *know* is true. God wants us to get our hearts and minds going in the right direction, and focused on the issues that are really important; he'll let us in on the smaller issues later, once we know how to think about him and honor him. We can't let little problems steer us: often we come up with "reasonable" answers to those problems that will contradict precious Biblical doctrines that we already believe. When that happens, we are putting the cart before the horse – we're letting our ignorance stand in the way of our faith!

The one-two punch

When you are explaining Creation to someone, you will have the most success if you use the weapons that God has given for the purpose. These weapons are tried and true; they have been effective in convincing people in the past, and they will still be effective in our present scientific age.

In fact, the best strategy in warfare is to use a weapon that the enemy doesn't have. For example, the United States brought World War II to an abrupt halt when it used the atomic bomb on Japan. If it hadn't, the war would have gone on much longer – the two sides had the same kind of weapons, and the same battlefield tactics, which means that the results depended on sheer willpower and how long each side could last. With the atom bomb, however, the odds swung immediately to one side and victory was certain almost overnight.

These weapons that God has given you to "fight the good fight of faith" have tremendous power in defeating ignorance and sin. Paul tells us about them in Corinthians:

> For though we live in the world, we do not wage war as the world does. The weapons we fight with are not the weapons of the world. On the contrary, they have divine power to demolish strongholds. We demolish arguments and every pretension that sets itself up against the knowledge of God, and we take captive every thought to make it obedient to Christ. And we will be ready to punish every act of disobedience, once your obedience is complete. (2 Corinthians 10:3-8)

The truths about Creation that we looked at are knock-out punches. There's simply no argument against them. Nobody can argue against the fact that there was an Eyewitness; how can you doubt the word of someone who saw what happened? There is no doubt that God does miracles; there have been too many eyewitnesses, hostile as well as friendly, who will testify to us that he does. The commands of Creation fit in so perfectly with the rule and order of the universe now, our moral responsibility to the Law-giver, the testimony of our own consciences, and the demands of Judgment Day to come, that it's an overwhelming argument to the manner of the Creation of the universe.

Focus on these strong points. Keep bringing the discussion back to them. Unbelievers naturally don't want to talk about such things, because they not only don't know much about them but they know, in their hearts, that such things – if true – would spell disaster to their own arguments. So, keep in mind that this is the battlefield, these are the weapons, that God has given us in our fight against unbelief. Use them and you will find that the Kingdom of God will grow under your hand, and the enemy will either run from you or surrender.

Paint the whole picture

I hope you realize by now that Creation isn't a simple matter. It isn't just the issue of how many days God took to make the world, or whether he used evolution to do it. The issue of Creation isn't just an argument against evolution or even science itself; it's the foundation for all the works of God throughout all time.

If we understand what happened at Creation, we will have answers to a great many problems in life. The Creator commanded the world into existence; that puts us in a definite position in the world – as responsible subjects who will be accountable to him on Judgment Day. God made the world through the Spirit, which means that we depend on God daily for our physical needs, and we will only see and know God through the further work of the Spirit. Christ made the world, which means that we must all come to terms with him as our King, and follow him as he destroys the first Creation and sets up a new Creation that will fulfill his eternal purposes.

All these points set a new agenda for us to study; they open up a panorama on the world that opens our eyes to vast realities that we didn't realize existed. Creation deals with issues that we all must come to terms with eventually: the wise will learn about them now, the foolish will be faced with them for the first time on Judgment Day. The better we master what God did in the beginning, the better chance we have of improving our lot in life as we live in God's world. The universe was designed in such a way that the person who knows the mind of the Creator will best succeed.

A miracle is a miracle!

There is one more point to make that will help with other issues in the Bible as well as Creation, which is this: don't get into the habit of looking for a natural explanation for a miraculous event. Too often we let science scare us away from the miracles of the Bible; we try to explain them by means of natural laws and principles because we want unbelievers to accept them. But when we do this we take away from their amazing quality of impossibility; we also degrade the glory of God who claims to be able to do the impossible.

What comes to mind in particular is the Flood account in Genesis 6-9. Scientific Creationists spend a great deal of time on this account. We've already seen the reason for this: the Flood is largely what made our present world the way it is – we actually have little evidence from Creation itself to work with. And they too often try to explain the Flood by means of normal scientific processes.

This is not to say that they don't do good work. They do us a great service when they show us that a Flood really did occur – there is overwhelming evidence left over for the Flood. They also do us a much-needed service when they show us how wrong the evolutionists' theories are in trying to explain the same physical evidence. There is a need for Creationists to do more work in this area.

What I'm objecting to is their tendency to explain the "how" of the Flood with reasonable scientific theories. I've already mentioned the "passing asteroid" theory. The fact is that God can very well send a world-wide Flood without resorting to natural means. In fact, that's the point we've been trying to make all along: God won't use natural means to do his miracles, simply because there's nothing in the world that is able to fulfill his requirements. He does a miracle because nothing else *can* do it.

When we read the account of the Flood, or any other miracle for that matter, what we should expect to see is *nothing whatsoever* that can explain what happened. The thing defies explanation; it couldn't have happened naturally unless God did a miracle out of Heaven, a logic-defying act that is contrary to all laws of nature. That's a description of his miracles. What we're looking for, in other words, is *a God who can do the impossible*, not a God who needs help to pull off his works. Is your God big enough to do that? Would you be satisfied if God turned out to be Baal, who operates *by means of* nature because he can't do anything contrary to nature?

The Bible isn't just a history of God's acts. It's also an interpreter of those acts. Here we see the glory of God, not his shame and weakness. We see a favorable review of God here, more than we'll see from other sources of information in our culture. The Bible isn't going to present God to us in such a way that we have to apologize for him. No, its account will glorify him as the only God, the Master and King, the Creator, the Miracle-Worker, the Judge of all the earth – the God to both fear and put our hope and trust in. Come to the miracle accounts looking for *that* God, and you'll truly understand what you're reading.

Appendices

A historical survey of Creationism's response to the findings of modern science

How to determine what is Truth

A historical survey of Creationism's response to the findings of modern science

Summary

The phrase "modern science" describes the scientific endeavors of Western man since the days of Copernicus and Galileo. Starting with these early pioneers, man discovered *how* to study creation and find ways to utilize it more effectively for his own purposes. And it was Galileo's case that set the stage for what would be the continuing struggle between the Church and science: in its quest for new discoveries, science would inevitably challenge traditions and beliefs held by the Church that were thought to be inviolable.

The Christian Church has been crippled for the last two centuries by its poor defense of Creationism. In short, Christians were caught off guard by the reasonableness and power of the scientific method. Since they had no well-developed theory of their own, aside from the simple statements of Genesis, they had one of two choices: to stubbornly resist science's claims by a bare appeal to the authority of the Bible; or to submit quietly to science's interpretations and discard their old beliefs. The first was difficult to hold, since the scientific evidence was so compelling. The second was troubling to the conscience but at least resolved the public conflict between society's two great authorities.

Without a clear platform from which to evaluate scientific theories critically, the Creationists found themselves helpless and isolated in an increasingly scientific culture. Conservative Christians have known from the beginning that a wholesale acceptance of evolution must necessarily lead to an anti-Christian world view, but they seemingly could never could put their finger on the antidote for the growing moral sickness. The results of scientific investigation proved to be overwhelming and impossible to deny.

We propose to examine here a portion of the battle between Creationists and evolutionists, and note what it was that the

Creationists relied upon to counter scientific skepticism in the Genesis account. In doing so, we will see how this "defense" actually played right into the hands of the anti-Creationists. We will not, at this point, critique the statement of the evolutionists, nor try to mend the holes in the Creationists' arguments; since the argument is simply on the wrong battlefield, the subject requires a new approach and no amount of "plugging the dike" will satisfactorily meet the need. Our only aim here is to see the *progression* of the debate that has led to the present situation. That in itself should demonstrate the inadequacy of the historical Creationist argument.

Science before Lyell

Science in seventeenth century England[34] probably best reveals the nature and excitement of science in its youth and vigor. Names such as Newton, Boyle, Hartlib, Flamsteed, Ray, Hooke, Bacon and Hobbes demonstrate that this was the era that provided the solid foundation for two subsequent centuries of scientific achievement. Known as "virtuosi" – a term made popular in Robert Boyle's *The Christian Virtuoso*, they reveled in the discovery of a world made by God, open to the mind of man and made, obviously, for man's enjoyment and use.

> The period had the privilege of revolutionary discovery in so many fields; it pioneered on so many fronts. No age before had understood how well the heavens do declare the glory of God, and no age since has known the untutored surprise of first uncovering the hidden beauty of nature ... Wherever they turned in the study of nature, they discovered new wonders which provoked ever new adoration for their Creator. Nothing was more true of the virtuosi's own experience than their repeated

---

[34] Much of the following material is based on Richard S. Westfall's excellent work, *Science And Religion In Seventeenth-Century England,* University of Michigan Press, 1958. His careful research into the *ideology* of the early scientists has revealed, in this author's opinion, the weakness inherent in the approach of natural theology.

assertion that the study of nature only leads the soul more surely to God. [35]

But their wonder at the beauties of Creation, as their scientific work uncovered them, were limited almost exclusively to the manifest *wisdom* of the Creator who could make such a complex variety in the physical world. They marveled at how he could make perfect structure and harmony *at the physical level* – hence, in Nehemiah Grew's words, in describing the microscopic structure of plants,

> The staple of the stuff is so exquisitely fine that no silkworm is able to draw anything near so small a thread. So that one who walks about with the meanest stick holds a piece of nature's handicraft which far surpasses the most elaborate woof or needlework in the world. [36]

Christopher Wren was amazed at the tremendous distance to the sun and other stars; Edmond Halley, writing a prefix for Newton's *Principia*, marveled at the "inviolable Law" that God set up to run the universe; Robert Hooke, inspired by microscopic views of plant life, wrote,

> So prodigiously various are the works of the Creator, and so all-sufficient is He to perform what to man would seem impossible, they being both alike easy to Him, even as one day and a thousand years are to Him as one and the same thing. [37]

Their wonder was drawn out to God's wisdom that could produce –

> ... the wonderful order, law, and power of that we call nature that does most magnify the beauty and excellency

---

[35] Ibid., 26-27.

[36] Nehemiah Grew, "Epistle Dedicatory" to chap. 2 of *Anatomy of Plants*, London, 1682; cited in Westfall, ibid., 27-28.

[37] Robert Hooke, *Micrographia*, Vol.13 of R.W.T. Gunther, *Early Science in Oxford* (14 vols. London and Oxford, 1920-1945), pp.134-135; cited in Westfall, ibid., 30.

of the divine providence, which has so disposed, ordered, adapted, and empowered each part so to operate as to produce the wonderful effects which we see; I say wonderful because every natural production may be truly said to be a wonder or miracle if duly considered.[38]

Robert Boyle was one of the best examples of the early virtuosi, because of both his scientific agenda and his Christian witness. However, he was so eager to pursue both that he unwittingly laid the groundwork for the demise of Creationism. He held to the then-popular belief that the universe was completely mechanistic, very much like a clock that God made, wound up, and stands away from.[39] The world system works so perfectly, according to Boyle, that it has no need of God's further intervention. His intention was to show God's infinite wisdom at being able to create such a system; but the scientific result was *a self-sufficient system which does not need God*. Science now pursues that very feature of the universe – that according to built-in laws and principles, we can understand and predict its movement without having to bring in outside, "divine" influences to account for anything; research is based upon that assumption of self-sufficiency.

Boyle's dilemma immediately became apparent as it collided with the doctrine of the Providence of God. If the universe is truly mechanical, and science can describe and account for all of its physical manifestations without relying on theological concepts, then how can we say that God "interferes" with our lives even to help us? Is not everything that happens to us, in a materialistic universe, scientifically and not theologically apprehended? In a controversy with Newton over the reality of Providence, Leibniz,

> ... denying the Newtonian conclusion that God must correct aberrations in the cosmic machine from time to time, ... attacked the idea that God intervenes in His

---

[38] Robert Hooke, *The Posthumous Works of Robert Hooke*, ed. Richard Waller (London, 1705), p.423-424; cited in Westfall, ibid., 31.

[39] Though the idea of clockwork did not originate with them. Jean Buridan, in the fourteenth century, suggested a theory of "impetus" that would eliminate the need for any Divine Intelligence to keep the universe running. See Herbert Butterfield, *The Origins of Modern Science 1300-1800*, New York: The Free Press, 1957, 20.

creation at all. Newton, he charged, had conceived of God as a watchmaker who must wind his piece now and then, even clean and mend it. Leibniz pointed out that the more often God must mend His work, the more unskillful He must be. Divine interventions in nature would imply self-contradiction on the part of the Almighty Himself. [40]

This of course would affect other Christian doctrines, most notably the possibility of miracles. A miracle could not happen in a strictly mechanistic universe in which God refuses to intervene. Scientists in later generations, true to the pattern set forth here in the birth of science, would take pains to impale the possibility of miracles on the rigid mathematics of inexorable physical law.

The Christian virtuosi painted themselves into a corner:

> The conception of mechanical nature involves the exclusion of spirit from the physical realm. God is thought of as the Creator Who built the machine originally and set it in motion; but once created, nature is an autonomous material order made up of senseless atoms blindly moved by other unconscious particles. Mechanical nature does not leave any function for God in His creation, and it excludes the spiritual soul of man as well. Although the human soul may observe the order and even at times act as a sort of mechanical force in moving bits of matter, it is not an integral part of the physical world. Mechanical nature can function equally well if the human soul is present or not. In a word, the virtuosi stripped away the defenses against materialism, although they were decidedly not materialists themselves. [41]

What we need to add to Westfall's assessment is that the virtuosi, though purposing to glorify God through their science,

---

[40] Westfall, *Science and Religion in the Seventeenth Century*, 75.

[41] Ibid., 77.

apparently did not realize the limitations imposed by the argument from design; and their error resulted from their exclusive focus on the physical universe instead of the larger spiritual superstructure of the Creation event. They could not foresee that the same argument from design could be used against them on the scientific playing field. They were looking at creation from the point of view of *physical* evidence – material signs that the Creator had been at work. But evidence can be interpreted in many ways, especially when the investigators have ulterior motives. This of course became apparent even in their day when non-Christian scientists started describing the world in purely materialistic terms and denying the existence of God – as in the philosophy of Hobbes. But the coup d'etat finally emerged with twentieth century physics, as we shall see below. Scientists eventually came to appreciate the *point* of design from a non-theistic point of view.

Creation, according to the virtuosi, revealed God's natural order – thus leading to the development of a "natural religion," or certain supposed proofs of God's direct involvement in Creation discoverable through scientific research. But natural religion did nothing to stem the tide of atheism; in fact, it actually lent support to those looking for a universe that did not require a God to keep it running. As long as the virtuosi focused their attention on scientific "proofs", there would be little or nothing forthcoming to "prove" to determined doubters that there really was a spiritual God.

> While the virtuosi concentrated vigorously on the demonstrations of natural religion and proved to their own satisfaction that the cosmos reveals its Creator, they came to neglect their own contention that natural religion is only the foundation. The supernatural teachings of Christianity received little more than a perfunctory nod, expressing approval but indicating disinterest. Although the absorption in natural religion and the external manifestations of divine power did not dispute or deny any specific Christian doctrine, it did more to undermine Christianity than any conclusion of natural science. [42]

---

[42] Ibid., 106-107.

This inattention of early scientists to the *supernatural* truth expounded in the Bible unfortunately surfaced in the greatest of the virtuosi, Isaac Newton. He did more than perhaps any of the others to demonstrate the mechanical nature of the universe with his laws of motion. "Newton's scientific work made the universe, as it was held in theory, neither more nor less mechanically inexorable." [43] And although Newton devoted a large part of his life to theological writings, ostensibly for the purpose of glorifying the Creator whose works he so eloquently made plain in his scientific work, he actually forced religion to wear the halter of scientific law. God, he asserted as a scientist, "endures forever and is everywhere present, and by existing always and everywhere, he constitutes duration and space." [44] A seemingly pantheistic view! Someone asked him, how are we to understand the Genesis account of Creation? God created the world according to physical laws, he claimed:

> Newton's answer involved the simple application of mechanics. Before the earth attained its present speed of rotation, it had had to be accelerated from rest; the first days of creation were much longer because the earth was rotating more slowly. As the earth was gradually accelerated under steady force, it finally reached its present velocity, at which point the force was withdrawn, leaving it to rotate forever at the rate of three hundred and sixty-five revolutions per year. [45]

Westfall perceptively points out that, although this explanation sounds plausible enough to a physical scientist, Newton equates God to a "mechanical force, bound, even in the act of creation, to the universal laws of the *Principia*." [46]

---

[43] Ibid., 201.

[44] Isaac Newton, *The Mathematical Principles of Natural Philosophy*, trans. Andrew Motte (2 vols. London, 1729), 2, p.390; cited in Westfall, ibid., 199.

[45] Ibid., 199-200.

[46] Ibid., 200.

Newton's orthodoxy, as would be expected, suffered from his thoroughgoing scientific world view. A little known aspect of his religious creed was that he was an Arian by conviction. He wrote that early Christianity was easily understood by everyone,

> ... untill men skilled in the learning of heathens Cabbalists & Schoolmen corrupted it with metaphysicks, straining the scriptures from a moral to a metaphysical sence & thereby making it unintelligible.[47]

What he meant by "metaphysical" and "unintelligible" was the doctrine that Jesus Christ was part of the Godhead, the Son of God – i.e., the doctrine of the Apostles. His explanation was that Christ was *Lord*, not God: "We are forbidden to worship two Gods but we are not forbidden to worship one God & one Lord."[48] The scientist could not allow "metaphysical" – or non-materialistic and anti-rational – truths in God's universe, no matter how the Scripture reads. Thus Newton, and others in his day, attempted to construct a model of the universe in purely materialistic terms; it was their intention to avoid at all costs any mention of spiritual concepts behind Creation – that is, anything that could not be described by the scientific method.

Inappropriate defenses of the Church

In this early age of scientific inquiry, conservative Christians committed understandable (as well as fanciful and inexcusable) blunders as they tried to explain the event of Creation. Generally they were attempting to square their current scientific knowledge with what they *thought* the Bible taught. The scientific community has never let the Church forget those early mistakes.[49]

---

[47] *Yahuda* MS 15.5, f.97ᵛ; cited in Richard S. Westfall, *Never At Rest: A Biography of Isaac Newton*, Cambridge University Press, 1980, 823.

[48] Ibid., 823.

[49] Though it is quite unfair for them to mock Christians because of those early errors, considering the roots of modern science itself! For example, no less a scientist than Newton wrote extensively for nearly thirty years on the subject of alchemy – over a million words! See Westfall, Ibid., 21, note 12.

Perhaps the most serious mistake was the idea that God created *immutable species*. What they meant by that was that the forms of life that we see now are absolutely unchanged from the first week when God made them; and there have never been, nor will there ever be, any *new* species other than what God first made. This idea was generally held throughout history until the nineteenth century, and was offered as visible proof that God created the world according to the Genesis account, which states that he made everything "according to its kind."

Not until Linnaeus did scholars begin to notice that perhaps the theory did not hold up under scrutiny. In his *Systema Naturae*, Linnaeus, due to his widespread observations and study, admitted that new species may arise through crossbreeding. From what he had been observing, he could not decide –

> ... whether all these species are the children of time, or whether the Creator from the very beginning of the world had restricted this course of development to a definite number of species. [50]

In later editions of *Systema*, Linnaeus removed without comment the earlier statement he had made about *no new species*.[51] Before long, it became obvious to naturalists that there were in fact many changes going on in the world of living things; and those changes apparently occurred as a response to a living organism's surroundings. The old doctrine of immutable species crumbled before the onslaught of scientific inquiry.

This concept is not a necessary element of the doctrine of special Creation, however. Creationists today freely admit that a species can undergo many changes in response to its environment. What they do not admit, and what modern evolutionists still cannot produce, is any actual example that one species changes into another species – or produces a change *in kind*, as Genesis would state it. Even under this stricture, we can expect a great deal of elasticity in the system, and naturally so, since God in his wisdom would certainly

---

[50] Carolus Linnaeus, *Systema Naturae*, quoted by Loren Eiseley, *Darwin's Century: Evolution and the Men Who Discovered It*, Doubleday, 1958, 25.

[51] Ibid., 25.

create a *living system* that would be capable of effectively handling any circumstances that would arise. There may be, in living things, a wider range for the capacity to change than we might know. The Scriptures did not say how much or how little change there would be, given the circumstances; it only says what God first made. The point of contention, as ever, is over whether God made, at the same time, through miracle, the original representatives of all living things on earth, or whether all currently living things are descendants, through the process of evolution, from a few or one original primal life form. To bog down over the technical question as to what degree the resulting organisms can change is to miss the point.

Another error was Archbishop James Ussher's date of Creation, set at 4004 BC, according to calculations made by him using the Biblical chronology of the patriarchs and their genealogies. But few Creationists now accept that interpretation of the Biblical text; the generations recorded there did not necessarily follow from father to son, but in some instances from the father to some better-known descendent from among many that he had. Because of this, we are not actually sure how many years are actually accounted for with the minimal information that the genealogies give us. Again, the point is whether evolution created the world over billions of years or whether God did it in recent history.

Another Creationist mistake was what is known as the "gap" theory. The claim is this: between verses one and two in Genesis 1, a vast geologic time transpired in which the world that God created in verse one existed and was destroyed – thus resulting in a wholesale destruction best described by the Biblical phrase "without form and void." Then verse three begins with the "second" creation of the world, in which God made a new world over the ashes of the first one.

An excellent representative of the "gap" theory was G. H. Pember. Not content to simply explain the mysterious phrase "without form and void" in Genesis 1:2 as the initial state of Creation, he describes a first earth peopled with an original race of sinners, led by diabolic forces that eventually forced God to destroy the entire planet in punishment. The only "proof" that he had for this sequence of ancient "history" is a series of deductions: since there evidently was "chaos" in verse 2, this means that it must have been the remains of a first earth; its destruction would *have* to have been the result of sin, since God does not capriciously destroy his own Creation without good reason. And sin, as we know in our present world, is the result of rebellious sinners – which gives us the liberty to fantasize about what that world must have been like.[52]

The primary reason for entertaining this theory was the overwhelming "evidence" that modern geology has forced us to take seriously. Starting with Lyell, the scientific data presented made it seem irrational to deny that mountains and rivers and oceans have taken eons to form. How else could we explain what was so obvious to see? In addition, how would we account for fossils – remains of life that were obviously extant millions of years ago and took vast periods of time to turn to stone? One easy way out of this dilemma was to create a long period of time within the Creation account, without disturbing the six days of the creation of the present heavens and earth. Thus the "gap" theory. However, we are still faced with the *six days* of the rest of the chapter! If *that* was a miracle, why then do we need the "gap" theory to explain naturally-occurring geologic events that took place over billions of years? And if the six days were symbolic of eras, then why go through the bother of creating and destroying a first world to account for geologic eras just to remake a world through normal evolutionary processes? The two "creations" do not fit together.

There have been many more theories to account for how Creation happened, and they have proved to be a constant embarrassment to the Church. Lyell, in the beginning of his work on geology, takes the time to list and mock the various "Christian" theories of Creation. For instance, he noted that –

> The reader should be informed, that according to the opinion of many respectable writers of that age [*here he means during the time of Newton, Boyle and Hooke*], there was good scriptural ground for presuming that the garden bestowed upon our first parents was not on the

---

[52] G. H. Pember, *Earth's Earliest Ages: A Study of Vital Questions*, Fleming H. Revell Company, 33-77.

earth itself, but above the clouds, in the middle region between our planet and the moon. [53]

What is common to all these mistakes is that they are still dealing with Creation through a strictly physical (in other words, scientific) point of view. One cannot successfully describe what was primarily a spiritual event using only materialistic concepts; neither Christian nor atheist can make it work. What we have to do, first, is drop what is wrong without giving up what is right. The Scripture really does give us the necessary insight into what God did in making the world; without it we will never understand what he did. But we must not insist on applying scientific methods to the Biblical account! What we will end up with, if we do so, are absurd fabrications which unsuccessfully attempt to reconcile what was primarily a work of the Spirit with a materialistic philosophy.

Charles Lyell and the new geology

In 1830 a young Scot named Charles Lyell published the first volume of an epochal work: *Principles of Geology*. In it he attempted to do two things: first, he wanted to set scientific endeavor on a firm footing by demonstrating true scientific methodology – through observation and hypothesis, not by recourse to divine revelation. Second, he wanted to remove the obscurantism that burdened science – promoted primarily by the medieval Church's tradition and ignorance – and replace it with a more enlightened and realistic understanding of our world. For example, he cites the following as a "popular delusion" and identifies it with deceitful practices of monks profiting from "doomsday" prophecies:

> It had been the consistent belief of the Christian world, down to the period now under consideration, that the origin of this planet was not more remote than a few thousand years; and that since the creation the deluge was the only great catastrophe by which considerable change had been wrought on the earth's surface. On the other hand, the opinion was scarcely less general, that

---

[53] Charles Lyell, *Principles of Geology*, Vol.1, The University of Chicago Press, 1990 reprint of 1st edition of 1830, 38.

the final dissolution of our system was an event to be looked for at no distant period. The era, it is true, of the expected millennium had passed away; and for five hundred years after the fatal hour, when the annihilation of the planet had been looked for, the monks remained in undisturbed enjoyment of rich grants of land bequeathed to them by pious donors, who, in the preamble of deeds beginning "appropinquante mundi termino" – "appropinquante magno judicii die," left lasting monuments of the popular delusion. [54]

The unique theory that governed all of his geologic research is known as the *principle of uniformitarianism,* or what he termed "the doctrine of absolute uniformity:"[55]

> The geologist who yields implicit assent to the truth of these principles, will deem it incumbent on him to examine with minute attention all the changes now in progress on the earth, and will regard every fact collected respecting the causes in diurnal action, as affording him a key to the interpretation of some mystery in the archives of remote ages. Our estimate, indeed, of the value of all geological evidence, and the interest derived from the investigation of the earth's history, must depend entirely on the degree of confidence which we feel in regard to the permanency of the laws of nature. Their immutable constancy alone can enable us to reason from analogy, by the strict rules of induction, respecting the events of former ages, or, by a comparison of the state of things at two distinct

---

[54] Ibid., 24. It is interesting that his criticism cites all three points that Peter says "scoffers" will "deliberately forget" in the last days – "But they deliberately forget that long ago by God's Word the heavens existed and the earth was formed out of water and by water. By these waters also the world of that time was deluged and destroyed. By the same Word the present heavens and earth are reserved for fire, being kept for the day of judgment and destruction of ungodly men." (2 Peter 3:5-7)

[55] Ibid., 87.

geological epochs, to arrive at the knowledge of general principles in the economy of our terrestrial system.⁵⁶

In other words, the processes of geology have always worked at the rate that they do now. So, if we observe that it takes a certain amount of time to create a geological feature in our day, we can use that rate to calculate backwards in time to the beginning – since our assumption is that it *always* takes that much time to create something. The rate of change is always uniform – from the very beginning of the universe. We don't need miracles to explain anything.

Basically Lyell wrote off all inspired revelation, saying that all of it was *unnecessary* to explain what natural processes could easily explain. This was the only real reason he gave for dispensing with Scripture, aside from the ludicrous theories that older Creationists often postulated. In fact, he felt that any attempt to discover the origin of the earth was arrogance:

> To assume that the evidence of the beginning or end of so vast a scheme [*he refers here to the geological and biological earth*] lies within the reach of our philosophical inquiries, or even of our speculations, appears to us inconsistent with a just estimate of the relations which subsist between the finite powers of man and the attributes of an Infinite and Eternal Being.⁵⁷

We do not have the room here to explore the system he created, nor why he was so satisfied with his results. But he truly impressed his generation with his new approach to doing science. The effect of his work was staggering. Virtually everyone in educated circles was amazed, convinced, and turned into an enthusiastic supporter of his theory. This included Christians of all persuasions. Lyell's work did more to undermine people's faith in the Creation account than any other single work in the history of modern scholarship, including that of Darwin's *Origin Of Species*.⁵⁸ The reasons ought to be clear. If our

---

⁵⁶ Ibid., 165.

⁵⁷ Ibid., vol.3, 385.

⁵⁸ Irvine states that "The Principles are perhaps the most important link in the long, tenuous, precarious chain that leads up to *The Origin of Species*. Lyell taught Darwin

world came into being by the *same processes* that are going on now (and not by miraculous causes), and if, therefore, there has been a tremendous amount of time so that such processes could take place, then obviously not only is the Genesis account untrue, but there is no need for God to create anything since the system will gradually provide for its own needs. The jump to biological evolution was only quantitative, not qualitative; Lyell had already laid the ax to the tree of Creation before Darwin had written anything.

The religious conservatives almost always had severe problems with Darwinism (although they were rarely consistent in their critiques), but none of them seems to have had any doubts that Lyell was accurate in his science. This happened in spite of the fact that Lyell's geology was the more original of the two, and that Darwin just accepted Lyellian principles and applied them to the animate world!

Darwin's model of evolution

Evolution was not a theory unique to Darwin. There had been several versions of it circulating in Europe for over a hundred years, but none of them satisfactorily explained the facts of nature. Jean Baptiste Lamarke, for example, also held that the earth was of great age and biological species have gradually developed in response to their environment. But he defined evolutionary change as the effort of an organism to meet its needs within its environment (known as the theory of "acquired characteristics"), whereas Darwin saw the environment selecting out the fittest and eliminating whatever is inadequate – a subtle but pivotal difference in outlook.

Charles Darwin acquired Lyell's *Principles of Geology* while on his famous *Beagle* voyage to South America. His contribution was the intuitive leap that Lyell's principles could be appropriately applied to the biological side of the world. As he observed the differences of

---

not only how to think about geology, but how to think ... he acquired the genetic or evolutionary point of view, for geology was then the most historical of the natural sciences." 56. "Nearly everything he [*Lyell*] said was at variance with the Mosaic narrative, yet he contradicted it with so much tact and dignity that sound Englishmen could not long withstand him." 106. William Irvine, *Apes, Angels, and Victorians: The Story of Darwin, Huxley, and Evolution*, New York: Time Incorporated, 1955.

species, and their geographical distribution, he could see Lyell's reasoning for the necessity of extremely long periods of time, and gradual changes in response to changing environments occurring during that time. His unique theory was the idea of *natural selection*: when an organism has become adapted to its environment in a way that is favorable to its existence and reproduction, then that organism survives; those that cannot develop survival characteristics will die out, and become extinct. Over time, those gradual changes produce new species. Evolution makes an important assumption about the world that Darwin saw and was reluctant to talk about, yet finally had to admit: this is, as the old virtuosi first taught us, a mechanistic world, more than any of us realize. He concluded that there is simply no need to introduce a God into the picture, or anything spiritual for that matter.

> He felt that the more divine guidance in variations, the less reality in natural selection … He saw that scriptures and mythology were part of the evolution of every people … He rejected Christian miracles because they were similar to those in other mythologies, because they rested on dubious and conflicting testimony, and because they contradicted the uniformitarianism he learned from Lyell. He also rejected the divinity of Jesus and doubted the supremacy of Christian ethics. [59]

Natural selection is incompatible with Theism, and Darwin knew that. So did Thomas Huxley, who took every opportunity to undermine the religious establishment of Victorian England with a rigid interpretation of evolution. Not all of their contemporaries saw the point, however; Christians attempted to marry the theory of evolution with a less literal interpretation of Genesis,[60] but with the result that theism had less and less credibility in the scientific community.

---

[59] Ibid., 132-133.

[60] For example, Darwin's contemporary, the American botanist Asa Gray, proposed "to attribute the inexplicable variations in Darwin's scheme to divine providence … Darwin announced that 'however much we may wish it, we can hardly follow Professor Asa Gray in his belief' in divinely guided evolution." Numbers, ibid., 4.

Darwin's theory of biological evolution put the solution in the hands of scientists for disentangling them from the Gordian knot of religion. From that point on, it was open war between materialistic science and Biblical Christianity. The first opted for a completely mechanistic universe, the second knew (without knowing specifically *why*) that such a world view did not accurately describe God's Creation.

Christian reactions to the theories of Lyell and Darwin

We would expect that the defenders of the faith would have risen up in protest to Lyell's world view, or at least expressed some doubts in light of plain Scriptural teaching; but even they succumbed to the new spirit of the age. Charles Hodge, for example, stated that –

> The geological objections to the Mosaic record are apparently the most serious. According to the commonly received chronology, our globe has existed only a few thousand years. According to geologists, it must have existed for countless ages. And again, according to the generally received interpretation of the first chapter of Genesis, the process of creation was completed in six days, whereas geology teaches that it must have been in progress through periods of time which cannot be computed. [61]

Reading this, one hopes that Hodge is simply laying out the current options and will adopt a conservative interpretation in the end. Instead, he turns to James Dana's *Manual of Geology* and offers a solution in which the Biblical days represent geological ages, and an inorganic earth gradually progresses to the state of an organic earth. [62] And in case anyone had problems of conscience trying to reconcile this scientific answer with the seemingly plain statements of the Bible, Hodge assured us that Dana and others who taught this theory belonged to "the first rank of scientific naturalists" (Darwin and especially

---

[61] Charles Hodge, *Systematic Theology*, Vol.1, Grand Rapids: Wm. B. Eerdmans Publishing Company, 1975, 570.

[62] Ibid., 570-572.

Huxley no doubt disagreed with this assessment!) and are of "a truly Christian spirit." [63]

The only thing that he could muster in defense of the historic faith was his criticism of Darwin's lack of teleological sensitivity:

> It is however neither evolution nor natural selection, which give Darwinism its peculiar character and importance. It is that Darwin rejects all teleology, or the doctrine of final causes. He denies design in any of the organisms in the vegetable or animal world. He teaches that the eye was formed without any purpose of producing an organ of vision. [64]

Again, Christians dropped back to the argument from design to prove special Creation, and that played right into the hands of the evolutionists. According to Darwin's theory, design is the *point* of evolution: things will not work unless the design is fitting and opportune. Design, we are shown by way of the principles of evolution and physics, happens on its own because the system naturally requires it. As circumstances impact an organism and probe its weak points, a surviving pattern will naturally emerge.

Hugh Miller, a self-made Scottish geologist and great popularizer of scientific discoveries, wrote in the same vein as Hodge. His only worry was that Darwin took the purpose out of Creation.

> Christianity, if the development theory be true, is exactly what some of the more extreme Moderate divines of the last age used to make it — an idle and unsightly excrescence on a code of morals that would be perfect were it away. [65]

---

[63] Ibid., 573.

[64] Charles Hodge, *What is Darwinism?*, New York: Scribner, Armstrong, and Company, 1874, 52.

[65] Hugh Miller, *The Footprints Of The Creator*, Boston: Gould & Lincoln, 1854, 41.

His main objection was not the fact of evolution, but that the soul of man – which he took to be a self-evident fact – would have evolved, if the development theory of life were correct, without the intervention of God.

> The difference between the dying and the undying, — between the spirit of the brute that goeth downward, and the spirit of the man that goeth upward, — is not a difference infinitesimally, or even atomically *small*. It possesses all the breadth of the eternity to come, and is an *infinitely great* difference. [66]

Miller also showed Lyellian influence in his geologic work: he thought that each day of Genesis was an age, elevations in the world order, in which "through an act of creation" each "dynasty" of predominant life form entered the scene. [67]

James M'Cosh, president of Princeton University in the latter half of the nineteenth century, also had no problem with evolution. He just wanted to be sure to include the idea of design in the creation of the world:

> The argument from final cause, properly understood, is derived from those concurrences and correspondences of agents to produce a given end, which everywhere fall under our notice. These mutual adaptations of different and independent powers are so numerous, so curious, and so beneficent, that they clearly show that there has been an Intelligent Being arranging them beforehand. They cannot proceed from chance, and we therefore conclude that they must proceed from design. [68]

Like a breath of fresh air, Charles P. M'Ilvaine, rector of St. Anne's Church in Brooklyn and professor in the University of the City

---

[66] Ibid., 38.

[67] Ibid., 330-332.

[68] James M'Cosh, *Typical Forms and Special Ends In Creation*, NY: George Dickie; Robert Carter & Brothers, 1856, 40.

of New York, came the closest to putting his finger on the kind of truth that would stop materialistic science in its tracks. Amazingly, almost alone he seemed to see that miracles can be raised to the level of a proof, sufficient to test and place opposite the results of the scientific method:

> There is nothing unreasonable or improbable in the idea of a miracle being wrought in proof of a divine revelation. [69]
>
> If miracles were wrought in attestation of the mission of Christ and his apostles, they can be rendered credible to us by no other evidence than that of testimony. There are various descriptions of evidence, as the evidence of sense — the evidence of mathematical demonstration — the evidence of testimony. Each of these has its own department of subjects. A question of morals cannot be demonstrated by mathematics, or proved by the senses. A question of historical fact can be settled only by testimony. It might as well be put to the tests of chemistry, as to have applied to it either the evidence of mathematical demonstration or the senses. [70]
>
> Miracles are capable of being proved by testimony. [71]
>
> The testimony in proof of the miracles of the gospel has not diminished in force by the increase of age. [72]

M'Ilvaine then turns to the Gospel miracles. In a penetrating insight, he sees the finality of the testimony about the miracles – as if such testimony is a more sure proof than any scientific inquiry could have given us!

---

[69] Charles M'Ilvaine, *The Evidences of Christianity in Their External or Historical Division*, 9th ed., American Tract Society, 1832, 173.

[70] Ibid., 176.

[71] Ibid., 178.

[72] Ibid., 196.

> In being called to examine the credibility of the gospel miracles by the evidence of testimony, we have a special advantage over those who were present to try them by the evidence of their senses ... they who believe the miracle of Christ's resurrection on the strength of testimony, have a blessing beyond those whose conviction came by sight. This will appear from the consideration, that evidence obtained by investigation, and appreciated by reflection, is more consistent with the state of probation, and of moral discipline and responsibility in which we are placed, than evidence forced upon us by the involuntary agency of the senses. [73]

In contrast, other writers of his age disappoint us with their limited view of Creation. For example, in volume III of the Bridgewater Treatises, William Whewell states impressively that –

> God is the author and governor of the universe through the laws which he has given to its parts, the properties which he has impressed upon its constituent elements: these laws and properties are, as we have already said, the instruments with which he works: the institution of such laws, the selection of the quantities which they involve, their combination and application, are the modes in which he exerts and manifests his power, his wisdom, his goodness: through these attributes, thus exercised, the Creator of all, shapes, moves, sustains and guides the visible creation. [74]

However, he gives no particular reason for believing that God did this to the world except by analogy to our own works; he just assumes that God was behind the laws of the universe. This virtually insures the success of the materialists, who simply take the word "God" out of his description and claim *the same kind* of universe that would

---

[73] Ibid., 199-200.

[74] William Whewell, *Astronomy and General Physics Considered with Reference to Natural Theology,* Treatise III of the Bridgewater Treatises on the Power, Wisdom, and Goodness of God as Manifested in the Creation, London: William Pickering, 7th ed. 1839, 357.

be a result of, for example, the laws of quantum mechanics in the first few seconds of the Big Bang, which, according to the theorists, are capable of producing the same kind of universe by sheer determinacy.

Many Christian writers, especially after Darwin's theory of biological evolution swept the world, essentially gave in and went along with the tide. They could hardly do otherwise and keep their positions of leadership in the modern Church. Though Darwin himself had no interest in integrating evolution and religion – he purposely maintained an agnostic stand – many others were interested in doing so. They were less honest than Darwin about the root idea of evolution and natural selection. They seemed terribly anxious to find a way to make the Bible seem to agree with the latest theories of science – almost always sacrificing the plain truth of the Bible in the process. For example, George Fisher, professor of Church History at Yale University, claimed that if science forces us to take a different interpretation of Scripture from that of our time-honored traditions, then it is time to do that. [75]

> No course could be better adapted to excite a general distrust of Scripture than that of making a stand at one point after another, only to beat a retreat at the first regular onset of the assailant. The policy which we here condemn rests upon the assumption that natural science is to be looked upon as an adversary bent on conquest, instead of a branch of human knowledge to be hailed as an ally and a friend. [76]

According to Fisher, the only point at which science must take a back seat to religion is the problem of whether God was behind Creation; otherwise, science, unaided by the Bible, can supposedly –

> ... describe the forms of being that exist, can trace them back to antecedent forms, can continue the process until

---

[75] George P. Fisher, *The Grounds of Theistic and Christian Belief*, NY:Charles Scribner's Sons, 1883, 456.

[76] Ibid., 457.

it arrives at a point beyond which investigation can go no farther.[77]

Another concept that the nineteenth century Christian writers were careful to point out was the correspondence between man's mind and his world. M'Cosh noted that there is obviously a special adaptation (how else but by God's design?) between man's mind and the universe:

> It is yet suited, by its structure and its organs, to all the objects by which it is surrounded, and which it is expected to contemplate and to use. When man appears on the earth, which had been so long in preparation for him, he comes with powers and aptitudes fitted to the scene in which he is placed. We have now before us a correspondence of a higher kind than any previously contemplated. It may be called the Archetypal correspondence connecting Homology with Teleology.[78]

However, modern science also has an answer to this defense: the *anthropic principle*. Basically it states that it is no wonder that man is at the "eye level" of the universe, able to know and use it for his purposes: it produced him, did it not? Man as the outcome of a materialistic universe must be the point of the universe, the self-expression of the universe as it unfolds according to strict scientific laws. In order to avoid this trap, Christians have traditionally backed up to defending the divine origin of the soul of man, and the obviously unique mind of man that lifts him up above materialistic principles into a dualistic world of matter and spirit. But even this route of escape is being closed by modern scientists with new theories about man's brain being the result of the operations of quantum mechanics,[79] not an interdependent relationship between gray matter and an ethereal soul. It has become increasingly difficult to mark out a specifically Christian domain in a world defined more and more as materialistic.

---

[77] Ibid., 479.

[78] M'Cosh, Ibid., 441-442.

[79] See Roger Penrose's thesis in *Shadows of the Mind: A Search for the Missing Science of Consciousness*, Oxford University Press, 1994.

By the turn of the twentieth century, Darwinism had so thoroughly conquered the minds of men that many in the Christian camp simply gave up. They changed whatever theological concepts necessary to fit in with the "facts" that science presented them. For example, one can sense the theological exhaustion in James Simpson's assessment of the new situation:

> The average man ... passes through courses of scientific instruction, and sooner or later — if he thinks at all — he is compelled to contrast the fundamentals of this discipline with the fundamentals of a theology which is still largely mediaeval. His endeavor is to reach an interpretation of Nature, to attain an account of things that will be consistent, not merely with itself but with this other record; but he soon realizes that there is much that is disparate in the two points of view, many things that are mutually destructive, and particularly in the regions where science and theology directly impinge is the incompatibility felt to be greatest.[80]

> Religion has her great mission, that of enabling man to overcome his surroundings and himself and to acquire that peace of spiritual content that will give him the victory over disquieting doubt and temptation: and in all this Science can help — Science in so far as she is truth, for it is the truth that sets men free from the prison of their fears. But Religion can never be Science, and still less can Science ever be Religion. Religion deals with the supernatural, it is said: but the supernatural is concerned with the whole world. We talk of the real and the ideal, different aspects of reality: but the natural and the supernatural stand to one another in an analogous relation. And our interpretation of the real is modified and governed by our interpretation of the ideal.[81]

---

[80] James Y. Simpson, *The Spiritual Interpretation of Nature*, NY: Hodder and Stoughton, 1912, 1-2.

[81] Ibid., 35.

As we add to the list of converts of Lyellian and Darwinian evolution, we are amazed at the roll call: men who were staunch "literalists" of the Bible in every area except, apparently, that of origins. Louis Agassiz, for example, the famous paleontologist at Harvard University, was far from the position of Creationism as we know it today. He held to a geologically old earth as well as a subdued theory of evolution, though most Creationists still insist on using him as a proponent of Biblical Creationism.[82] C. H. Spurgeon, the London Baptist preacher, known for his untiring efforts at combating modernism in the Church, strangely gave way in the area of geology and accepted the old-earth theory.[83] B. B. Warfield, the preeminent theologian of Princeton Seminary and one of the last defenders of old-school conservative Christianity in our century, also clearly allowed for a geologically old earth[84] and the role of evolution in the development of man.[85]

To summarize, Christian intellectuals, for the most part, were at a loss to know how to critique the new science, so they changed their old assumptions and began looking at their own foundations instead. They limited their remarks, when defending the idea of God creating the world, to areas in which science (at least then) had no interest: to the argument from design, to the perfect fit between the world and man's mind which understands and uses the world to his advantage, and only rarely to the incontrovertible fact of miracles.

The rise of modern physics

At the end of the nineteenth century, physicists thought that they had found all there was to discover in their field – that it was just a matter of cleaning up a few loose ends in their theories.[86] But there

---

[82] Numbers, 7.

[83] C. H. Spurgeon, *What the Stones Say, Or, Sermons in Stones*, Pilgrim Publications, 1975, 2-3.

[84] Benjamin B. Warfield, "On the Antiquity and the Unity of the Human Race", *Biblical and Theological Studies*, Philadelphia: Presbyterian and Reformed Publishing Company, 1968; 247.

[85] Ibid., p. 255.

[86] Steven Weinburg, *Dreams of a Final Theory*, Vintage Books, 1993, p. 13.

were a few nagging details about the real world that refused to fit precisely into the well-developed systems of nineteenth century physics. Several investigators, determined to pursue these anomalies down whatever trail they might find, discovered the new world of the atom that nobody had previously even imagined – a world in which the classical laws of physics no longer applied.

We need not review that process of discovery here – the work done by Bohr, Einstein, Schroedinger, Dirac, and others – although it makes a fascinating story of a small group of individuals laying the foundations for a new world view that would quickly topple man's understanding of the universe and put our feet on "slippery ground," so to speak. Through quantum mechanics and the relativity theory, a scientific understanding of *how* the world works has changed qualitatively since just the last century. However, Christians have not been keeping up very well with the changes in scientific thinking, and consequently their rebuttals to modern science's arrogant claims are ignored as irrelevant – and too often they are.

The two nails in the coffin of old Christian cosmology that modern physicists have delightedly applied are the mathematics and symmetry of their new systems. Non-physicists do not seem to understand the power of the complex equations behind modern physics. The various concepts involved in special relativity, and the strange, irrational characteristics of the atom at the quantum level, are not artificial constructs that physicists made up to satisfy idle minds. In fact, many of these ideas, especially in quantum mechanics, were unearthed in spite of the fact that scientists did not want to believe they were true! What they could not argue with, however, was that these characteristics are there in the equations. The math drove the discoveries; the equations predicted, even demanded, the strange world of relativity and quantum mechanics. Basically, the scientists "invented" a new world on the chalkboard by means of complex mathematics, and then went out and "discovered" that their math was right – the world *is* like the mathematical predictions.

This is tremendously comforting to a physicist. It means that, at the very bottom of existence, the universe really is mechanistic, determinate, and completely knowable. No longer does he have to rely on the hope and hunch that science is the key to knowledge; now he has the tools to prove it. The math not only predicts the world's behavior, down to the sub-atomic level, it predicts its very makeup. This is one of the most important discoveries of twentieth century science. Gravitation, for example, *has* to be true for the math to work out right; the math predicts the existence of gravity. "Thus the symmetry among different frames of reference requires the existence of gravitation."[87] To the non-technical student, this may seem a strange way of looking at the universe, but to a physicist it means a dream come true. He finally has a closed, predictable system that is self-fulfilling, self-consistent, and self-existent where even the laws are mathematically defined – *and there is no longer any need to reach out of the system for a God to explain anything.*

Steven Weinberg, a Nobel Prize winning physicist, has discussed at length the importance of symmetry – or what he alternatively calls a "beautiful theory" – in science.

> Symmetry principles have moved to a new level of importance in this century and especially in the last few decades: there are symmetry principles that dictate the very existence of all the known forces of nature.[88]

Again, this is not the whim of a hopeful scientist, but the force of mathematics. It *predicts* a world that is self-consistent.

> I have been referring to principles of symmetry as giving theories a kind of rigidity ... We are on the track of something universal – something that governs physical phenomena throughout the universe – something that we call the laws of nature. We do not want to discover a theory that is capable of describing all imaginable kinds of force among the particles of nature. Rather, we hope for a theory that rigidly will allow us to describe only those forces – gravitational, electroweak, and strong – that actually as it happens do

---

[87] Ibid.,144.

[88] Ibid., 142.

exist. This kind of rigidity in our physical theories is part of what we recognize as beauty.[89]

Modern physicists have taken to writing whole chapters about whether there is a God – they feel now that they have something to say about that. Weinberg concludes that we do not need the God of tradition in a quantum world.[90] Stephen W. Hawking, Lucasian professor of mathematics at Cambridge University, states that the quantum theory reveals a self-contained universe:

> ... the quantum theory of gravity has opened up a new possibility, in which there would be no boundary to space-time and so there would be no need to specify the behavior at the boundary. There would be no singularities at which the laws of science broke down and no edge of space-time at which one would have to appeal to God or some new law to set the boundary conditions for space-time ... The universe would be completely self-contained and not affected by anything outside itself. It would neither be created nor destroyed. It would just BE.[91]

Carl Sagan, in his introduction to Hawking's book, concludes:

> Hawking embarks on a quest to answer Einstein's famous question about whether God had any choice in creating the universe. Hawking is attempting, as he explicitly states, to understand the mind of God. And this makes all the more unexpected the conclusion of the effort, at least so far: a universe with no edge in space, no beginning or end in time, and nothing for a Creator to do.[92]

---

[89] Ibid., 147.

[90] In fact, he takes offense that anybody would believe in the traditional doctrines of the Biblical God in light of, for instance, Nazi atrocities – which to him are reason enough not to take that God seriously. Ibid., 250-251.

[91] Stephen W. Hawking, *A Brief History of Time From the Big Bang to Black Holes*, introduction by Carl Sagan, Bantam Books, 1988, 136.

[92] Ibid., x.

The gauntlet has been thrown down. Before this crushing certainty of modern physics, Christians have either crumbled helplessly or simply ignored the results. They have no good platform from which to critique the apparent success of science as it reveals the way the world really works. It clearly does little good to go back to the old argument from design, because that is precisely what the physicists claim about *their* system – the math predicts the design; the design is inherent to the system, not imposed from without. To say that *God* imposed the design upon creation is to add an "unnecessary" outside element for which we must (but cannot) provide some sort of proof, because for scientists the world can be explained just as easily without introducing that factor.

The sole witness for Creationism

Evolution made such a clean sweep through the intellectual West that, by the beginning of the twentieth century, very few Christians were willing to admit that they believed in the literal interpretation of Genesis 1-3, and certainly no one was comfortable challenging geology's claim of an old earth. But one interesting holdout was the Seventh Day Adventist Church. Prompted by a supposedly direct revelation of its visionary founder Ellen G. White, who claimed to have been transported back to the time of Creation and witnessed the event,[93] the SDA laid the groundwork – all new – for the twentieth century phenomenon of Biblical Creationism.

The SDA's principle spokesman was George McCready Price, a normal school teacher who was self-taught in geology. His main work was *The New Geology*, published in 1923 by the SDA publishing house. His approach has been closely emulated by modern Creationists (not of the SDA Church) such as Henry Morris and John Whitcomb in their book *The Genesis Flood*.

Price's main thesis is that the Flood, or Universal Deluge, that occurred during Noah's time is the key to understanding geology, and

---

[93] Ellen G. White, *Spiritual Gifts: Important Facts of Faith, in Connection with the History of Holy Men of Old*, Battle Creek, MI: Seventh Day Adventist Publishing Association, pp.64-96; cited in Numbers, 74.

therefore of God's Creation in general. He heaps up evidence for the Flood from all over the world in an impressive show of geological insight. In other words, *physical evidence demonstrates the truth of Scripture.* There ought to be unmistakable signs, he asserts, that such an event occurred.

This is appealing as far as it goes, but it does not really address the "how" of Creation, nor whether Genesis 1-3 is myth or fact. The inference is that if the Flood story is literally true, then the Creation account must also be true. But that does not necessarily follow, at least to a scientist who wants more facts than mere suppositions. The problem for Flood Creationists is that there are almost no facts from the event of Creation to build a case for a six day event without dropping into a contrived scientific model that can easily be picked apart by the experts; on the other hand, the physical evidence at hand seems, on the surface, to overwhelmingly support the deductions of modern physics instead.

This weakness still pervades modern Scientific Creationism. For example, Morris, in an attempt to get Creationism accepted into public school curriculum, purposely eliminated any Biblical references in his textbook on Creation:

> ... Most creationist books treat the subject of origins from the Biblical point of view, as well as the scientific, and, therefore, are not appropriate for instructional purposes in the public schools ... The purpose of *Scientific Creationism* is to equip the teacher to treat all of the more pertinent aspects of the subject of origins and to do this solely on a scientific basis, with no references to the Bible or to religious doctrine.[94]

This tactical move did *not* meet with approval from all of his colleagues. John Whitcomb, co-author with Morris of *The Genesis Flood*, took exception to the idea that Biblical Creation can be sufficiently understood apart from specifically Biblical concepts. [95]

---

[94] Henry Morris, *Scientific Creationism*, Creation-Life Publishers, 1974, 3.

[95] Numbers, 246.

But Creationists, for the most part, have continued to follow Morris' lead and refuse to see the necessity of shifting the debate from its scientific footing to a more theological focus.

Not only that, they are still focusing on the Flood instead of Creation, even when they are ostensibly attempting to explain the Creation event. For example, Seventh Day Adventist author Harold Coffin, in his work *Origin by Design*, first covers the Creation story in 16 pages – basically recounting what is already spelled out in Genesis 1 with a few interpretive comments on how several of the events could have happened according to established scientific principles. For the rest of the book (430 pages) he spends most of his time discussing the Flood, supposedly (revealed by his chapter titles) because the Flood was the primary formative agent of our present world.[96] One can only assume that the author does not find any solid evidence that would demonstrate the process of Creation, whereas there are many opportunities to interpret present physical evidence in light of the Deluge.

---

[96] Harold Coffin, *Origin by Design*, Review and Herald Publishing Association, 1983.

How to determine what is Truth

Because man is a rational creature, he works with truth – with knowledge, understanding, and wisdom – in order to carry out his purposes in the world. Truth is important to a human being because it forms the basis for all his judgments and actions. To make a *judgment*, he has to be able to determine the value of a thing, its purpose, its true character, and whether it's of use to him; therefore he must be able to learn the facts, the details involved and their ramifications, so that he can make a sound judgment on it. And in order to know what *action* to take, when to act, the necessary steps in acting, and how to integrate his action with the actions of others, he must again know the facts involved in the situation.

Truth, then, is the constant goal of human endeavor. The problem is that we must be able to discern the difference between truth and error; we have to have reasonably fail-safe ways of getting the truth so that we can act on that knowledge with confidence and get the results that we expect. Not every form of "knowledge" is true, trustworthy, or useable, because we can easily be misled by appearances, held back by ignorance, or deceived by opponents. If we act on a distortion of the truth, our work will fail, because we live in God's specially designed Creation; only by knowing the truth will we live in God's world with any degree of success.

Scientists, for example, have developed a way of obtaining truth that they can trust – the *scientific method*. The steps of the scientific method can be outlined as follows: [97]

Idea-generating phase: Identify a topic of interest to study.

---

[97] These steps are taken from Anthony M. Graziano & Michael L. Raulin, *Research Methods: A Process of Inquiry*, Harper Collins Publishers, 1989, 33.

Problem-defining phase: Refine the vague and general idea(s) generated in the previous step into a precise question to be studied.

Procedures design phase: Decide on the specific procedures to be used in the gathering of the data.

Observation phase: Using the procedures devised in the previous step, collect your observations from the subjects in your study.

Data-analysis phase: Analyze the data collected above using appropriate statistical procedures.

Interpretation phase: Compare your results with the results predicted on the basis of your theory. Do your results support the theory?

Communication phase: Prepare a written or oral report of your study for publication or presentation to colleagues. Your report should include a description of all of the above steps.

The tremendous success of the scientific method over the centuries has been due to several factors:

- **The results are adaptable to our senses** – since our physical senses are our primary means of both understanding the world we live in, and guiding our actions in this world, the scientific method acts as an extension to our senses in our search for the truth. We naturally don't trust whatever "truth" that someone might present to us that's contrary to our sense perceptions; scientific research, however, deals with the very stuff that our senses crave.

- **The results are easily verifiable** – which means that when someone follows the strict procedures of the scientific method in their research, any other researcher can follow the same steps and get identical results. This demonstrates the predictability of nature and its laws. It's also the basis of our works that rely on the unchangeable principles of matter and energy: we know that if we follow procedures already discovered by others in their research, we can build up an economic and social and political structure that will be useful and reliable for everyone.

- **The results are acceptable to the entire community of human beings** – that is, the results conform to the common experience of sense and rationality of humanity. This idea of the common consent of the community insures that scientific research is conducted not according to the idiosyncratic traits of the researcher, but in ways that anybody can understand and utilize. Campbell states that "Science is the study of those judgments concerning which universal agreement can be obtained." [98]

- **The results account for reality** – scientists want to describe the real world, therefore the aim of scientific research is to describe principles that accurately account for the events in our physical universe. Thus we can understand *why* events happen because the scientific theory successfully explains the processes behind them. In other words, the results and success of the scientific method in correctly describing the universe, and giving us the power of prediction and use of its principles, justifies the method used to discover those principles.

---

[98] Norman Campbell, *What Is Science?*, New York: Dover Publications, 1953; p.27.

But for all the successes of the scientific method over the last several hundred years, it has some obvious weaknesses.

First, it makes man the standard of truth, and the judge of what is the truth. In so far as it addresses man's responsibility and sphere of action, this is in part justifiable; but it makes the obviously false assumption that there is no higher standard or Judge who dictates ultimate truths. There are many things that are true whether man knows it or not, and they impact the world of man in powerful ways. The scientific method is blind to that spiritual dimension by choice.

Second, the scientific method can bring us no further in our pursuit of the truth than sense perception. Philosophically this is a weak position to take, because it has always been a point of contention as to whether our senses truly represent the characteristics of the universe or simply act as an artificial interface to the universe, making it impossible to know its true nature. More important, however, is the fact that, again, the scientific method addresses the capability of the creature while totally ignoring the point of view of the Creator, who would have a point of view unique to himself. We can only know reality *after* the fact of Creation, as a part of and on the same level as the Creation, through our senses that are designed to discern its present form. God, however, knows the inner nature and cause of Creation in a way that we can't.

Third, the scientific method puts us at odds with any truth outside the physical universe. As we have seen, the scientific method lacks the ability to deal with spiritual realities; therefore a strict adherence to it will inevitably skew the truth process. But the problem is more serious than that: to the unspiritual man, the truth about God and his spiritual world is nonsense and therefore not real. "The man without the Spirit does not accept the things that come from the Spirit of God, for they are foolishness to him, and he cannot understand them, because they are spiritually discerned." (1 Corinthians 2:14) Scientists who are thoroughgoing about their scientific method reject God and spiritual categories; science caters *too well* to the senses, and leads people to believe that there is no other truth than what the scientific method can give them. But this is a circular argument: if the scientific method, by common agreement, only deals with what our senses can handle, and if it correctly describes the way our physical universe works so that we can make accurate predictions about its behavior, that doesn't force us to then state that God isn't real because he doesn't appear to be part of the process. The scientific method itself eliminates God from the system; it's no wonder, then, that those who refuse to depend on anything other than the results of the scientific method can't see God.

Fourth, the scientific method provides no final statement on the truth. Ironically, this isn't an admission of failure on the part of scientists, but a point upon which they hope for the victory of science over traditional authority. "Our knowledge of the universe is incomplete because new knowledge can alter current knowledge. Therefore, all knowledge is tentative."[99] With that sweeping statement they include religious knowledge – for which they have no proof other than mere assumption. On the contrary, the lack of a final statement on the truth behind reality is perhaps the most inhibiting and upsetting aspect of modern man's life. If we will never know the truth about God and how the spiritual world affects the physical, then we will never be free from the devastating effects of sin and death – which show themselves in very real ways in the physical world. (John 8:32)

---

[99] Graziano and Raulin, ibid., 23.

Therefore, God in his wisdom has provided man with *several* ways of knowing truth. Man isn't only a creature of physical senses, he's a psychological, social, moral and spiritual creature as well. When scientists limit reality to strict materialism, that's an artificial constraint that violates not only the full scope of Creation but the character of man himself. Just as there are different senses to adequately handle the different types of properties of matter, there are different faculties in man's nature to handle different *kinds* of data in the world – besides materialistic data. In order to form judgments and carry out actions as a responsible creature in God's Kingdom, man has to *use* and *rely on* various ways for discovering truth – not just one way.

Even scientists who claim to adhere strictly to the scientific method for determining all truth also have to rely on other methods to get along in life, whether they admit it or not. They may say that other methods aren't so dependable for determining truth, but they can't totally ignore them. This is by God's design: he created a world in which we have several reliable methods of knowing when something is the truth and when something isn't the truth. Atheists depend on the way God's system works, and borrow what they need from it, without giving due credit to his wisdom in the design of it.

The flaw in this viewpoint is that it assumes that other methods of determining truth are not so reliable as the scientific method. They aren't objecting to the fact that there are alternative methods of knowing truth, but to the *reliability* of those methods; in their opinion, only the scientific method can yield the kind of truth that fits their requirements as scientists. They often describe the function of religion as smoothing out our personal lives; but they are only resorting to the typical ploy of appeasing the religious community with a deferential nod to their obscure role in society without giving them any credit for knowing truth in a way that science can't. They don't want the religious to claim any certainty of "knowledge" apart from the scientific method.

But Christians need not succumb to the claims of the modern scientific method as the sole arbiter of truth. *Our* certainty is based on what God has undeniably done, his works that underlie even the world of the scientists, as recorded in God's own revelation – the Bible.

There are at least five other ways at our disposal for knowing the truth besides the scientific method. We can only briefly mention them here. But in reviewing these methods, we need to keep three things in mind: **first**, the feeling of certainty that the scientific method gives us rests on its success factors listed above; but the certainty that we feel as a result of these other five methods aren't based on our physical senses, nor do they depend on our acceptance before they can be considered reliable sources of truth. Sensual data requires *our* powers of discernment and judgment; spiritual data requires only belief in, and obedience to, God's authoritative statement and work. God never allows man to be the ultimate judge and standard of his spiritual truth – hence the discomfort of sinful man when being forced to rely on them. But when God gives us certainty in his truth, and we don't have to doubt and test its validity because he assures us that *it is* absolute truth, then we have something rock solid to work with.

Second, these five other methods free us from the artificial constraint that a slavish dependence on the scientific method imposes upon us. The old saying that "to a carpenter, every tool is a hammer" aptly describes those who submit every fact to scientific scrutiny. But we aren't forced to submit all questions of truth to the scientific method; information that we get from these other sources is just as reliable and useable, and in fact can't be learned through science.

Third, they necessarily deal with a reality bigger than the material universe. The scientific method is useful when measuring and using matter and energy; but there's more to the world than matter and energy. For proof of this statement, most people would readily admit that not everything man does can be traced back directly to a few basic principles of physics and chemistry (though scientists *claim* that they could do such a thing, they have yet to do so, and their claims don't convince the philosophically and religiously astute[100]). Furthermore,

---

[100] Nor do they convince all scientists. Lindley states that "Modern cosmological theories are built on ideas that have no proven validity, if one insists on the old-fashioned standard of empirical evidence. The hope of the cosmologists is that, in the

there are significant realities in life that obviously don't have any basis in scientific principles, realities which scientists scorn to acknowledge and Christians point to as proof of their claims. To be specific, these sources of truth point out that God is real, that we have spiritual duties as creatures of God and therefore are responsible to him, that we are surrounded by, and are ourselves filled with, dangerous conditions that threaten our relationship with God, and that Heaven is a storehouse of spiritual treasures that are available to us for our spiritual needs and service.

God's Word: proof by source

The Word of God is the very foundation of the universe. God created the universe through his Word, he sustains it by his Word, the command of Creation was according to the specifications of his Word and will, and the Spirit enabled Creation to obey the Word by bringing it into conformity to it.

God also communicates with man, unique among all the creatures of earth, through his Word. Man is a rational creature and therefore lives on the plane of thought and language; most of his actions, certainly all those pertaining to his calling in God's kingdom, stem from the activities and operations of his mind. So we find God accommodating himself to the mind of man through the medium of human language: both the written Word, or the Bible, and the living Word which is Christ himself.

The Word addresses fundamental issues for man that cannot be discovered through any other means. The spiritual nature of the

---

fullness of time, observations and theory will come together in one particularly neat arrangement so elegant that it will be persuasive despite the lack of solid evidence. Nothing in cosmology encourages this hope. Simple theories have been replaced over the years by more complicated theories, which nevertheless do not work very well. Perhaps the universe really is a hugely complicated place; perhaps there are fifty-seven varieties of dark matter in the universe, coming from fifty-seven broken symmetries in particle physics. Perhaps there never will be a compellingly simple theory of galaxy formation, and we will just have to make do with the simplest theory we can think up." Lindley, ibid., pp. 205-206.

Creation, the holiness of God, sin and lawlessness, death and suffering, redemption and eternal life, final judgment, reward and punishment – all these matters and more are issues that we must have answers for. Without this truth, we will not even be aware of our duties before God, let alone know how to carry them out.

But there are many other sources of so-called truth in our sin-filled, ignorant world that claim our attention. Our spiritual enemies make a point of deceiving us at every turn, and our hearts are all too quick to believe everything that we hear and want. Therefore, it is of utmost importance to establish a reliable source of any information about God.

For this reason, when the true God speaks to us from his Word, he reveals *who it is* that speaks these things to us. He identifies himself in two ways: by means of his Name, and the works he has done. For example, in Isaiah we read:

> This is what the LORD says – your Redeemer, the Holy One of Israel: I am the LORD your God, who teaches you what is best for you, who directs you in the way you should go. (Isaiah 48:17)

Only the God who claims *these* names, and backs them up with works done in history that demonstrate the validity and power of those names, can demand our attention and faith in what he has to say to us. No other gods can claim these names for themselves, and therefore cannot be a sure and certain source of revelation of spiritual matters.

For example, we have already seen the importance of miracles in the process of Creation. Often when God spoke to Israel, therefore, he reminded them of how he made the world:

> This is what the LORD says,
>
> he who appoints the sun
> to shine by day,
> who decrees the moon and stars

> to shine by night,
> who stirs up the sea
> so that its waves roar—
> the LORD Almighty is his name:
> "Only if these decrees vanish from my sight,"
> declares the LORD,
> "will the descendants of Israel ever cease
> to be a nation before me."
> This is what the LORD says:
>
> "Only if the heavens above can be measured
> and the foundations of the earth below be searched out
> will I reject all the descendants of Israel
> because of all they have done,"
>   declares the LORD. (Jeremiah 31:35-37)

The one who made the world through command, who created all things by means of miracles, has the authority and power to address the issues of sin, redemption, and the future of his people.

The source of the Word carries its own proof. At no point does the Bible attempt to "prove" that its information is from God; there is no proof possible. To what would we appeal as a higher authority? Nobody can validate the authority behind the Creator's words other than the Creator himself. When God speaks as the Creator, as the Redeemer, as the Fortress, as the Provider, he appeals only to himself, and to his own works, to convince us of what he is saying. "Even if I testify on my own behalf, my testimony is valid, for I know where I came from and where I am going." (John 8:14) The words of the "I am who I am" (Exodus 3:14) are the source of all truth, and therefore cannot be submitted to any proof process. Therefore to deny the truth of the Word of God is to deny God himself, since his Word comes from his very nature and his actions upon the world.

Miracles: proof by demonstration

A miracle reveals the identity and nature of the God who performed it, and does it in such a convincing way that we are, again, forced to admit that only the God of Israel could have done such a thing.

Miracles serve three purposes: *first*, they show us what yet needs to be done in our lives. Without the miracles of God, we are prone to think that the world will continue in its present state without any significant change other than the little we can do by our own efforts. But God has consistently addressed the brokenness, the failure, the emptiness, the suffering, and the death that our world is filled with. We cannot solve these problems, yet we desperately need solutions for them. Miracles are the only way that these problems can be solved. Without them we must resign ourselves to the inevitable consequences of sin and death.

Second, they show us what God is capable of doing. The nature and extent of the miracles convince us that God is bigger than we imagined. The primary purpose for the recording of God's wonders in history is so that we will learn who our God is, and the kinds of things he can do for his people. The miracles, therefore, provide material to pray about. Habakkuk well expresses this hope based on the knowledge of God's former works:

> LORD, I have heard of your fame; I stand in awe of your deeds, O LORD. Renew them in our day, in our time make them known; in wrath remember mercy. (Habakkuk 3:2)

Third, miracles show us how the Lord builds his Kingdom. He prefers to work by means of miracle, precisely because the natural world does not have the means nor the necessary materials for his purposes. The beginning of the nation of Israel, for example, and the beginning of the Christian Church both required extensive miraculous activity, without which none of the promised Kingdom would have transpired.

Jesus used miracles to prove his identity and calling throughout his ministry. For example, when John the Baptist wondered whether Jesus was the Messiah that was prophesied, Jesus responded by saying:

> Go back and report to John what you hear and see: The blind receive sight, the lame walk, those who have leprosy are cured, the deaf hear, the dead are raised, and the good news is preached to the poor. Blessed is the man who does not fall away on account of me. (Matthew 11:4-6)

The fact that he performed these miracles showed that he was the Creator, the Redeemer, the LORD (Yahweh) of Exodus 34:6-7, the Covenant keeper, the King, the Righteous One, etc. Not only did they reveal his identity, they also outlined his program during his ministry: to set up a new Kingdom, to call the wicked to repentance, to destroy the works of the Devil, to redeem God's people, and to set up a new standard of righteousness. To Jesus, miracles were a proof of his authority, where he came from, and what he came to do:

> Do not believe me unless I do what my Father does. But if I do it, even though you do not believe me, believe the miracles, that you may know and understand that the Father is in me, and I in the Father. (John 10:37-38)

The power of the demonstrative truth of miracles is seen in the fact that a single miracle, proven beyond any doubt as having actually occurred, would forever alter our scientific, religious, and historical view of the world. It would demonstrate that there *is* a God, that he is the Creator, that he can and does interact with his Creation in whatever way he pleases, that natural processes which we learn through science and history are only temporary (relatively speaking, in contrast to eternity past and future) measures between the miraculous beginning and ending of the world. Given the fact of a miracle, scientists would have to dispose of their materialistic philosophy as a result, and acknowledge the reality of God's spiritual world and the dependence of the material world on the spiritual.

Eyewitnesses: proof by legal obligation

We have already seen the importance of an eyewitness in respect to God's actions in the world. (See above, "The Proof of

Creation: Eyewitness".) The witness saw God at work, or heard his voice, and testifies to us about the reality of God and the nature of his works. Furthermore, no one can doubt the eyewitness without calling him a liar; they must provide witnesses of their own to contradict him and convince the court.

The importance of the eyewitness is that his testimony is *legally binding*; it is not a matter for scientific or philosophical analysis. God picked certain people to be witnesses of his truth, for the purpose of revealing the truth about himself to mankind. We will eventually be judged by God on whether we believed what these special witnesses have told us about him. The reality of Judgment Day is what gives their testimony such persuasive power.

Jesus warned that we are obligated to take the testimony of God's witnesses seriously; we have no sanction to doubt or change anything in God's Word:

> As for the person who hears my words but does not keep them, I do not judge him. For I did not come to judge the world, but to save it. There is a judge for the one who rejects me and does not accept my words; *that very word which I spoke will condemn him at the last day*. For I did not speak of my own accord, but the Father who sent me commanded me what to say and how to say it. I know that his command leads to eternal life. So whatever I say is just what the Father has told me to say. (John 12:47-50)

> His master replied, 'You wicked, lazy servant! *So you knew* that I harvest where I have not sown and gather where I have not scattered seed? Well then, you should have put my money on deposit with the bankers, so that when I returned I would have received it back with interest. (Matthew 25:26-27)

> That servant *who knows his master's will* and does not get ready or does not do what his master wants will be

> beaten with many blows. But the one who does not know and does things deserving punishment will be beaten with few blows. From everyone who has been given much, much will be demanded; and from the one who has been entrusted with much, much more will be asked. (Luke 12:47-48)

> If you were blind, you would not be guilty of sin; but *now that you claim you can see*, your guilt remains. (John 9:41)

Again, we do not place the burden of proof on the witness – what is there to prove? Anyone who saw God in action simply states what he or she saw or heard; trying to prove such an event actually takes away from its credibility. The thing cannot be proved, since, as we have seen, God is outside the world and is not subject to our analysis. The only thing that the witness can do is simply to state the fact of God's presence and actions. We who have received their testimony are now *obligated* to believe him; our actions in life will be judged against the backdrop of what we have heard of the reality and truth of God.

Fruit: proof by development

By God's design, we can know the nature of a person's heart by his actions. This fact is not only a result of God's wisdom in the way he made man, it is a result of God's active judgment as he brings out the secrets in the depth of our hearts so that all can see.

> Watch out for false prophets. They come to you in sheep's clothing, but inwardly they are ferocious wolves. By their fruit you will recognize them. Do people pick grapes from thornbushes, or figs from thistles? Likewise every good tree bears good fruit, but a bad tree bears bad fruit. A good tree cannot bear bad fruit, and a bad tree cannot bear good fruit. Every tree that does not bear good fruit is cut down and thrown into

the fire. Thus, by their fruit you will recognize them. (Matthew 7:15-20)

> They are the kind who worm their way into homes and gain control over weak-willed women, who are loaded down with sins and are swayed by all kinds of evil desires, always learning but never able to acknowledge the truth. Just as Jannes and Jambres opposed Moses, so also these men oppose the truth — men of depraved minds, who, as far as the faith is concerned, are rejected. But they will not get very far because, as in the case of those men, *their folly will be clear to everyone.* (2 Timothy 3:6-9)

The reason this is such a reliable way of knowing someone's character is that the heart is the "wellspring" of a person's life. (Proverbs 4:23) We naturally act according to our will, and the will is the inclination of the heart toward or away from God's truth. Eventually a person's heart will become plain by his actions.

Judging a person's heart by the fruit that they produce gives us much valuable information which we could not know by any other means. For instance, we know whether someone really loves others – and God, for that matter – by their actions toward that other person:

> Suppose a brother or sister is without clothes and daily food. If one of you says to him, "Go, I wish you well; keep warm and well fed," but does nothing about his physical needs, what good is it? In the same way, faith by itself, if it is not accompanied by action, is dead. But someone will say, "You have faith; I have deeds." Show me your faith without deeds, and I will show you my faith by what I do. (James 2:15-18)

We also can know whether someone's religion is superficial by noting the actions they take in their worship and spiritual obedience:

> Woe to you, teachers of the law and Pharisees, you hypocrites! You clean the outside of the cup and dish, but inside they are full of greed and self-indulgence. Blind Pharisee! First clean the inside of the cup and dish, and then the outside also will be clean. Woe to you, teachers of the law and Pharisees, you hypocrites! You are like whitewashed tombs, which look beautiful on the outside but on the inside are full of dead men's bones and everything unclean. In the same way, on the outside you appear to people as righteous but on the inside you are full of hypocrisy and wickedness. (Matthew 23:25-28)

We know whether someone is capable of handling spiritual responsibility by whether they were responsible and capable in past duties:

> Then he sent for the servants to whom he had given the money, in order to find out what they had gained with it. The first one came and said, 'Sir, your mina has earned ten more.' 'Well done, my good servant!' his master replied. 'Because you have been trustworthy in a very small matter, take charge of ten cities.' (Luke 19:15-17)

Finally, we can know whether the Word of God takes hold in someone's heart by watching what happens when they hear it:

> When anyone hears the message about the kingdom and does not understand it, the evil one comes and snatches away what was sown in his heart. This is the seed sown along the path. The one who received the seed that fell on rocky places is the man who hears the word and at once receives it with joy. But since he has no root, he lasts only a short time. When trouble or persecution comes because of the word, he quickly falls away. The one who received the seed that fell among the thorns is the man who hears the word, but the worries of this life and the deceitfulness of wealth choke it, making it

unfruitful. But the one who received the seed that fell on good soil is the man who hears the word and understands it. He produces a crop, yielding a hundred, sixty or thirty times what was sown. (Matthew 13:19-23)

Not only can we learn the state of a person's heart by the fruit of their lives, we can also know the nature of many other things – for example, the worth of a righteous man's advice:

> The mouth of the righteous is a fountain of life,
> but violence overwhelms the mouth of the wicked.
> (Proverbs 10:11)

One important application of this source of truth is to test the claims of the materialists against real life. A strictly materialistic philosophy, and any science built upon it, can only result in failure in a universe designed primarily to glorify God. The suffering and failure of our godless and wicked century is eloquent proof of that fact. On the other hand, it is well known that faithful Christians are the most valuable citizens if one wants a peaceful, moral, and well-ordered community. The fruit that they produce is conducive to life, not death.

The Spirit's enlightenment: proof by personal experience

The above methods of determining truth are pressed upon us from the outside, so to speak. Others may tell us the truth that they have learned, and we may be obligated to take seriously what we have heard. But it is still only "second hand" information; we may not be inclined to believe it in spite of our obligation. For instance, it is possible to accept, for the sake of peace, the testimony of an eyewitness without actually believing him; it is possible to learn the oracles of God without knowing for a fact that there is a God who said such things. All human beings are born ignorant of God in a personal way; we are all separated from the presence of God, so that nobody by nature knows God in person. Therefore, until we actually meet God in person, our information about him is necessarily "second-hand."

However, this particular method – experiencing the reality of God first-hand – yields truth that will be absolutely convincing to the mind and heart, though it can only be related to others, not used as a proof that will necessarily convince them. Personal experience of God is a strictly individual matter, but it is convincing nevertheless.

> No longer will a man teach his neighbor, or a man his brother, saying, 'Know the Lord,' because they will all know me, from the least of them to the greatest," declares the Lord. (Jeremiah 31:34)

The eyewitnesses – including the prophets and apostles themselves – experienced God first-hand. For example, Moses saw the "form" of God: "With him I speak face to face, clearly and not in riddles; he sees the form of the LORD." (Numbers 12:8) Isaiah said that "I saw the Lord seated on a throne, high and exalted, and the train of his robe filled the Temple." (Isaiah 6:1) The disciples "heard," "saw," and "touched" the "Word of life." (1 John 1:1-4) Paul heard the voice of Christ during his conversion. (Acts 22:6-10)

This same encounter is necessary to bring a sinner into the Kingdom of God and enable him to walk in the light of life. When a person is born again (John 3:3) he sees the reality of God and his world. A person who walks in faith (Hebrews 11:1) knows the reality of Heaven, and he knows that God really does exist. (Hebrews 11:6)

A person who meets God in person discovers an inner "witness" that confirms the reality of God in that encounter, and this infuses a vitality and hope in the heart as a result of this personal relationship with God through Christ. This is the purpose of Christ sending his Spirit to live in us. "The Spirit himself testifies with our spirit that we are God's children." (Romans 8:16) When this happens, we can no more doubt the reality of God and his spiritual world than we can our own existence.[101]

---

[101] At this point we need to point out that, since there is only one God, the God that one meets personally had better match the Bible's description of him – that is, God's own revelation of himself – or we have reason to doubt the claim behind the encounter. Since there are deceiving forces working to turn us away from the true

This method of learning about God is so utterly convincing because God gives it as a gift to his children. In a world full of doubt and ignorance, we need the assurance that we are children of God, that his promises to us are certain and sure, and that Christ does have our well-being at heart, so that we have something solid to hope for. He does not necessarily give us an assurance about all things relating to him, but he does open himself to us just enough to keep us interested spiritually and equipped to carry out our responsibilities in obedience to his will.

The person who rejects the truth of God that is based on the other four methods will no doubt suffer from the ignorance that he imposes upon himself; but the person who rejects the God that they have personally experienced has no other hope. Such an action is not a denial that God is real (as one might do with information from the other methods); on the contrary, through the Spirit he *has* experienced God's reality. What he rejects is the life that this personal knowledge brings:

> It is impossible for those who have once been enlightened, who have tasted the heavenly gift, who have shared in the Holy Spirit, who have tasted the goodness of the word of God and the powers of the coming age, if they fall away, to be brought back to repentance, because to their loss they are crucifying the Son of God all over again and subjecting him to public disgrace. (Hebrews 6:4-6)

God, we must take all precautions to insure that the God we meet is the one who revealed himself by Name in his Word.

NOTES

NOTES

www.ingramcontent.com/pod-product-compliance
Lightning Source LLC
Chambersburg PA
CBHW022002160426
43197CB00007B/233